New Uses for Obsolete Buildings

Principal Author

Jo Allen Gause
ULI–the Urban Land Institute

Contributing Writers and Advisers

Bruce M. Hoch
Development Concepts Group

John D. Macomber
George B.H. Macomber Company

Jonathan F.P. Rose
Affordable Housing Construction Corporation

D1597486

**Urban Land
Institute**

About ULI–the Urban Land Institute

ULI–the Urban Land Institute is a nonprofit education and research institute that is supported and directed by its members. Its mission is to provide responsible leadership in the use of land in order to enhance the total environment.

ULI sponsors educational programs and forums to encourage an open international exchange of ideas and sharing of experience; initiates research that anticipates emerging land use trends and issues and proposes creative solutions based on this research; provides advisory services; and publishes a wide variety of materials to disseminate information on land use and development.

Established in 1936, the Institute today has some 13,000 members and associates from more than 50 countries representing the entire spectrum of the land use and development disciplines. They include developers, builders, property owners, investors, architects, public officials, planners, real estate brokers, appraisers, attorneys, engineers, financiers, academics, students, and librarians. ULI members contribute to higher standards of land use by sharing their knowledge and experience. The Institute has long been recognized as one of America's most respected and widely quoted sources of objective information on urban planning, growth, and development.

Richard M. Rosan
Executive Vice President

Project Staff

Senior Vice President, Research, Education, and Publications
Rachelle L. Levitt

Vice President/Publisher
Frank H. Spink, Jr.

Project Director
Jo Allen Gause

Managing Editor
Nancy H. Stewart

Copy Editor
Barbara M. Fishel/Editech

Book Design/Layout
Helene Y. Redmond
HYR Graphics

Production Manager
Diann Stanley-Austin

Recommended bibliographic listing:
Gause, Jo Allen. *New Uses for Obsolete Buildings*. Washington, D.C.: ULI–the Urban Land Institute, 1996.

ULI Catalog Number: N03
International Standard Book Number: 0-87420-802-5
Library of Congress Catalog Card Number: 96-61393

Cover photo: Lake Union Steam Plant, Seattle, Washington
Photo credit: James F. Housel

Contents

Foreword

The Urban Land Institute has been interested in adaptive use—converting a building originally designed for one purpose to an economically viable new purpose—for a number of years. In 1978, ULI published *Adaptive Use: Development Economics, Process, and Profiles,* a book containing case studies of adaptive use projects and an overview of the economics and process of adaptive use. The book's intent was to inform the real estate community of what was then an emerging development opportunity: the reuse of historic buildings for economic market-rate purposes. Until then, most adaptive use projects had been initiated by public and quasi-public interest groups in an effort to preserve historically and architecturally significant buildings. As many preservationists had discovered, however, only so many museums or related public uses can be supported in a given community. It was becoming apparent that if historic buildings are to be saved, more conventional, economic functions must be found for them. The real estate community, striving to widen development opportunities, was beginning to turn its attention to this arena. The private sector's interest in historic buildings had been heightened by the federal rehabilitation tax credit that had been enacted in 1977 to encourage

private investment in historic rehabilitation and to promote urban and rural revitalization. The tax credit had an enormous effect on stimulating privately initiated restoration and adaptive use of historic properties.

The tide changed a decade later, however, with the passage of the Tax Reform Act of 1986. Among other changes, the act reduced the tax credit for preservation rehabilitation and, more significant, tightened the passive activity rules that effectively eliminated major sources of capital flowing into real estate investment. The changes in the tax code abruptly halted uneconomic, tax-driven investment in all types of real estate, which, painful as it was in the short term, most would agree was a necessary correction. While public and private interest in preserving historically important buildings remains strong, newly completed rehabilitation/reuse projects that qualify for the tax credit today are about 20 percent of what they were before 1986, according to the U.S. Department of the Interior.

The environment for adaptive use in the mid-1990s is at once more complex and more opportune than in the late 1970s. Since the late 1980s, the real estate community and other non–real estate–oriented owners and users of buildings have been responding to a new potential for

redevelopment—the increasing number of functionally obsolete buildings that have limited future market potential for their intended uses. Half-empty and vacant outmoded buildings have become a familiar sight in most urban environments and, more recently, are an emerging suburban issue as well. A number of interrelated factors over the last ten to 15 years have played a part in causing relatively modern (and often structurally sound) buildings to become obsolete, including fundamental changes in the economy, and in the workplace.

To what extent is the real estate community finding opportunities to adapt obsolete buildings for economically viable new uses? While no reliable statistics are available that show the magnitude and types of adaptive use activity, renovation of existing buildings (which might or might not involve a change of use) is clearly gaining in significance. According to U.S. Department of Commerce statistics, additions and alterations of existing buildings accounted for 42 percent of the dollar value of all private nonresidential construction permits issued in 1994, up from 32 percent in 1988. A growing body of descriptive and technical material on individual adaptive use projects provides compelling evidence that building owners, managers, users, and developers, driven by the need to become more productive with fewer resources, are increasingly finding inventive ways to reuse existing buildings. Moreover, there is good reason to believe that the need and opportunities for adaptive use will be even greater in the next decade than ever before.

During 1995, ULI convened a series of six roundtable discussions in Baltimore, Seattle, Washington, D.C., New York, Chicago, and Boston to examine issues related to adaptive use. ULI staff, in conjunction with ULI District Councils in these cities, invited real estate practitioners, officers of financial institutions, and public officials with expertise in adaptive use development to participate in two-hour discussions. Participants presented brief overviews of recently completed local adaptive use projects, generally highlighting project initiation, feasibility, planning, financing, and implementation. Following the overviews, a moderator introduced the following types of questions for general discussion by the participants:

▼ What conditions drive the need and opportunities for converting existing buildings to new uses?
▼ What is the nature and scale of recent adaptive use activity? What is the outlook for future opportunities?

▼ What are the major advantages of and constraints on adaptive use development?
▼ What are the key factors that determine the success of adaptive use projects?

This publication is an outgrowth of the roundtable discussions. Part 1 presents a synthesis of the major themes, insights, and conclusions from the roundtable sessions; it includes contributions by roundtable participants and other experts on various aspects of reusing existing space. Part 2 presents eight case studies documenting successful strategies for converting a variety of existing building types to new uses. The case studies expand on the issues discussed at the roundtables and illustrate the broad range of opportunities that can be found in reusing buildings. To provide a feel for the diversity of recent adaptive use activity throughout the United States, Part 3 catalogs 83 brief profiles of adaptive use projects representing a wide array of old and new uses, sizes, costs, and financing techniques. Project descriptions and tables in Part 3 are based on information supplied by developers, architects, and other project representatives in response to a survey conducted by ULI. Appendix A contains cross-references of case studies and project profiles arranged according to old uses, new uses, and geographic locations.

It is rare that any one form of development offers so many economic, social, and environmental advantages as adaptive use; everyone benefits. Despite the wide acceptance in the marketplace for redeveloped buildings, however, adaptive use is by no means a feasible option for every underutilized structure. Unlike conventional real estate development in which location follows market demand, both the location and the local market are fixed in adaptive use development. Sadly, local market demand will not support the reuse of some structurally and architecturally desirable buildings. But as the case studies and project profiles presented in this book demonstrate, wonderful opportunities exist for those willing to look.

The special challenges of adaptive use are many, but in the final analysis, successful adaptive use development hinges on the same skills that real estate practitioners have always needed: creativity, problem solving, and the ability to deliver the right product to the right market. ULI hopes this publication will encourage practitioners in all facets of real estate to consider adaptive use as a development option and will stimulate ideas for future projects.

Acknowledgments

This book evolved from a series of roundtable sessions that ULI staff, in conjunction with members of six ULI District Councils, convened to discuss issues related to adaptive use development. ULI extends its gratitude to members of the councils for the considerable time and effort that went into organizing the discussions and to the many roundtable participants for their generous contribution of time and their thoughtful insights.

Although this project required the time, effort, and cooperation of many people too numerous to list, a number of individuals deserve special acknowledgment. First, thanks go to the three individuals who served as advisers, valuable resources, and contributors: Bruce Hoch, principal of Development Concepts Group, who wrote the feature box on project feasibility and finding a new use for an existing building; John Macomber, chair and CEO of George B.H. Macomber Company, who provided most of the material on sharing the risk of an adaptive use project; and Jonathan Rose, president of Affordable Housing Construction Corporation, who candidly shared his considerable experience in a feature box on insights and lessons learned from adaptive use development. Thanks are also

due Eric Anton of Starrett Corporation, who contributed the feature box, "Solving the Empty Building Syndrome in Lower Manhattan."

I am indebted to the owners, developers, managers, and architects who provided information, data, and photographs of the many adaptive use projects described in this book. It is our hope that the information will assist many others. Appreciation and thanks also go to those individuals who wrote all or part of the eight case studies in Part 2, including Ken Braverman from Truman Annex Properties; Steven Fader, an independent consultant; Terry Lassar, a planning consultant and writer; David Mulvihill from ULI; Eric Smart from Bolan Smart Associates; and Joe Steller from the Maryland Department of Transportation.

Several individuals or firms went to great lengths to provide background material and current information about the initiatives their respective organizations have undertaken to encourage the reuse of obsolete commercial buildings, including Nancy Goldenberg from Center City District in Philadelphia, Mary Fishman from the Chicago Department of Planning and Development, Anne Job from the Downtown Denver Partnership, and Jerry Doctrow from Legg Mason Realty

Group. It was a pleasure to work with these individuals.

Numerous ULI staff were instrumental in getting the book published. Former staff members Andre Bald and Beth Williams deserve full credit and appreciation for so capably conducting the survey that is the basis for the project profiles featured in Part 3. Their task involved mailing nearly 200 letters requesting recommendations for current adaptive use projects, locating representatives of the projects and sending them questionnaires, and summarizing the responses. And special thanks go to ULI's publication staff for bringing the book together: Frank Spink, who oversaw the publication process; Nancy Stewart, who coordinated the manuscript's editing; Barbara Fishel, who edited the manuscript; Helene Redmond, who designed the book's layout, Diann Stanley-Austin, who handled the printing schedule; and Meg Batdorff, who designed the cover.

And to the many others who contributed to this project and could not be mentioned specifically in this limited space, I am truly grateful.

Jo Allen Gause
Director, Office and Industrial Development Research/Education

ULI Adaptive Use Roundtables

Baltimore, Maryland
March 23, 1995

Jerry L. Doctrow
Roundtable Coordinator
Legg Mason Realty Group, Inc.
Baltimore, Maryland

Shubroto Bose
City of Baltimore Development Corporation
Baltimore, Maryland

Dennis Jankiewicz
Design Collective
Baltimore, Maryland

Stan Keyser
Keyser Development Corporation
Baltimore, Maryland

Ed Kohls
Design Collective
Baltimore, Maryland

Jeff Middlebrooks
City Works
Baltimore, Maryland

Betty Jean Murphy
Savannah Development Corporation
Baltimore, Maryland

William J. Pencek, Jr.
Maryland Department of Housing and Community Development
Crownsville, Maryland

Peter Ponne
Loyola Federal Savings & Loan
Glen Burnie, Maryland

Ted Roth
Struever Brothers, Eccles & Rouse
Baltimore, Maryland

David Stein
Downtown Partnership
Baltimore, Maryland

Barbara Wilks
Cho, Wilks & Benn
Baltimore, Maryland

Seattle, Washington
March 29, 1995

Caroline Roberson
Roundtable Coordinator
Bellevue Downtown Association
Bellevue, Washington

William R. Eager
TDA, Inc.
Seattle, Washington

Karen Gordon
City of Seattle
Seattle, Washington

William Justen
Koll Real Estate Group
Bothell, Washington

David Schooler
Sterling Realty Organization
Bellevue, Washington

Washington, D.C.
April 6, 1995

Eric Smart
Roundtable Coordinator
Bolan Smart Associates, Inc.
Washington, D.C.

Michael E. Hickock
Hickock Warner Fox Architects
Washington, D.C.

Gary Klacik
Federal Realty Investment Trust
Bethesda, Maryland

John Payne
Fairfax County Department of Housing and Community Development
Fairfax, Virginia

Traies Haydon Roe
Price Enterprises, Inc.
Arlington, Virginia

New York, New York
April 25, 1995

Alexander C. Twining
Roundtable Coordinator
Avalon Properties
New Canaan, Connecticut

Irwin Cantor
The Cantor Seinuk Group
New York, New York

Scott Coopchick
The Galbreath Company
New York, New York

Philip Johnson
Philip Johnson, Ritchie & Fiore Architects
New York, New York

Costas Kondylis
CK Architects
New York, New York

Charles Reiss
The Trump Organization
New York, New York

Ysrael Seinuk
The Cantor Seinuk Group
New York, New York

Michael Simmons
GE Investments
New York, New York

Louise Sunshine
The Sunshine Group
New York, New York

Donald Trump
The Trump Organization
New York, New York

Bruce Warwick
The Galbreath Organization
New York, New York

Andrew Weiss
The Trump Organization
New York, New York

Chicago, Illinois
July 11, 1995

Donald A. Shindler
Roundtable Coordinator
Rudnick & Wolfe
Chicago, Illinois

Norris R. Eber
Tucker Properties Corporation
Chicago, Illinois

Albert M. Friedman
J.A. Friedman & Associates
Chicago, Illinois

Elizabeth Hollander
DePaul University
Chicago, Illinois

James Martell
The Prime Group
Chicago, Illinois

Mary Nelson
Bethel New Life, Inc.
Chicago, Illinois

Boston, Massachusetts
October 12, 1995

John D. Macomber
Roundtable Coordinator
George B.H. Macomber Company
Boston, Massachusetts

Mark Barnard
MIT Real Estate Office
Boston, Massachusetts

James F. English
Raymond Property Company
Boston, Massachusetts

Frederick M. Gibson
Taylor & Partners, Inc.
Boston, Massachusetts

Franklin B. Mead
Mead Consulting, Inc.
Boston, Massachusetts

Myron Miller
Miller Dyer Spears, Inc.
Boston, Massachusetts

Part 1

New Opportunities For Adaptive Use

*The only real voyage of discovery consists
not in seeking new landscapes,
but in having new eyes.*
—Marcel Proust

Conditions Creating New Opportunities

Development patterns in urban environments have always been extremely fluid. City neighborhoods and commercial districts often decline over time in response to economic ups and downs and demographic shifts. By the same token, changing conditions bring new markets and economic development to deteriorated areas. Cities that developed before the widespread use of the automobile are usually characterized by dense mixed-use development with built-in flexibility for land uses and building uses to adapt to changing markets. Economic changes, demographic shifts, new transportation systems, and other external influences precipitate transitions in urban neighborhoods; existing and newly constructed buildings respond to new market demands. In the second half of this century, the transition from an industry-based economy to knowledge-based industries eliminated the market demand that many

Cho, Wilks & Benn

Cho, Wilks & Benn

An outdated 450,000-square-foot factory in the heart of Baltimore's old industrial waterfront, Tindeco Wharf has been revived for a mix of new uses: 240 luxury apartment units, a health club, an HMO, office space, and a parking garage. The pier was redeveloped with a pool, greenspace, a restaurant, and a promenade at the water's edge connecting to Baltimore's Inner Harbor. Lofts were added to all units to increase the leasable area, with dramatic double-height spaces where existing high ceilings remain. New penthouses with decks were added on the roof to take advantage of the views.

Blakeslee, Lane, Inc.

The former factory's courtyard before redevelopment (top) is now a focal point for the interior offices and apartments (bottom). The courtyard fountain and pool flow into the building's lobby.

3

When the Annie E. Casey Foundation, the nonprofit arm of UPS, relocated its headquarters to Baltimore, it chose to convert a 52,000-square-foot 1960s building into five stories of office space and two levels of parking—all designed and constructed within six and one-half months.

Cho, Wilks & Benn

industrial districts. Like outmoded buildings from past eras, many of these buildings can and will be economically adapted for new uses, and a wider range of players than ever before are finding opportunities to create value by reusing existing buildings for new uses. Ten years ago, the majority of adaptive use projects were speculative and generally initiated by developers. Today, buildings are just as likely to be reused by *user organizations* looking to satisfy the need for building space with unusual characteristics, constraints, or flexibility; a *building owner* attempting to protect or liquidate an investment; *corporations* that, under pressure to maximize the productive use of their assets, see adaptive use as a way to turn surplus properties into income-producing investments; an *institution* looking to realize the highest and best use for a building that it owns or controls; *public agencies* that, facing an eroding tax base, encourage or undertake the reuse of underused assets to stimulate

urban industrial districts depended upon, propelling areas like SoHo and TriBeCa in New York City and the Dallas downtown warehouse district into decline. Now fashionable arts districts, these areas are just two of many examples across the country of the enduring ability of existing buildings to meet new market demands. Functionally obsolete office and other commercial buildings in city centers are the modern equivalent of these older inner-city

The low, dark corridors that characterized the existing building (left) were enlivened with construction of a light-filled atrium (right).

Cho, Wilks & Benn

Cho, Wilks & Benn

revitalization and economic growth; and *developers* who find opportunities to modify existing buildings to attract different types of occupants. Regardless of who sponsors the project, under the right set of circumstances adapting an existing building can prove to be a better alterative than buying, building, or leasing a new building.

In most cases, the factors that determine the economic feasibility of a specific adaptive use project are the same today as they were 20 years ago: adequate demand in the local market; manageable public approvals; the physical characteristics and location of an existing building; and the availability of financing. New influences on these familiar economic fundamentals, however, are creating conditions favorable for adaptive use. This section looks at some of the conditions that are giving rise to the need and opportunity to find productive uses for obsolete buildings.

Smith, Hinchman & Grylls Associates, Inc.

Surplus Buildings

A combination of interrelated conditions has rendered many buildings *functionally obsolete* —that is, no longer productive for their intended use. Overbuilding in the 1980s, the economic recession and subsequent real estate crash in the late 1980s and early 1990s, structural changes in the economy, large-scale corporate restructuring and downsizing, innovations in communications and information technologies that have revolutionized the way business is done worldwide, changing preferences for how and where we work and live: all have changed the world in many ways.

Gary Quesada, Korab-Hedrich/Blessing

Focus: HOPE's Center for Advanced Technologies (CAT) is the dramatic transformation of a surplus automotive plant donated by Ford Motor Company (top) into a state-of-the-art training facility. CAT's intensive six-year work/study curriculum prepares graduates from inner-city Detroit high schools for careers as manufacturing engineer/technologists. The $22 million adaptive use renovation was paid for by a variety of public and private grants. From the outside, the renovated CAT (middle) is not much different from the original structure. The inside, however, bears no resemblance to the old. A 180,000-square-foot single-level computer-integrated manufacturing area is connected by a sawtooth roof (bottom) to a 40,000-square-foot, three-story wing (the former plant office) containing an electronic library, interview rooms, and a conference center.

Figure 1-1. Maytag Corporation Training Center and the Des Moines Area Community College Polytechnic Campus

Newton, Iowa

Before: *The surplus manufacturing facility on the Maytag Corporation campus in Newton, Iowa.*

After: *The newly renovated Maytag Corporation Training Center and the DMACC Polytechnic Campus.*

Maytag Corporation explored various alternatives for a surplus manufacturing facility at its Newton, Iowa, headquarters, eventually choosing an innovative strategy to dispose of its unproductive asset. The result benefited a great number of people.

Maytag donated the building and eight acres to a foundation headed by the Des Moines Area Community College (DMACC), with the understanding that the building would be redeveloped as a multipurpose community asset whose primary uses would be a much-desired campus of higher education and a community center. Because the building was larger than DMACC would need, Maytag planned to lease back the excess space from the foundation and redevelop it into a corporate conference and training center for its private use. Through creative financing and engineering, the 54,000-square-foot, single-story factory was reincarnated into a 108,000-square-foot community college and corporate conference center eight months after work began.

Additional space was needed to accommodate the different uses. The Alter Group, the project developer, determined that adding a second floor was a better use of the site than doubling the building pad. But because some of the soil underneath the building could not support the weight of a second floor, the existing six- to 24-inch concrete floor was replaced with a 12-inch "raft slab." The new, heavily reinforced slab floor distributes weight equally throughout the building, placing excessive weight on key support footings.

Functionally obsolete buildings come in all types in all kinds of settings. The most endangered building types, those with the least promising market potential for their intended uses, are found among Class B and C office buildings in urban centers; suburban office parks; downtown department stores; corporate-owned surplus manufacturing, warehouse, distribution, and other industrial properties; closed military facilities; and surplus educational facilities. The

Figure 1-1 *(continued).*

Access to the college and conference center is through a dramatic two-story atrium. Crossing tile patterns in the lobby suggest a unification of different interests, a concept that underscores the project's evolution.

DMACC required sophisticated fiber-optics teleconferencing equipment so that classes could be broadcast from other DMACC sites and viewed by students at Newton. Interactive technology allows instructors to view classrooms and students to speak directly with off-site teachers.

The developers also had to consider the users' sophisticated telecommunications requirements. DMACC required sophisticated fiber-optics teleconferencing equipment to broadcast classes from other DMACC sites to Newton, and it needed its computer systems to be linked via a Local Area Network with other campuses. Maytag also required additional power to operate test kitchens, a simulated retail store environment, and a video production studio.

The project involved several private and public entities that contributed to and benefited from the renovation. Iowa Governor Terry Branstad acknowledges that this project was the first real example of a public/private partnership in Iowa. Financing came from a number of sources. Maytag donated the building and eight acres to the DMACC Foundation along with $1 million in cash. Considering the tax benefits realized from the donation and relief from property taxes, Maytag's net cost for its new training center was far less than the cost of building a new facility. The city of Newton contributed $1 million and also benefited from the in-stallation of water and sewer lines compatible with the city's street improvement program. Site landscaping was provided with a grant from the city and the local public utility. With two creditworthy leases in place (DMACC and Maytag), the Foundation secured a mortgage from a local bank for the balance of the development costs. The careful selection of construction materials and value engineering enabled the project to finish $60,000 under budget.▼

sheer volume and variety of underutilized buildings that retain only a fraction of their former value has prompted many investors, users, and developers of real estate to scrutinize these assets for redevelopment opportunities. As roundtable participants pointed out, however, the *availability* of surplus buildings has created a greater *potential* for adaptive use than ever before, but the real opportunities depend on a project sponsor's ability to match the asset's

Figure 1-2. Cavanaugh's Inn

Seattle, Washington

Cavanaugh's Inn, a privately initiated, market-driven reuse of a vacant 20-story bank building, shows the hidden economic potential of many aging underused office towers.

Jimi Lott/Seattle Times

Cavanaugh's Inn, a recently opened 300-room hotel in downtown Seattle, is a shining example of transforming an obsolete downtown office tower into a productive new use.

When Spokane-based developer Goodale & Barbieri Companies (G&B) became interested in entering Seattle's hot hotel market (only three other cities in the country topped Seattle's hotel occupancy rate in 1995 and the city's tourism industry is poised to grow even stronger), it scoured the area for a well-located site on which a new hotel could be opened as quickly as possible. Having successfully undertaken adaptive use development in the past, the diversified developer of hotels, offices, and retail space was open to considering unconventional alternatives. Thus it was with an open mind that G&B considered acquiring and converting a vacant 20-story former U.S. Bank headquarters building on Fifth Avenue to a midpriced hotel.

G&B soon realized that reusing the 1974-vintage office building offered some exceptional advantages. First, the site is ideal for a hotel. It is within easy walking distance of downtown Seattle's retail and entertainment districts and the Washington State Convention and Trade Center, and within a two-block radius of 12 million square feet of office space. It is also in a four-block business improvement district where property owners pay for extra security and cleanup. Second, the building was built before enactment of an ordinance limiting height for that part of downtown to 85 feet. At 240 feet, the existing building offers open views of downtown and Puget Sound. The prevailing zoning allowed the new hotel use and permitted G&B to take advantage of the height bonus by reusing (but not adding to) the existing structure. Don Barbieri, G&B's president, says that reusing the existing building shortened the public approval process and construction so much that the company was able to open the hotel a full three years earlier than if it had constructed a new building elsewhere.

A third advantage of adapting the older bank building to a hotel was the existing building's suitability for the new use. The structure occupies an entire block and is massed so that the upper 15 floors sit atop a wider base formed by the first five floors. The large lower floors have been converted to a mix of uses: 23,000 square feet of shops and restaurants, 25,000 square feet of offices, and a 23,000-square-foot banquet and corporate meeting space. The smaller floorplates on the upper floors were conducive to an efficient configuration of larger-than-average hotel rooms around the windowed perimeter, with the elevator banks and cleaning and storage space in the center. While the building's well-maintained exterior required minimal renovation, the interior floors were essentially gutted to make way for construction of the new guest rooms, offices, and retail space.

The bank's existing building systems were well suited to the needs of the new hotel. While new air terminals were needed to control individual guest rooms, the entire central HVAC system was reused. The elevator cabs were remodeled and upgraded to comply with requirements of the Americans with Disabilities Act, new plumbing risers and domestic hot water generators were installed to serve the residential occupancy, and new fire sprinkler and high-rise alarm systems were installed. The emergency generator system had to be replaced to handle the building's updated life safety demands, but the original electrical distribution system had more than enough capacity to handle the hotel loads. Parking in a two-level underground garage yields an above-average hotel parking ratio.

Funding for the renovation of Cavanaugh's Inn was a combination of debt financing from a pension fund and the developer's equity. G&B has just completed another mixed-use reuse project in downtown Spokane that used bank financing.

Barbieri says that the total cost of acquiring the bank building and converting it to Cavanaugh's Inn is probably comparable to constructing a new hotel. But the value of the location, density bonus, and three-year time savings—advantages realized only by reusing the existing building—is beyond measure.▼

physical potential to a willing market. The following paragraphs discuss some of the issues related to various categories of obsolete surplus real estate.

Office Buildings

In the late 1980s and early 1990s, overbuilding, a weak economy, and a soft real estate market allowed tenants in older Class B office buildings to move to newer Class A space for lease rates comparable to what they had been paying in older buildings. These market factors, compounded by rapidly advancing standards for communication and information technology in office environments, the changing nature of work and the workplace, and modifications in building codes and safety requirements, have left many Class B buildings unable to meet the needs of current office tenants.

Although some functionally obsolete but structurally sound office buildings in good locations can be repositioned to compete successfully with newer, high-tech buildings, the high cost of upgrading many of these older properties, even in an improving market, cannot be justified by the expected new rent levels.

It is difficult to estimate the amount of Class B office space that has slipped or is in danger of slipping into obsolescence, and no reliable estimate of Class C space exists. SIOR (Society of Industrial and Office Realtors)/Landauer statistics show that at the end of 1994, 1.1 billion square feet of Class B office space, representing 35.6 percent of the total office inventory, was available in the United States. The vacancy rate for Class B space in central business districts was 21 percent, compared with 14 percent for Class A buildings in the same locations.[1]

Schlitz Park, a thriving 1.5 million-square-foot, 40-acre office park near downtown Milwaukee, is the modern reincarnation of a 110-year-old Schlitz brewery complex. Nine of 13 existing buildings have been converted to multitenant office and some warehouse use. These before and after photos show the new home of Blue Cross & Blue Shield United of Wisconsin. The Brewery Works, the project developer/owner, took a phased, low-risk approach to redevelopment. When a building was identified for conversion, it was cleared of any remaining equipment, cleaned up, and renovated just enough so that prospective tenants could see the potential for office space. Once a tenant was secured, long-term leases allowed the renovation to be completed according to the tenant's needs. Sources of financing for the $87 million project included industrial revenue bonds, conventional first mortgages, tax increment financing, and the developer's equity.

Even under the most optimistic scenario for office demand for the remainder of the decade, the market potential for the current glut of underused office buildings, especially in urban business districts, appears to be limited. It does not suggest that the demand for office space will be stagnant in the future. In fact, according to projections by the U.S. Bureau of Labor Statistics in November 1993, the service-producing sector, comprising mostly office-based jobs, is expected to capture 91 percent of the total increase in jobs over the period from 1992 to 2005. Employment in managerial, professional, technical, and administrative support occupations is projected to increase by roughly 14.6 million jobs, or 30 percent, from 1992 to 2005, accounting for about 55 percent of the total increase in jobs.

Despite continuing corporate consolidations and downsizing, the bulk of the office market is expected to continue to be Class A space for the foreseeable future. Much speculation exists about the impact that current trends, such as telecommuting and "hoteling," will have on the overall size of the office market, but such departures from the traditional corporate workplace will almost certainly affect the configuration and location of office space.

Morris Architects

Industrial Properties

After rising steadily for five years, the industrial market vacancy rate declined for the second year in a row in 1994 to 8.4 percent, down from 10.2 percent in 1993. Like the office real estate market, the industrial market is closely connected with national economic cycles. Yet a surplus of 876 million square feet of vacant industrial space still exists in the United States.[2] Even though production is expanding, many older industrial properties cannot be upgraded to accommodate modern manufacturing operations, because many of them do not meet

Proving that a successful new use can be one that is radically different from a building's original use, Facilities Development Group of Houston converted a massive cold storage warehouse (above) into one of the nation's largest jail facilities (right) for Harris County, Texas. The addition of four new levels to the six-story building increased its size from 350,000 to 620,000 square feet. The 4,000-bed jail was redeveloped for a cost of $20,000 per bed (a total cost of $85 million), less than half the national average. The large floorplates of the warehouse proved to be cost-effective by accommodating more beds per floor than other options, thereby reducing operating costs.

Morris Architects

Figure 1-3. Great Mall of the Bay Area

Milpitas, California

Hawkeye Aerial Photography

An aerial view of the former 2 million-square-foot Ford auto assembly plant. Five hundred thousand square feet of the original facility was demolished to achieve adequate parking for a 1.5 million-square-foot shopping mall.

Ford Motor Land Development Corporation and retail developer Petrie Deirman Kughn (PDK) joined forces to convert a dormant Ford Motor Company assembly plant into a retail outlet mall. At 1.3 million square feet of retail space, the Great Mall of the Bay Area in Milpitas, a suburb of San Jose, is one of the largest reuses of a major industrial facility in the United States.

After turning out automobiles and trucks for nearly 30 years, the 2.1 million-square-foot assembly plant was idled in 1983 and since then had served as a painful reminder of lost employment within the community. In 1992, after remediating the effects of PCBs, asbestos, and soil and water contamination, Ford Land began evaluating development options for the 150-acre property. The company determined that little chance existed of finding an alternative manufacturing use of comparable size. Office, R&D, and warehouse uses were ruled out because of substantial vacancy levels prevailing in

the market area; conventional regional shopping centers were already well represented. Multifamily housing was rejected because of the enormous size of the parcel and the proximity of existing rail lines.

Retail developer PDK approached Ford Land about the possibility of re-

developing the abandoned factory into an outlet mall. In late 1992, Ford Motor Company's board of directors approved Ford Land's 75 percent partnership with PDK to convert the plant into a retail mall. The project's pro forma cash flows and return on equity competed favorably with other alternatives for capital investment within Ford.

The project team sought to retain as much of the 2.1 million square feet of existing building space as possible while developing appropriately sized retail spaces and well-balanced parking areas. To reach this objective, over 500,000 square feet of space had to be demolished before new construction could begin. Still, 1.6 million square feet of the original structure (approximately three-quarters) was retained. In addition, the project team salvaged 12,000 tons of steel, tin, and copper and recycled over 75,000 cubic yards of asphalt and concrete for reuse in paving the mall parking lot.

Another major challenge was meeting an extremely tight construction schedule (completion within 15 months of demolition) so that retail tenants could be open for the holiday shopping season. This constraint was further exacerbated by the need to incorporate substantial seismic upgrading

New store space being constructed within the existing structure.

Figure 1-3 *(continued).*

into the construction schedule. Through proactive involvement from the entire project team and an aggressive approach to problem solving, the project was completed on time in September 1994.

Because lenders were unwilling to provide nonrecourse loans for the project, Ford Land financed it internally. The city of Milpitas agreed to reimburse the developers for $7 million of off-site improvements through a funding mechanism in which the developer receives 50 percent of the incremental sales tax generated by the mall each year until costs are fully amortized.

Appropriately enough, the mall's theme is travel, developed in four main entry courts heralding the glory days of different modes of transportation: automobiles, ships, trains, and planes. The mall is configured in an oval "race-track" layout, all on one level. About half the leasable retail tenant space is designed to accommodate large value-oriented anchor tenants; the other half is targeted for smaller off-price stores and outlets. The mall attracts people

The Great Autos Court, one of four entrance courts to the Great Mall of the Bay Area.

from a wide area, not only to its stores but also to its restaurants, food court, and entertainment facilities.

One and one-half years after opening, the project is approximately 70 percent leased. After losing some smaller tenants to a downturn in the retail mar-

ket during the mall's first year of operation, Ford Land is gradually changing the tenant mix to include more upscale fashion tenants, such as Off Saks Fifth Avenue Outlet, a 25,000-square-foot anchor store.▼

---

the physical requirements of larger equipment or the infrastructure capabilities for flexible customized production. Thus, like office buildings, much of the currently vacant industrial space is functionally obsolete.

Some manufacturing facilities have been abandoned for the same reason that textile mills built in New England during the last century were abandoned: new technologies forced them into obsolescence. In recent years, corporate America has been getting back to its core businesses and divesting non–value added business lines. In the process, corporations have declared a record number of underutilized manufacturing plants, distribution centers, and other industrial facilities surplus. On most corporate balance sheets, these unneeded properties are high-value assets and as such cannot be disposed of lightly.[3] Faced with surplus

industrial assets they cannot use and cannot easily dispose of, businesses are increasingly finding creative ways to generate income from these properties through adaptive use.

Military Base Closures

The realignment and closure of military bases, which began in 1988, has contributed a wide variety of surplus buildings available for adaptive use. Already more than 100 facilities have been closed around the country, and dozens of other operations are slated to be curtailed or closed in the next several years. Because the actual release of the facilities is often 18 months or longer after being designated for disposition and a lengthy land planning process is involved, the long-term effect of base closings on the real estate market is yet to be felt.[4]

Some closed or soon-to-be-closed bases are in prime metropolitan locations offering access to transportation facilities, high-quality infrastructure, workers of all skill levels, and educational institutions. To date, dozens of former bases have been redeveloped, usually as industrial parks or research, educational, or aviation facilities. The Charlestown Navy Yard in Boston, for example, closed in the mid-1970s, now supports over 2 million square feet of research and office development, as well as hospitality, residential, and recreational uses.

Future real estate opportunities look especially attractive in the San Francisco Bay Area. Since 1993, nine military bases have closed or are scheduled for closure; all are in the process of planning and marketing their reuse. These facilities—which range from a few hundred acres to nearly 5,500 acres—represent large tracts of developable land in one of the most sought-after real estate markets in the world. Three bases scheduled for closing before 1997—Alameda Naval Air Station, Mare Island Naval Shipyard, and Treasure Island—are located on islands in San Francisco Bay and offer spectacular views of the bay, the city of San Francisco, and surrounding costal mountains.[5] All of the bases offer a wide variety of old and new structures, including numerous special-purpose facilities.

Experts assembled at a recent panel, "Successful Base Reuse Concepts," sponsored by E&Y Kenneth Leventhal Real Estate Group and *Real Estate Forum* magazine believe that with the continued growth of the U.S. economy, companies will increasingly take advantage of

Presidio of San Francisco, formerly the Presidio Army Base, encompasses 1,500 acres between the Golden Gate Bridge and San Francisco. The National Park Service is presently leasing over 400 historic commercial and residential buildings to tenants and developers who will rehabilitate and manage the properties.

the "opportunity" space becoming available as a result of closing military bases. "Banks are back in the lending business, real estate is a desired asset, and the Navy, Army, and Air Force are learning to deal with base reuse better than they did when they had one or two coming on at a time," says Michael Evans, national director of E&Y Kenneth Leventhal. "The convergence of those factors will accelerate the process and the transfer of closed facilities to the private sector."

The panelists discussed a number of financing options that are coming into play for base redevelopment. Tax increment financing, for example, is being used successfully across the

The Tides Foundation and Equity Community Builders, Inc., a San Francisco developer, formed a joint venture to convert this complex of 73,000 square feet of medical space in the historic Letterman Hospital at the Presidio to offices and public exhibition space. The renovation qualified for rehabilitation tax credits.

Figure 1-4. Truman Annex

Key West, Florida

The historic gate and entrance to Truman Annex.

Originally an old industrial building, The Foundry was redeveloped into a three-story, 26-unit condominium complex.

Harbor Place, a luxury apartment complex, combines the adaptive use of an existing naval administration building with new construction.

The Truman Annex is a private, market-driven redevelopment of a surplus military installation into a mixed-use community. The 43-acre former strategic naval station is located at the western end of Key West, Florida, adjacent to the city's historic downtown and commercial district. After some false starts and financial shortfalls, largely the result of the recession of the early 1990s, the redeveloped Truman Annex is close to completion, comprising 60,000 square feet of commercial space, 525 residential units, 244 hotel rooms, and 22,000 square feet of museum space.

After acquiring the property through a General Services Administration auction in the mid-1980s, the project's principal developer, Pritam Singh, faced many of the formidable challenges and obstacles commonly encountered by private developers pursuing the redevelopment of military bases, including environmental contamination and remediation, the need to replace obsolete or noncompliant infrastructure, extensive and unpredictable entitlements, a national economic recession, and intensive community involvement.

Singh purchased the surplus naval station in 1986 for $17 million with financing secured through a Florida savings and loan. The developer then spent the next 18 months obtaining the necessary regulatory approvals to redevelop the property, a task made extremely complex as a result of the state's "development of regional impact" (DRI) legislation requiring review and coordination from several agencies, amendment of the city's future land use map, master plan approval, and amendment of the city's planned redevelopment district.

The developer, who was responsible for all environmental cleanup, was in fact one of the first private developers to successfully negotiate with the U.S. Department of Defense to receive financial reimbursement for the environmental cleanup of a former military installation. Surprisingly, the extent of contamination was fairly limited, considering the industrial activities that once took place on the site. Cadmium, lead, chromium, PCBs, and asbestos required remediation at a cost of approximately $1.5 million.

Given the project's considerable size, Singh divided the property, by use, into 12 distinct parcels and financed each parcel individually. Unfortunately, the initiation of the redevelopment project coincided with a severe downturn in local residential sales triggered by the national economic recession, forcing the primary lender to take control of the project. By using equity capital raised from several third-party investors, however, Singh was able to buy back the project's residential component. Truman Annex's commercial waterfront district was sold to Ocean Properties, which is completing construction of a hotel, timeshare units, marina, and streetfront retail shops.

While a majority of the project's development involved new construction, a significant component involved adaptive use. Several of the former naval station's existing structures, both historic (the property has over 15 structures that are listed on the National Register of Historic Places) and nonhistoric buildings, have been converted into residential, retail, office, and museum uses. For example, Harbor Place, a 64-unit multifamily complex, combines both old and new. The residential complex comprises the redeveloped naval administration building and a newly developed residential structure. The developer also redeveloped two three-story buildings originally used for industrial purposes into The Foundry, a 26-unit condominium complex.▼

Mare Island Naval Shipyard, a 5,400-acre base located on the northern reaches of the San Francisco Bay, was scheduled to be transferred to the city of Vallejo, California, in spring 1996. The plan for reusing the property, which was adopted in 1994, targets residential, retail, industrial, and educational uses. Many of Mare Island's 960 existing buildings, such as those in the shipyard industrial complex, the Marine barracks, and the historic building used by the Navy for offices and blueprinting, have the potential to be adapted for civilian use.

Treasure Island Naval Station (aerial view), a 403-acre artificial island in the middle of San Francisco Bay, is slated to be closed in 1997 and turned over to the Redevelopment Agency of San Francisco. The installation, a self-contained small town, includes 903 apartment units, a large theater, a conference center, and a small boat marina. A plan for reuse of the island, to be developed by the private sector, is being formulated. Interim leases include approximately 60,000 square feet of hangar space, which has been leased to two film production companies and converted for use as set construction facilities and sound stages (below).

Bay Area Economics

Bay Area Economics

country for the costs of demolition, environmental cleanup, and infrastructure associated with the redevelopment of military bases. States might also be willing to provide some financing for military base reuse if the new use is perceived as salable and something that will further economic development. Some Californians are interested in developing a cohesive state policy on economic development that could benefit locally initiated base redevelopment programs. David De Roos, deputy director of the California Redevelopment Association and publisher of *Base Reuse Report,* says he looks forward to something that involves a state infrastructure bank or participation in a national infrastructure bank.[6] The federal Department of Defense has agreed to lend

money against future revenue streams on a case-by-case basis. Residential uses also offer financing options. According to James Meadows, executive director of the redevelopment authority overseeing the conversion of Lowry Air Force Base in Denver, 500 housing units of an existing 800 units at Lowry have been leased, creating an income stream of about $2 million, which was used as the basis for funding a $34 million revenue bond issue.

While closed military bases present enormous opportunities for local economies and for the real estate community, the process of redevelopment is time-consuming and full of uncertainties. Many base conversions share common obstacles, including costly environmental cleanup and the need to improve infrastructure. Base redevelopment must be cultivated through a collaborative effort of the many community and private interests at stake. Successful redevelopment requires an upfront realistic assessment of the strengths and liabilities of the community and the base itself, broad community agreement as to what the goals of the redevelopment are, thorough market feasibility analyses, and the use of master planning and zoning to achieve those goals. Notwithstanding the formidable challenges encountered in the redevelopment of military bases, the history of base redevelopment to date and the number and location of future closures suggest a great many more opportunities for adaptive use development in the coming decades.

Effective Initiatives for Adaptive Use

Most major cities in the nation have experienced a multitude of economic and social problems resulting from the steady exodus of businesses and residents to the suburbs over the last two decades. The economic recession and real estate depression of the late 1980s and early 1990s added further downward pressure to already eroding tax bases in the urban core. Now that we are well into the second half of the 1990s, a decade shaped by economic change and uncertainty, the increasing presence of Class B and C office buildings and other functionally obsolete commercial facilities in many U.S. cities continues to sap the economic vitality from many central business districts (CBDs).

Most municipal governments today recognize that rehabilitation and reuse of existing properties by the private sector is the key to the economic revitalization of urban centers. But given the economic and political realities of the day—less federal funding for urban revitalization and more demands on already strained budgets—direct subsidization by state and local governments for redevelopment of underused commercial buildings is limited. Roundtable participants, however, are encouraged by increasingly proactive and collaborative public, quasi-public, private, and nonprofit efforts taking place to stimulate urban economic development and revitalization.

Public Support of Adaptive Use

Recognizing the effect of a downward spiral that clusters of underused and vacant commercial buildings represent for urban centers, local governments have been stepping up to the plate with incentives designed to encourage the private sector to renovate them for viable new uses and thereby stimulate the rejuvenation of CBDs. Unlike the cash subsidies of the past, many newer incentives involve removing institutional obstacles that serve as disincentives to private redevelopment and offering tax abatements and other reductions in cost to enhance financial feasibility. Such incentives include changes in zoning ordinances and building codes that remove some of the risks and

costs of renovating older buildings, zoning variances, flexible application of building code requirements, property tax abatements, assistance in financing, environmental cleanup, and improvement of the infrastructure. Some recent municipal actions have helped pave the way for market-driven adaptive use:

▼ The Lower Manhattan Economic Revitalization Plan, Mayor Rudolph Giuliani's package of incentives aimed at making commercial space (mostly office) in lower Manhattan more competitive with Midtown and promoting the conversion of functionally obsolete commercial buildings into housing, was signed into law in October 1995 (see Figure 1-5).

To make buildings in lower Manhattan more attractive to tenants currently outside the one-square-mile area, new commercial tenants can take advantage of tax abatements and energy cost savings, effectively lowering their rent. A twofold program of tax benefits and zoning changes is designed to encourage the private sector to convert commercial buildings to residential and mixed uses (primarily apartments on the upper floors of buildings and retail and office space on the ground floor). Tax benefits for adaptive use include a 14-year phased tax abatement for conversion of office properties to residential use and a 12-year phased tax abatement for mixed-use conversions and commercial renovations. Zoning changes serving to enhance the economic feasibility of converting buildings to housing include reduced minimum average floor area per dwelling unit, which enables greater density; home offices in apartment units, with up to three employees allowed per unit; and the provision for more parking.

The Lower Manhattan plan was actively supported by a private interest—the Alliance for Downtown New York, a business improvement district (BID) formed in early 1995 to foster economic revitalization in lower Manhattan. It seeks to improve the lighting, safety, sanitation, transportation, marketing, and image of the area. Improvements managed by the BID are financed through a tax assessment of property owners

Figure 1-5. Solving the Empty Building Syndrome in Lower Manhattan

Tenants, brokers, and owners of real estate became aware in late 1992 that the commercial office space market in lower Manhattan faced serious structural problems. Unlike downturns during the previous three decades, downtown office space had become technologically, locationally, and financially obsolete.

In 1992, no solution was in sight, and office vacancies in the Wall Street district continued to climb. Today, Mayor Rudolph Giuliani's administration, with the support of the Alliance for Downtown New York, is trying to spur economic revitalization in lower Manhattan with the conversion of prewar office buildings to housing, incentives for commercial tenants, and tourism. For adaptive use of these buildings to become a reality, though, developers will need to be creative in both design and financing.

What Is Empty Building Syndrome?

Empty Building Syndrome describes buildings that no longer accommodate the needs of the tenants for which they were designed. Many buildings in lower Manhattan are technologically obsolete. Floor-to-floor heights are not adequate for commercial banks or trading firms, and antiquated electric wiring and plumbing are costly to replace. Toilets must be upgraded to meet the requirements of the Americans with Disabilities Act. A lack of column-free space to accommodate trading operations and inadequate heating, air-conditioning, and ventilation systems are extremely costly to fix. For these reasons, it is estimated that lenders have foreclosed on at least 45 buildings, all over 100,000 square feet, in lower Manhattan during the past five years. And any owners who are willing and able to invest the capital required to reposition these prewar and early-post-war office buildings face a declining office market.

Unlike Midtown, which saw substantial net growth in 1994, downtown's net absorption was a negative 300,000 square feet.

City Incentives

After several years of decline, the situation in lower Manhattan may be turning around. Through passage of the Lower Manhattan Economic Revitalization Plan in October 1995 and actions taken by the Alliance for Downtown New York, a solid foundation has been laid to encourage the conversion of downtown commercial buildings to residential uses.

The Lower Manhattan plan is a comprehensive package of tax abatements and exemptions, energy savings, and zoning changes aimed at making commercial space downtown more competitive and encouraging the reuse of obsolete commercial buildings for housing. Although to date no conversions of substantial size (over 100,000 square feet) have been completed, up to two dozen projects are either under construction or planned.

The Alliance for Downtown New York, a business improvement district (BID) formed in 1995, has been instrumental in improving the perception of downtown as a revitalized center for shopping and tourism. The BID is actively supporting the mayor's plan to stimulate the production of new housing units through the reuse of obsolete office buildings.

America's Third Largest CBD

Lower Manhattan, the traditional financial and insurance district of New York City, is surrounded by water on three sides and bounded by Chambers Street to the north. Some of the country's most well-attended tourist attractions are within one square mile. With 93 million square feet of privately owned office space, the area constitutes the nation's third largest

CBD (behind Midtown New York and Chicago's Loop). Today, the overall office vacancy rate in downtown New York is above 22 percent, and the vacancy rate for Class B and C space is over 30 percent, perhaps higher. Almost 40 percent of the vacant office space downtown is in pre–World War II buildings. Corporate real estate directors and senior managers responsible for making decisions about real estate confirm that Class B and C office space cannot even be rented at a cost that would cover taxes and operating expenses. Banking and trading companies typically occupy only Class A space for their front-line operations and locate back-office operations in lower-cost areas throughout the metropolitan area. Thus, most of these secondary downtown properties will never again serve as corporate office buildings.

The Adaptive Use Strategy

The challenge to property owners in the downtown district is to create desirable space by reinventing the use of these buildings. Market demand clearly points to residential use as the highest and best opportunity for conversion of lower Manhattan's obsolete office buildings.

Demand for rental units in New York City is as strong today as it has ever been during the past 20 years. The vacancy rate for market-rate rental units in Manhattan is 1 percent, closer to 0.4 percent on the desirable Upper East and Upper West Sides. The downtown residential market, principally in Battery Park City, is also close to being fully occupied. Half of the inhabitants who live downtown, work there.

Approximately 1,500 units were expected to be built in New York City in 1995, with a similar number expected in 1996. Considering that about 8,000 new households are expected to be created during the two-year period from 1996 through 1997,

Figure 1-5 *(continued).*

with 75 percent of these households renting apartments in New York City, this rate of housing production is extremely low.

With infrastructure in place and discounted values, lower Manhattan's outmoded office buildings can be converted to affordable, nontraditional residential space cheaper than current standard new construction. Pricing could realistically be 15 to 20 percent less than comparable space in Battery Park City, for example. Collateral businesses and attractions can be planned simultaneously with apartment developments. Naturally, for these projects to become reality, the rates of return must be compelling. Starrett Corporation targets 12 to 15 percent cash-on-cash returns for the first stabilized year of residential operation. As the demand for housing in the downtown neighborhood grows, the opportunity to convert rental apartments to condominium ownership could become extremely profitable.

Obsolete office skyscrapers like these prewar buildings typify the Empty Building Syndrome in lower Manhattan. The Lower Manhattan Economic Revitalization Plan includes tax incentives and zoning changes aimed at encouraging the conversion of commercial buildings to residential use.

The Challenges

Commercial office buildings in lower Manhattan, often built between 1890 and 1933, are difficult for developers and investors to evaluate. Adaptive use projects in other cities are likely to present similar challenges for developers. The challenges typically fall into four categories: predicting demand, financing, design, and construction.

Predicting Demand. Quantifying future demand for apartments from rehabilitated office buildings can stump even the most experienced broker. Although demand is strong and construction of market-rate units is predicted to be slow in the coming years, a significant degree of market risk is involved. A major setback on Wall Street, for example, could hurt new conversion projects, as a significant component of the target market for rental units is young investment bankers.

Financing. The ability to finance speculative construction in New York City, like most other parts of the country, is extremely difficult. A variety of creative financing methods, however, could be applicable to downtown projects, one of which is the issuance of tax-exempt bonds. Even so, it is likely that any adaptive use project in the district will require a large amount of equity to move forward.

Unlike urban redevelopment programs of the past, the city and state will make no outright cash investments in projects. The city is clearly committed to the process of adaptive use; however, the financing of projects and the purchase of real property is the private sector's domain. The city and state governments have provided incentives for redevelopment. It is now up to the development community to use these programs creatively.

Design. Predicting the proper distribution of apartment types and sizes is never easy, but converting Wall Street skyscrapers to housing is especially difficult. Although architects can create wonderfully interesting two-, three-, and four-bedroom apartments within the large floorplates of these buildings, it might not be the proper mix for the market. A key design challenge of converting Wall Street office towers is to increase the ratio of usable space by making productive use of the interior space near the building's core.

The creativity and problem-solving abilities of architects and engineers are also put to the test by the challenge of designing appealing and economically feasible apartments within the shells of prewar "cathedrals of commerce." Many of these buildings have the advantage of smaller floor-

Figure 1-5 (continued).

plates, large, operable windows, high ceilings, elegant lobbies, and good views. The apartments and lofts created within former downtown office buildings, both large and small, can become a new type of urban residence that combines living and working space.

Construction. Estimating the cost of converting an existing building to a new use is many times more difficult than estimating the cost of new construction. To evaluate the financial feasibility of a potential project, the development team must thoroughly understand all of the building's components. A great deal of collaboration and creative problem solving is required from the project architect, engineer, and construction estimator to determine the best type of mechanical systems for the building. Starrett Corporation attempts to derive as much value as possible from a building's existing systems. Typically, the heating, cooling, and ventilating systems are

the most costly components of the project. Replacing windows is often a major cost, but in some instances, operable, double-pane, energy-efficient commercial windows can be adapted to residential use, saving substantial cost. The cost of removing asbestos and lead-based paint is also significant and should be carefully estimated; Starrett, for example, has found concrete slabs containing asbestos in a project.

Conclusion

The very strong market for rental apartments and the weak commercial office market suggest adaptive use and mixed-use residential conversion projects could be the right solution to lower Manhattan's Empty Building Syndrome. The business improvement district and incentives in the Lower Manhattan plan have helped spark interest in adaptive use, but the risks of converting these

office buildings to housing are formidable. Understanding market dynamics and the supply/demand equation, and assembling a team of experienced design and construction professionals are essential.

As New York and other cities begin to reuse obsolete office buildings, success will depend on the ability of creative developers to analyze vast amounts of information and make informed judgments regarding conversion. But the rewards could be well worth the effort.▼

Source: Eric Michael Anton. In 1993, Anton organized a conference entitled "Solving the Empty Building Syndrome of Lower Manhattan." That conference helped stimulate debate about the future of downtown as a mixed-use district. He is now putting these ideas into practice as an employee of Starrett Corporation, one of New York City's oldest and largest firms engaged in developing, building, and managing multifamily properties.

---

in the district. The alliance is trying to boost activity downtown through increasing tourism, attracting more retailers, and creating a larger after-hours population and new tax dollars through the conversion of commercial buildings to housing. The alliance is also promoting the extension of commuter rail lines into the downtown district.

Public incentives and efforts made by the alliance and other organizations interested in revitalizing lower Manhattan are having a positive effect. As of mid-1996, the redevelopment of approximately ten commercial buildings of varying sizes to residential use has been initiated by private developers, and negotiations and planning for another dozen conversions have begun. The combination of a tight citywide residential market, low prices for empty downtown office buildings, and the city's financial incentives can make the economics

of converting lower Manhattan buildings attractive. Some developers say they can produce stylish lofts and apartments at prices at least 20 percent lower than in more established neighborhoods uptown.[7] The alliance estimates that 1,200 to 1,500 converted residential units will be completed by the end of 1997. The BID has set a target of 5,000 residential unit conversions, to be completed at the rate of about 1,000 per year.

▼ Bellevue, Washington, has revised the measure that determines whether improvements made to a building will trigger the need to bring the building and site into compliance with codes for new construction. Presently, if the value of the improvements exceeds the building's *replacement value*, it is considered new construction, which allows for considerably more renovation and reuse than the previous measure of *assessed value*, which is often low for older properties.

▼ Baltimore, Maryland, will donate certain properties that it owns to developers willing to rehabilitate and convert the properties to new uses. The city has given away several surplus school buildings to be converted into housing.

▼ Seattle has added new language in its building code that gives building officials more discretion in interpreting the requirements of building codes. Building officials are now specifically authorized to modify code requirements for individual cases that they determine to be impractical.

Most local building codes regulate the design of existing and new buildings based on a building's use. When a change of use is proposed, the definitions distinguishing renovations from new construction can sometimes require reuse projects to conform to site and building standards for new construction that can be so costly that they make an otherwise feasible project uneconomical. Many local building codes do include provisions that allow flexibility in the application of regulations for renovation of existing structures, although some jurisdictions have not used the provisions ex-

Two conversions of large-scale office buildings to residential uses are in progress in lower Manhattan and expected to be completed in mid-1997. Rockrose Development Corporation is redeveloping 45 Wall Street (left), a 28-floor building built in 1961, into 440 rental apartments. Units at 45 Wall Street will have polished oak floors, large thermopane windows, contemporary kitchens and baths, a high-tech security surveillance system, and an on-site garage. Crescent Heights Investments is converting 25 Broad Street (above), a 21-floor building built in 1896 known as the Broad-Exchange Building, into 345 rental units. The apartments at 25 Broad Street will range in size from 1,032 to 1,500 square feet; half will be one-bedroom units, the rest two- and three-bedroom units. The lowest ceilings are ten feet, and five floors have 15-foot ceilings. All units will have large, double-hung windows.

tensively. Chapter 32 of the Philadelphia Building Code, for example, provides for such flexibility. Entitled "Existing Structures," the chapter describes a scoring system to rate a building's performance related to height, area, fire resistance, exiting requirements, and fire protection systems. "Safety scores" are applied to a series of life safety features, such as sprinklers and maximum distances between fire exits. This scoring system allows buildings to achieve a "passing grade" by addressing some but not all areas of noncompliance with the code, thereby making development significantly less expensive while still ensuring the safety of commercial buildings. But even though Philadelphia's evaluation and scoring provision has been in place for several years, it has rarely been used, perhaps because of architects' and engineers' lack of awareness, an incomplete understanding of its advantages, or a lack of clarity over exactly how the Department of Licenses and Inspections would interpret the system.[8]

In the absence of specific language in the building code that allows for flexibility in the requirements for renovation of existing buildings (or the unwillingness to apply what is already on the books), local authorities often find something on which to base less restrictive interpretations if the project is considered beneficial for the city.

The city of Boston's flexibility in interpreting zoning and building code requirements for Emerson College's conversion of the Little Building, a 200,000-square-foot medical office building built in 1917, into college dormitories contributed to the project's economic feasibility. The city allowed Emerson to extend exist-

Many older commercial buildings in downtown Philadelphia have wooden rooftop water tanks that can be used today for fire protection. Rooftop tanks can supplant the need for a fire pump, saving a significant amount, especially for smaller buildings.

Old-fashioned standpipes can become part of new fire protection systems in older, smaller commercial buildings adapted to housing. Pressure from Philadelphia's water mains is sufficient to pump water up several stories.

Structures built in the early 1900s often have wood floors and ceilings. Covering these combustible structural elements with drywall can be an inexpensive way to improve the building's "safety score."

22

The adaptive use renovation of the Exchange Building, a 1925 office building, into apartments was made possible, in part, by flexible interpretation of building codes.

The Exchange Building's original steel trusses and concrete ceiling were left exposed in this tenth-floor apartment unit.

ing but incomplete winder stairs (common in older buildings but prohibited in new buildings) as one of two required egress stairs in the building. The Boston Redevelopment Authority, the city's planning agency, supported Emerson's plan as a project that would add much-needed activity and vitality to a neglected section of midtown Boston and helped push the project through the approval process.

Flexible code inspectors and creative financing and design made the conversion of the Builders' Exchange Building, a 1920s ten-story office building in downtown San Antonio, Texas, possible. To meet stringent fire code requirements, the converted Exchange Building is now fully sprinklered with a central fire alarm system, but the city approved the existing exterior fire escape and relatively narrow fire stairs. When the developers showed that a hospital gurney would fit in elevators deemed too small by contemporary building codes, the city also approved the elevators.[9]

Roundtable participants agreed that, although local regulatory agencies are increasingly willing to interpret zoning and building codes less restrictively for certain reuse projects, the pro-

cess still deters development if prospective project sponsors expect the process to be arbitrary. To facilitate adaptive use development, local regulatory authorities at a minimum should standardize the application of building code requirements. And to significantly affect private investment, municipalities can adopt code provisions (or apply already existing provisions) that enable flexible application of regulations.

Proactive Private Initiatives

Among the most effective efforts to spur urban economic development and revitalization are those being carried out by private nonprofit organizations that combine public and private resources to promote community development. Some organizations are primarily concerned with providing affordable housing in deteriorated inner-city neighborhoods; others are more generally focused on promoting economic development and revitalization in their downtown areas. One strategy common to most all civic and business organizations that strive to revitalize center cities is to mobilize

Alcott Place, before being rescued and converted to 44 one-bedroom apartments for low-income seniors, was a run-down 44,000-square-foot school building in a deteriorating Baltimore neighborhood. The developer purchased the building from the city for a nominal fee and was able to use low-income housing tax credits and the federal rehabilitation tax credit to help finance the project.

community assistance of all kinds to cultivate private sector redevelopment of obsolete buildings for productive new uses. Often the most valuable role of such organizations is to act as an intermediary among private developers, investors, local businesses, building owners, lenders, local regulatory agencies, and other interests that play a part in redevelopment.

Nationally, nonprofit housing and community development organizations like Local Initiatives Support Corporation and the Enterprise Foundation provide a wide range of financial and technical assistance to hundreds of local community development corporations (CDCs) whose purpose is to provide affordable housing and economic development to deteriorated neighborhoods. Such organizations are responsible for tens of thousands of renovations of existing buildings. Private developers often form joint ventures with CDCs for individual projects and are able to take advantage of the myriad forms of assistance they offer.

Locally, business improvement districts, funded by assessments from property owners

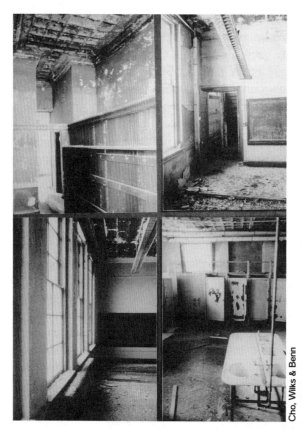

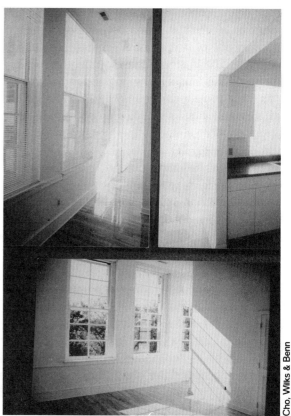

The interior of the vacated school building (left) was gutted to create new apartment units at Alcott Place (right). Access for the handicapped, security, and energy conservation were top priorities in the renovation.

Community involvement was the key to visualizing and ultimately realizing the reuse potential for a seven-building hospital complex in Chicago's West Side. When St. Anne's Hospital closed its doors in the mid-1980s (top left), Bethel New Life, a community development corporation that had been fighting the inner-city neighborhood's spiral of decline, realized that if left to rot, the full block of empty buildings would devastate the already blighted area. In 1989, after raising funds for partial collateral, Bethel was able to obtain a conventional mortgage to purchase the hospital property for $3.2 million. As funds became available from various public and private sources, approximately 335,000 square feet (80 percent) of the former hospital facilities, renamed the Beth-Anne Life Center (middle left), has been redeveloped for such community-empowering uses as a small business center and training facility, 125 residential units for seniors (created from the main hospital unit), an office building for professionals with branch bank and drugstore, a performing arts center (housed in the former hospital chapel), and administrative offices for nonprofit health care and family service organizations. Bethel plans to convert the remaining space in the main hospital building into a 78,000-square-foot regional primary health center.

When the hospital chapel was turned into a cultural and performing arts facility, Bethel New Life took pains to preserve interior features that reflect its early prairie school–style architecture.

One of the former hospital buildings now houses a small business center that provides assistance and incubator space for community economic development.

Figure 1-6. Historic King Place

Milwaukee, Wisconsin

Conversion of the old Homer Savings Bank and adjacent office building to the multiple-use Historic King Place served as an anchor and catalyst for further redevelopment and economic revitalization of the surrounding Third Street neighborhood.

Designers paid particular attention to the durability and energy efficiency of finish materials, resulting in an attractive living environment at affordable prices in an improving central city neighborhood.

A newly constructed storefront benefits ground-floor commercial tenants of Historic King Place.

Historic King Place is notable not just for the physical rehabilitation and reuse of two architecturally and historically significant commercial buildings, but also as a model public/private partnership for improving a blighted central city neighborhood. The former Homer Savings Bank building, a five-story structure originally constructed in 1930, and the adjacent four-story Dorsen office building were renovated into 41 units of affordable housing with commercial space on the first floors. The redevelopment of these vacant buildings has galvanized Milwaukee's Third Street historic district for economic revitalization by bringing residents, retailers, and business activities back into the area.

Over half of the $4 million project's financing came from investors who used a variety of low-income housing tax credits and historic rehabilitation tax credits in exchange for equity contributions. Viewing the conversion of Historic King Place to housing as the first step in redeveloping the surrounding district, a host of local utility companies and private foundations contributed funds to help finance the project. The city of Milwaukee, also highly supportive of the project, created a tax increment financing district to provide additional incentives to attract new businesses and retailers to the area, which also benefited Historic King Place. Based on the availability of equity financing and the positive operating cash flows in the project's pro forma, First Wisconsin National Bank provided a $1.2 million first mortgage.▼

A number of measures incorporated into the architectural design of Historic King Place enhance tenants' security—keyed, secured elevators, door buzzers, security cameras, and wide corridors.

within their downtown boundaries to supplement municipal services, and business-backed economic development and civic organizations concerned with improving the economic vitality of their center cities are opening up new opportunities for adaptive use through their downtown redevelopment initiatives.

The Downtown Denver Partnership, Inc., for example, demonstrates how effectively business leadership organizations can bring about interest in urban redevelopment. Established 40 years ago, the Downtown Denver Partnership is a nonprofit business organization, funded mostly through memberships and grants, that unites businesses, civic organizations, and governments to improve downtown Denver's viability as a regional center for employment, entertainment, and living.

Among the partnership's many services and programs is the Center City Housing Support Office (HSO), created with the goal of adding 10,000 residents to downtown Denver in ten years. Downtown already has a residential base of 9,000 people, and 60,000 people live within two miles of the CBD. The HSO's housing development strategy is market-driven and project-oriented to encourage the development of housing of mixed types and prices.

In 1993, the HSO identified 35 vacant or nearly vacant commercial buildings in downtown Denver that it believed could be economically converted to housing. To attract private investment, the HSO established itself as a "one-stop shop" for developers. The organization vigorously marketed the buildings to prospective developers and acted as a liaison among developers, building owners, lenders, public agencies, neighborhood organizations, and other interest groups. The HSO directly assisted developers in obtaining acquisition and construction financing, including finding any public financial assistance for which a project might be eligible, and provided technical assistance, such as conducting market and feasibility studies for specific projects. Today, 17 of the buildings have been converted to rental or for-sale housing or are undergoing renovation. Given the accelerating momentum of demand for urban living, the HSO believes it is only a matter of time until the remaining vacant buildings will be converted to productive new housing.

Center City District

Center City District

Philadelphia's Center City District has undertaken a demonstration program to stimulate the reuse of these and other underutilized older commercial buildings to meet a strong demand for downtown housing.

Another innovative private initiative to encourage the conversion of underused downtown commercial buildings to housing is being spearheaded by Philadelphia's Center City District (CCD), an assessment-funded business improvement district whose downtown boundaries cover an 80-block area.[10] In addition to its focus on cleaning and security, CCD looks for new opportunities to enhance downtown Philadelphia's potential as a place to live, work, and visit.

One of CCD's most recent efforts has been to lay the groundwork for owners and investors to rehabilitate underused, outdated yet structurally sound, commercial buildings scattered throughout the downtown area for new residential uses. These early 20th century buildings are typically five to eight stories high and have long, narrow footprints. In recent years, the ground floors of these buildings have often been used for retail purposes, sometimes quite successfully, but the upper floors are almost always vacant. CCD has concluded that the obsolete configurations of the upper floors cannot be economically adapted to modern office space, even if demand for office space were strong, which it is not. The demand for housing in the Center City area is strong, however, and rehabilitated older buildings have proven market acceptance. CCD believes the physical configuration of the upper floors of the older commercial buildings could be adapted to meet the demand for housing.

CCD recently received a grant from The Pew Charitable Trusts to jump-start the rejuvenation of the downtown area east of Broad Street through a demonstration program designed to encourage owners to convert the upper floors of selected commercial buildings to rental apartments. CCD hopes that the demonstration program will serve as a model and a catalyst for the conversion of other underused buildings. Its role is not to subsidize the redevelopment but to identify any significant economic constraints that owners and investors would face, to reduce these barriers as much as possible, and to shepherd selected projects through conversion. CCD convened an advisory group comprising Center City property owners, developers, real estate professionals, and city officials experienced with adaptive use to help develop the demonstration program. A sidewalk survey was conducted to identify buildings that might be suitable for residential conversion. The initial list of two dozen potential buildings for conversion was eventually narrowed to ten properties. All of the subject building owners want to retain retail uses on the ground floors but are willing to consider making the investment to convert the upper floors to residential space if it is economically feasible to do so.

The team of consultants developed detailed architectural and code analyses for each building and concluded that all ten buildings could be made economically viable as apartment units. They analyzed one building, the Delong Building, in greater detail than the others, prepared preliminary specifications for the renovation of the building, and asked two general contractors for bids. The resulting cost estimates served as the basis for a detailed financial pro forma prepared for the building (see Figure 1-7).

The target market for the apartments includes students, young professionals, empty nesters, artists, and others willing to take some risks in location in exchange for attractive, affordable housing downtown. The project consultants believe a substantial demand exists for such units at rents of approximately $500 to $600 per month. The success of the initial conversions should pave the way for future projects to command higher rents. According to CCD, "While any number of public incentives would be strongly advisable, the aim was to make the economics work without them. The project thus has to be a 'no-frills' renovation with total development costs limited to under $45,000 per unit."[11]

CCD has identified three major barriers to the successful conversion of these buildings to apartments at reasonable costs. One impediment is the complexity of municipal codes that regulate the renovation of older buildings; wading through and understanding them is so time-consuming that the building owner generally must hire a consultant. A second barrier is the high cost of complying with certain requirements of the building code, such as requiring two exits from each unit, a particular problem in smaller buildings. The third factor constraining the economic feasibility of the conversions is the high cost of unionized construction labor

Figure 1-7. The Delong Building: An Adaptive Use Feasibility Analysis

The Delong Building is one of several turn-of-the-century commercial buildings in downtown Philadelphia whose mostly vacant upper floors could be economically converted into residential uses.

ties and using the ground floor for retail space.

Dating from 1900, the seven-story Delong Building features dark-colored brick trimmed in limestone. The projecting bay windows and wide cornices give the building a strong profile; its fire escape is one of the most distinctive in the city. The building is not protected by local historic ordinances, but it is significant to the Center City East Historic District and as such is eligible for rehabilitation tax credits.

From 1900 through the late 1970s, the Delong Building was occupied continuously with offices and street-level retailers. In 1978, the owner converted the ground-floor lobby to a small retail space, blocking the only access to the upper floors. Since then, the upper floors have remained completely vacant. Presently, the ground floor is fully occupied with retail space. One of the retail tenants occupies the elevator lobby of the building and would have to relocate to restore access to the upper floors.

The Delong Building's footprint is too long and narrow for most office use, but it would be ideal for apartments. Each 2,200-square-foot floor

would make two generous living spaces, divided by the existing stair core. The apartments would be flooded with natural light from the bay windows, which offer views of Chestnut and 13th Streets. The strong image of the building facade, the corner location, and the loft-like interiors could easily be made attractive to prospective tenants.

Despite standing empty for decades, the Delong Building's shell is in relatively solid condition. It is constructed of masonry walls with wood and steel floor framing in good condition. The wood window frames need some repair, and a water leak has damaged the plaster and flooring on the top level.

Typical of structures left vacant for any length of time, conversion to apartments will require a significant amount of interior work, including removal and replacement of existing partitions, dropped ceilings, and damaged plaster. Only the mechanical, electrical, and plumbing systems serving the ground floor can remain in place; new electrical service, wiring, plumbing, and heating units are required for the other floors. The existing standpipes are in good condition and should remain, although the standpipe system would not

The Delong Building occupies a corner lot at 13th and Chestnut Streets in Center City Philadelphia in what was once the heart of the city's office and financial district. Starting in the 1950s, office tenants began leaving the area for new office buildings being built in the northwest quadrant of downtown Philadelphia. The older area began a long period of decline, until 30 to 40 percent of the office space is currently vacant. Many architecturally prominent but deteriorated buildings in the old commercial district are vacant, and some owners are hanging on, maintaining their proper-

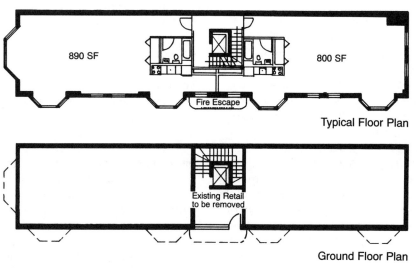

890 SF   800 SF

Fire Escape

Typical Floor Plan

Existing Retail to be removed

Ground Floor Plan

Floor plans for the proposed new use.

Figure 1-7 (continued).

Estimate of Probable Construction Costs

General Conditions	$ 34,550
Exterior Allowance	21,500
Demolition	38,600
Millwork and Carpentry	35,490
Doors, Frames, and Hardware	10,400
Glass and Glazing	0
Gypsum Wallboard	56,600
Flooring	21,500
Painting	19,900
Appliances and Equipment	12,210
Window Treatment	0
Specialties	2,200
Elevator	60,000
HVAC (included in electrical)	0
Sprinklers	0
Plumbing	57,500
Electrical	45,100
Subtotal	$415,550
Add Overhead and Profit (5 percent)	20,780
Total (without sprinklers)	$436,330
Add Sprinklers	69,000
Total (with sprinklers)	$505,330

Construction Cost per Unit

Without Sprinklers	$36,360
With Sprinklers	$42,110

be considered a true sprinkler system under the city's building codes. The elevator car and hoistway can be reused, but they require a new motor, control panel, and wiring to be operational. A larger accessible elevator car would not be mandated by the current city regulations, because the building is under 12,500 net square feet. Presently, the building owner may legally use only the ground floor of the building. To reopen the upper floors, the Department of Licenses and Inspections would have to evaluate the building before an occupancy permit could be issued.

The Philadelphia Building Code includes a provision that allows a flexible application of regulations for adaptive use. "Safety scores" are applied to a series of life safety features, allowing a building to achieve a passing grade by addressing some but not all of the areas of noncompliance with the code. The Delong Building has a relatively high negative safety score because of its interior wood construction, open exit stairs, and lack of fire protection systems. These problems can be corrected in two ways:

▼ Without sprinklers, the building can achieve a passing score through repair of the existing fire escape as a second exit, addition of drywall to protect the exposed wood and steel structure on all floors, and provision of fire-resistant walls, egress lighting, and a new detector and alarm system throughout the building.
▼ With sprinklers, drywall ceilings would not be required for street-level spaces, and the existing manual-pull fire alarm system could be reused.

An estimate of probable construction costs compares the renovation costs for conversion, both with and without sprinklers. The table shows the tradeoff between providing a sprinkler system and the installation of additional drywall and fire alarm equipment. A new sprinkler system would increase the construction cost per unit 16 percent, from $36,360 to $42,110 per unit. The additional cost of $6.60 per square foot is more than twice as high as normal because of the inefficiencies of providing a fire pump, diesel power source, and a hookup to the city's water main for such a small structure. Clearly, converting the Delong Building to apartments by providing additional drywall and no sprinklers results in significant savings in construction costs.

Project Budget

Hard Costs

Acquisition	0
Construction (without sprinklers)	$436,330
Contingency at 5 Percent	21,815
Subtotal	$458,145

Soft Costs

Architecture	$28,720
Legal	8,000
Financing Fees	9,600
Construction Interest	10,000
Insurance during Construction	3,000
Development Supervision	10,000
Subtotal	$69,320

Total Project Cost (without sprinklers)	$527,465
Total Cost per Unit (without sprinklers)	$43,955

The pro forma for the Delong Building (on facing page) is based on the following assumptions:

▼ There is no cost of acquisition. The existing owner rehabilitates the building with technical assistance from the development consulting team.
▼ The rehabilitation includes no frills.
▼ All pro forma income is net of current retail income.
▼ All pro forma expenses are net of current expenses.
▼ Conventional financing is available at 9 percent.
▼ The rental occupancy rate is similar to that in the neighborhood.
▼ Six one-bedroom lofts rent for $550 per month.
▼ Six two-bedroom lofts rent for $650 per month.▼

Source: Center City District, *Turning On the Lights Upstairs: A Guide for Converting the Upper Floors of Older Commercial Buildings to Residential Use* (Philadelphia: Author, 1996).

Figure 1-7 *(continued).*

Delong Building Pro Forma[1]

	1996	1997	1998	1999	2000	2001	
Revenue							
Residential Rent	$86,400	$89,856	$93,450	$98,123	$102,048	$106,130	
Minus 8 Percent Vacancy	−6,912	−7,188	−7,476	−7,850	−8,164	−8,490	
	$79,488	$82,668	$85,974	$90,273	$93,884	$97,639	
Application Fees	240	120	120	120	120	120	
Interest	500	500	500	500	500	500	
Laundry	1,200	1,200	1,200	1,200	1,200	1,200	
Total Revenue	$81,428	$84,488	$87,794	$92,093	$95,704	$99,459	
Expenses							
Repairs	$ 2,000	$ 2,080	$ 2,163	$ 2,250	$ 2,340	$ 2,433	
Maintenance	4,300	4,472	4,651	4,837	5,030	5,232	
Supplies	1,000	1,040	1,082	1,125	1,170	1,217	
Insurance	3,000	3,120	3,245	3,375	3,510	3,650	
Management at 6 Percent	4,886	5,069	5,268	5,526	5,742	5,968	
Cleaning	2,400	2,496	2,596	2,700	2,808	2,920	
Electricity	2,000	2,080	2,163	2,250	2,340	2,433	
Water/Sewer	2,000	2,080	2,163	2,250	2,340	2,433	
Trash Removal	2,400	2,496	2,596	2,700	2,808	2,920	
Legal and Accounting	1,000	1,040	1,082	1,125	1,170	1,217	
Real Estate Taxes	–	–	–	4,000	4,160	4,326	
Local Business Taxes	262	272	283	295	307	319	
Licenses and Permits	400	416	433	450	468	487	
Miscellaneous	1,000	1,040	1,082	1,125	1,170	1,217	
Advertising	1,000	1,040	1,082	1,125	1,170	1,217	
Total Expenses	$27,648	$28,742	$29,887	$35,130	$36,531	$37,987	
Cash Flow before Debt	$53,780	$55,746	$ 57,907	$56,963	$59,173	$61,472	$345,042
Less Interest on $527,465 at 9 Percent	−47,470	−47,470	−47,470	−47,470	−47,470	−47,467	−284,817
Net Cash Flow	$ 6,311	$ 8,276	$10,438	$ 9,494	$11,704	$14,002	$ 60,225

[1]The applicable inflation rate for rental revenues and expenses is 4 percent.
Note: Columns might not add because of rounding.

in the area. These constraints would likely be insurmountable to many building owners acting independently, especially those with no experience in real estate development—enter CCD. CCD, on their behalf, has initiated discussions with the Department of Licenses and Inspections, the agency that administers and enforces Philadelphia's zoning, building, and fire codes, and the Philadelphia Build-

ing and Construction Trades Council to seek mutually beneficial, cost-effective compromises. CCD also created a guide book, *Turning On the Lights Upstairs: A Guide for Converting the Upper Floors of Older Commercial Buildings to Residential Use,* for owners and developers interested in converting older commercial buildings to residential use. The publication presents a concise, practical overview of the regulations that govern existing buildings and a number of recommendations for economically adapting the upper floors of older commercial buildings for housing. The publication also includes suggestions directed to the city's review agencies regarding flexible interpretation and application of existing codes, accessibility guidelines, and preservation policies that could significantly reduce renovation costs without compromising the city's objectives.

In an era when growth means finding new ways to make more with less, both public and private interests are beginning to recognize that some of their institutional inflexibility is counterproductive to their own objectives. CCD believes the city, the unions, the building owners, and the Center City business and residential community all have a great deal to gain from the conversion of underutilized buildings to apartments and that acceptable compromises and solutions will be found. In fact, as of the publication of this book:

▼ The Department of Licenses and Inspections has expressed its willingness, for the buildings in the demonstration program, to apply the provision for flexible interpretations regarding renovations that is on the books but rarely used. Doing so opens up a major opportunity for the cost-effective redevelopment of these structures.
▼ The Philadelphia Building and Construction Trades Council has agreed to hold down renovation costs for the buildings in the demonstration program.
▼ A local bank is committed to supporting reinvestment in Center City's older buildings.

The Chicago Department of Planning and Development, the agency that oversees the city's economic and physical development, including efforts to redevelop historical and landmark structures, is also preparing a publication it hopes will encourage the reuse of obsolete buildings blighting many of the city's streets. The project was made possible through a grant from the National Endowment for the Arts and assistance from the Illinois Historic Preservation Agency. The publication, *Making a Store a Home: Converting Storefronts to Housing,* will be an illustrated guide for converting older storefront buildings into housing. The publication looks at who benefits from con-

verting stores to housing; who lives in such housing; the advantages and disadvantages of converting different building types; and key issues, such as meeting zoning and building codes, ensuring energy efficiency, and creating privacy and security. It also includes case studies with floor plans, facades, and cost summaries.[12]

Baltimore Heritage, Inc., a nonprofit, membership-based preservation and urban revitalization advocacy group in Baltimore, Maryland, is also taking a proactive approach to facilitate the reuse of urban buildings. The organization is raising private funds to analyze the extent of functional obsolescence of Class B office space in downtown Baltimore and to formulate strategies for matching the physical potential of the buildings with the local market. Like CBDs across the country, downtown Baltimore experienced an oversupply of new office buildings in the late 1980s and early 1990s. Rents in Class A office buildings declined to Class B levels, enabling tenants to leave Class B buildings for Class A space. Rents in Class B space downtown are now so depressed and vacancy rates so high that most buildings are worth little more than the land they are built on. Very little opportunity exists to reposition these office buildings, because the income from the upgraded office space, even if the buildings could command Class A rents, could not provide an adequate return on the costs to redevelop the properties.

The purpose of Baltimore Heritage's analysis is threefold: 1) to create a thorough inventory by building size of Class B office space in downtown Baltimore; 2) to quantify potential sources of demand for the space; and 3) to identify specific strategies for matching the supply to the demand. The study will also make recommendations for public policies that would encourage private redevelopment.[13]

Suburban Revitalization

Increasingly, the first generation of suburbs in this country, those mature jurisdictions on the fringes of cities, has begun to experience some of the same problems that larger cities are all too familiar with: aging and inadequate infrastructure, deficient educational systems, high crime rates, and deteriorated residential

Figure 1-8. River Village at Liberty Park

Birmingham, Alabama

Torchmark Development Corporation purchased a dilapidated, abandoned 40,000-square-foot strip shopping center outside Birmingham, Alabama, with preliminary plans to resurrect the facility as a retail center. The existing structure and its location at the front door of a residential community of 300 dwellings suggested that retail space was the most appropriate use for the center. A detailed market analysis indicated, however, that the location could not yet sustain the project as a shopping center. Instead, the site's scenic setting overlooking the Cahaba River, easy access to a major interstate highway, and Birmingham's growing economy pointed to office space.

With its own funds, Torchmark proceeded to convert the structure to an office and limited retail center, known as River Village at Liberty Park. The long one-story building was gutted, leaving the steel structural systems intact. A second story was added to a portion of the building, allowing nine-foot finished ceilings on both floors and increasing the net rental area by 20,000 square feet. A 4,200-square-foot restaurant, the River Market and Deli, occupies the end of the building nearest the street; the balance of the project is office space.

Once an inescapable eyesore and security threat for the neighboring housing community, River Village is now a thriving complex of small professional offices. The restaurant serves the office tenants during the day and the residential community in the evening. As evidence of the project's economic viability, River Village is appraised at $6.9 million, compared to the total redevelopment cost (including tenant improvements) of $4.2 million. Based on 1994 net operating income, the project yielded a 12 percent return on investment.▼

Bud Hunter 1995

Bud Hunter 1995

A defunct suburban shopping center (top) has been converted to office space and a restaurant (bottom).

33

and commercial corridors. Because they are often densely populated and no longer have that "next piece of land" on which to expand and grow, close-in suburbs—like their inner-city neighbors—must look to revitalization of their older corridors.

The suburbs were by no means immune from the tax- and easy capital–driven commercial overbuilding of the 1980s and the subsequent real estate crash experienced in large CBDs, but empty buildings pose somewhat different problems in suburban locations than in cities. Historically, suburban development has been shaped by the practice of single-use zoning, which designates certain areas for exclusive uses. The suburban landscape is characterized by separate residential communities, office and industrial parks, shopping malls, and commercial zones located along major

thoroughfares. Single-use zoning was intended to protect suburban lifestyles and land values, but ironically entire business parks stand half vacant with buildings whose only permitted use has limited market potential. Although the office and retail markets continue to be strongest in the suburbs, less desirable suburban office buildings and obsolete big-box retail centers face the same fierce competition in attracting new demand as CBDs. The cost of rezoning such properties often precludes cost-effective adaptive use.

Resistance to change and fear of the consequences of mixed-use zoning among public officials, lending institutions, landlords, potential tenants, and neighbors are still prevalent, although these attitudes may be changing. Roundtable participants noted that increasingly sophisticated public officials are starting

One of 20 apartments converted from surplus municipal office space.

The Fairfax County Redevelopment and Housing Authority turned surplus space in its own suburban office building into single-room-occupancy units for transitional housing. The office entrance (above) is separate from the entrance to the residences (top right).

to recognize the problems that inevitably result from segregating land uses and are questioning the conventional wisdom of suburban zoning. Searching for ways to rejuvenate declining suburban business corridors, some municipal authorities are exploring ways to introduce concepts of mixed-use planning into established suburban settings.

The Fairfax County Redevelopment and Housing Authority (FCRHA) exemplifies a new willingness by some local governments to rethink traditional planning concepts. The authority's primary role is to administer public housing and redevelopment programs in Fairfax County, a northern Virginia suburban jurisdiction outside Washington, D.C. FCRHA, whose mission also includes the revitalization of the county's older residential and commercial areas, believes many underused office buildings have strong physical and market potential to be converted to mixed-use facilities, but the agency admits that it will take time to overcome political and legal obstacles.

When FCRHA needed additional office space a few years ago, it found a vacant 55,000-square-foot office building in a distressed office park that it had purchased from the Resolution Trust Corporation at about 50 percent of its appraised value. The building had more space than FCRHA required for its own needs, so the agency began thinking about how the surplus space could be used for affordable housing and also serve as a model for mixed-use adaptive use. Thus was created a new concept called the Working Singles Program. Twenty single-room-occupancy units were fitted into the ground floor of the commercially zoned building. Designed for occupancy by one adult, an apartment can be rented for successive two-week periods. John Payne, senior design and construction manager for FCRHA, says the program's success has opened many eyes in the Fairfax County government regarding the potential for reusing surplus office buildings built during the boom of the 1980s. Payne says reusing office buildings for housing has several advantages: significantly lower site development costs than new construction; adequate existing parking; and, in many cases, proximity to transportation and employment centers. As for the regulatory requirements, even the staff of FCRHA, a county agency, had to wind its way through the zoning process and overcome initial skepticism from the neighborhood. Had the Working Singles Program not been granted a special zoning exception as a motel use, the project would have required rezoning and probably could not have been implemented.

Astute Players

Adaptive use development is initiated by owners and developers, by space users, asset management firms, public agencies, and corporate real estate departments, among others. All of these interests face the same pressures from their customers, lenders, shareholders, boards of directors, and taxpayers to run leaner and more efficient operations.

In the past, corporations tended to view their real estate costs as fixed, despite their being the second largest cost after wages on the corporate books. Today, they are focused on reducing their real estate occupancy costs and using space more efficiently. Businesses and institutions can no longer afford to retain surplus assets and marginally productive facilities. Corporate America has realized the substantial impact that more productive use of real estate can have on the bottom line and is aggressively looking to increase the economic benefits from its use of facilities. As businesses take a more strategic approach to real estate, more companies are scrutinizing a range of options, including nontraditional alternatives like adaptive use, for the most economic way to meet their own space needs and when dealing with surplus real estate assets. Enterprising developers, asset managers, and other real estate practitioners might find opportunities to match a building with a tenant by proposing potential options for adaptive use, even to those who are not actively looking to reuse an existing building.

If the circumstances are right, reusing an existing building can satisfy a user's locational, timing, program, or financial needs better than new construction. The financial feasibility of adaptive use for such an organization can sometimes be greater than for a real estate developer, because the user controls the revenue side of the feasibility equation. The "tenants"

Figure 1-9. Kennedy Biscuit Lofts

Cambridge, Massachusetts

The F.A. Kennedy Steam Bakery (left), once one of New England's busiest bakeries, has been transformed into the Kennedy Biscuit Lofts (right), a mixed-income housing community.

Originally known as the F.A. Kennedy Steam Bakery, this five-story brick factory in Cambridge, Massachusetts, was constructed in 1875 by Frank A. Kennedy to manufacture his family's biscuit products, including the renowned Fig Newton. The company was eventually sold to Nabisco, and the building continued to function as a bakery until 1952. MIT purchased the building in 1978 as part of its effort to assemble approximately 27 acres of land adjacent to the university for fu-

An unsightly loading dock was removed from the center courtyard to create. . .

. . .a handsome front entry to the Kennedy Biscuit Lofts apartment building.

ture development and leased the biscuit factory to a series of manufacturing users until the late 1980s.

Forest City Enterprises subsequently leased the entire 27-acre parcel from MIT to develop it as a mixed-use commercial R&D park, now known as University Park. In 1989, Forest City Enterprises formed a joint venture with Keen Development Corporation to transform the historic mill-style building into mixed-income housing, a certain amount of which is required by the master plan for University Park. After seven months of renovation, Kennedy Biscuit Lofts opened in early 1990 with 142 units of one- and two-bedroom apartments, three-bedroom townhouse duplexes, 28 live/work artist lofts, and a daycare center. Of the 142 units, 25 percent are reserved for low-income residents, 20 percent for moderate-income residents, and the remaining 55 percent for market-rate occupancy.

The building shell was completely restored. All proposed alterations to the former bakery, a certified historic structure, had to be approved by local, state, and federal historic commissions. The development team took care to incorporate historic elements of the building into the construction of living spaces, including integration of the original brick baking ovens into the design for the first-floor corridor and the adjacent apartments. A loading dock was removed from the cen-

ter courtyard to create the front entry. All exterior brickwork was cleaned and repaired to restore its original integrity, and the original oversized windows, which were in total disrepair, were replaced. A previously blank wall on the east side of the building was fenestrated in a manner complementary to the mill-style construction.

The conversion of the Kennedy Biscuit Lofts to housing was made possible by a combination of public and private funding sources, including tax-exempt bonds issued by the Massachusetts Housing Finance Agency, funds secured under Massachusetts's SHARP (State Housing Assistance for Rental Production) program designed to increase the number of affordable rental units, and the syndication of rehabilitation tax credits.▼

No two apartments at the Kennedy Biscuit Lofts are exactly alike. Designers restored and left exposed many of the original interior features, such as the old baking ovens and overhead beams, incorporating a glimpse of the building's history into the new living spaces.

are already part of the user's audience and their creditworthiness known.

Leahy Clinic typifies the aggressive approach that many non–real estate development companies are taking to get more economic benefits from their real estate assets. In 1992, Leahy Clinic, a group of physicians providing primary and secondary care in the Boston area, decided to open an ambulatory specialty care satellite facility that could draw specialty referrals to its hospital outside Boston. Leahy looked at a range of options for a 40,000-square-foot facility, including new construction and renovating an existing hospital building. An unexpected opportunity presented itself with the availability of a 150,000-square-foot, early-1970s-vintage bank headquarters building on nine acres of land in Boston's North Shore area. Although much larger than Leahy was looking for, the solidly built structure was extremely well suited for the proposed new clinic's needs: it had ample parking, flexible floorplates, and an extraordinary mechanical system, including a boiler, chiller, and generator, that could be renovated and reused.

After exploring the market, Leahy decided it could sustain its venture by leasing the surplus space in the bank building to health care and other related tenants. At about the same time Leahy acquired the bank building and hired Taylor & Partners to manage the conversion, the organization submitted a successful bid to acquire J.B. Thomas Hospital, a small municipal hospital in dire financial straits in a nearby town. After closing on the hospital, Leahy reformulated a comprehensive business plan for its health care operations that would take full advantage of its two new facilities. Eventually, Leahy transferred emergency and in-patient surgery services from J.B. Thomas Hospital to Leahy Clinic North, the converted bank building, using all 150,000 square feet of the facility for Leahy's patient programs. This efficient health care facility is now a model satellite operation. The cost of $162 per square foot to convert the bank building (all internally financed), including acquisition and construction costs, compares favorably to the approximately $200 per square foot to construct a similar facility from the ground up. In addition to cost savings, Taylor & Partners estimates that the conversion shaved ten months off the other

Converting a 1970s bank headquarters building into the Leahy Clinic North, a 150,000-square-foot health care clinic, saved the owner approximately $40.00 per square foot and ten months of construction time compared to other options considered, including a build-to-suit clinic.

The waiting room at the Leahy Clinic.

options considered—of considerable value to Leahy because the programs transferred from the hospital to the clinic were operating at a loss.

Price Enterprises, Inc., owner and operator of the Price Club warehouse stores, was also able to take advantage of excess space when it converted a 1950s-era warehouse and office facility owned by AT&T in Arlington, Virginia, to a Price Club store (see the Pentagon Centre case study in Part 2). Reusing the AT&T facility had several advantages over other potential development or redevelopment sites from which Price could serve Washington, D.C., and the affluent neighboring suburbs of northern Virginia. First, the site is in a prime retail area accessible by car and public transportation.

An existing subway stop on the site was one of the advantages of turning a vacant 320,000-square-foot AT&T warehouse and office building (left) into this retail power center (right). Because of a zoning variance pertaining to the existing building, reusing the structure enabled the owner/developer/user to realize its goal of quickly entering this prime retail market.

Second, because of a zoning variance that applied to the existing structure, reusing the building would eliminate a lengthy public approval process and enable Price to achieve its primary objective of entering the market as quickly as possible. Third, the facility was relatively inexpensive to acquire.

The only apparent negative factor in the deal was that the 320,000-square-foot industrial building was more than twice the space needed for the Price Club store. Ultimately, Price decided to take advantage of the economic potential of the remaining space by developing and managing an interior power center that now includes four big-box retailers and four restaurants.

Growth of Startup Companies

Because reusing existing buildings is often less expensive than conventional new construction, adaptive use can have a significant price advantage over newer competitive products. One price-sensitive market segment—one that roundtable participants believe represents a significant unmet demand for leasable office and laboratory space in adapted buildings—is high-tech startup companies. These small ventures typically need lower-cost efficient office and research and development space, and they often want to be located near major medical centers or universities, or in high-tech corridors. The difficulty in delivering existing space adapted for this market is the result more of

a lack of capital for this type of redevelopment than a shortage of demand or suitable buildings in the right locations. Project sponsors often have difficulty in securing conventional financing for adaptive use projects that target smaller startup tenants, even with lease commitments in hand, because the prospective tenants have a high risk of failure and lack established credit histories.

Roundtable participants discussed several speculative adaptive use projects initiated by building owners or developers that were all or mostly privately financed because of the high-risk nature of the tenants. Some of the projects were initiated by building owners who funded the redevelopment from internal resources; some were the result of innovative financing schemes. In most cases, project sponsors were willing to take a calculated risk to finance the improvements, expecting to receive a return over and above profit from real estate development.

BioLease, Inc., an affiliate of the Raymond Company, a Boston-based real estate developer, developed such a project in Boston's Charlestown Navy Yard that was as much a financing transaction as it was a traditional real estate development. Health Care Ventures, a venture capital group that holds a majority interest in some 44 startup biotech companies nationwide, asked BioLease to build (and provide financing for) facilities as needed for those companies in the Boston/Cambridge area. The first of these facilities was for BioTransplant, Inc., a biotech research company founded to

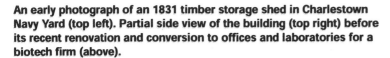

An early photograph of an 1831 timber storage shed in Charlestown Navy Yard (top left). Partial side view of the building (top right) before its recent renovation and conversion to offices and laboratories for a biotech firm (above).

As the only remaining example of four sheds originally built to store timber used to make spars, masts, and wooden components for Navy vessels, the building is a historic structure. As such, the developer was required to restore 40 original wood doors, each 14 feet high and set in pairs between stone piers on each side of the shed. As shown above, the building was literally taken apart and put back together again.

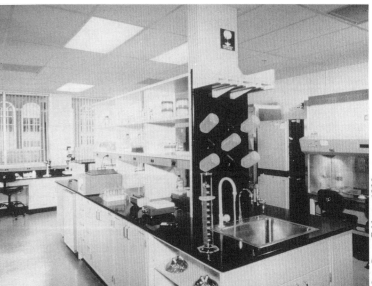

New office and lab space inside the former timber shed.

Originally an automobile assembly plant located on the Charles River, 640 Memorial's 40,000-square-foot floorplates and ornate facade, and Boston's growing biotech market created an exceptional opportunity for the owner to redevelop it for multi-tenant laboratory and office space.

supplement research being conducted at Massachusetts General's research facility. BioLease had previously developed Mass General's 650,000-square-foot research facility in the Navy Yard. Because BioTransplant's founder wanted to be near Mass General's research facility, site selection was not difficult. BioLease was able to obtain a long-term lease from the Boston Redevelopment Authority on a site across the street from the Navy Yard research facility. The site had an 1831 timber storage building that BioLease planned to convert to a state-of-the-art biotech laboratory and office.

The Boston Redevelopment Authority openly supported the project by expediting permits and approvals. Finding financial support was another story, however. BioTransplant is a privately held company that is not in the traditional sense "bankable." The company's primary research (developing drugs to combat the body's rejection of organ transplants) is sponsored by Health Care Ventures, with the expectation that BioTransplant will ultimately develop patentable drugs.

Although BioTransplant does occasionally receive research fees from pharmaceutical companies, the company might have only one month's operating capital in the bank at any one time. It is not surprising that BioLease had to raise a large amount of equity capital to redevelop the old timber storage facility. The developer's decision to become involved in this high-risk project was based in large part on its confidence in Health Care Ventures's ability to select companies engaged in scientific research with a high potential for com-

mercial success and its willingness to make a significant investment in the future of these companies.

BioLease eventually obtained a construction loan from the Bank of Boston (not guaranteed by Health Care Ventures) for 50 percent of the construction cost. The remainder of the financing came from two venture capital funds that were not real estate investors but were sold on BioTransplant's future prospects. BioTransplant's lease payment to BioLease includes two components—return on venture capital and a lease—and is calculated as total development costs plus the developer's cost of debt and equity funds, paid back over an agreed-upon term and interest rate. BioLease also holds warrants for BioTransplant stock should the company go public. BioLease, Inc., and BioTransplant both took a leap of faith regarding the project. Although it is likely that another biotech tenant could be found for the research space, BioLease had to be confident that BioTransplant would still exist when the building was completed. And because BioTransplant's rent is a function of total building costs, it had to believe that BioLease would manage development costs wisely.

Like BioLease, the Massachusetts Institute of Technology also took a calculated risk when it funded the conversion of one of its properties into space for emerging high-tech companies and underwrote the financing for tenant improvements. MIT had owned 640 Memorial Drive (see the case study in Part 2), originally an automobile assembly plant and later used by Polaroid, since 1956. When the facility became vacant, MIT explored several new uses for the deteriorated plant, including academic-related facilities, and concluded that the building had a strong potential to generate income that could be used to leverage the construction of campus housing and classrooms.

When the project was initiated in 1992, MIT recognized that pent-up demand existed for high-quality office and R&D space for emerging bio-tech companies. Because most of the startup firms were unable to obtain conventional financing, MIT was willing to finance buildout for the tenants. That the building tenanted so quickly—92 percent before completion in 1994 —attests to the fact that bio- and high-tech companies were not able to find less expensive, comparable space. Nevertheless, MIT hedged its bets by designing flexibility into the facility's layout so that it can be converted to alternative uses if the need ever arises.

Advantages and Challenges of Adaptive Use

The case studies and catalog of recent adaptive use projects presented in Parts 2 and 3 indicate the great variety of situations in which owners, users, and developers have chosen to reuse existing buildings for new purposes. Although each adaptive use project has a distinct set of structural, market, and financing variables that will determine whether the project sponsor's objectives are met, reworking an existing building can offer some advantages over developing the same type of product from the ground up. By the same token, working with an existing building presents risks and challenges that do not arise with new development.

The Advantage of Timing

Reusing an existing building can expedite the predevelopment process and enable a project to open in a significantly shorter period of time than new development. This factor is vitally important to many project sponsors; in fact, roundtable participants cited beneficial timing as one of the most influential factors in the decision to initiate a project. If a proposed new

A badly deteriorated 30,000-square-foot early 1900s factory/warehouse building in Baltimore's evolving Inner Harbor was transformed into 45 market-rate apartments for the elderly. The low acquisition price and a tight budget allowed the developer to keep rental rates low.

In addition to providing safety and comfort, designers made an effort to create a stimulating environment inside and out. Once an unneeded storage building (middle) was demolished, a community garden was created, using the existing structure as a trellis to frame outdoor activities (bottom).

use for an existing building conforms to the prevailing zoning, as was the case for Price Enterprises's Pentagon Centre project, public approval and permitting can be accomplished much more quickly and less expensively than new development without exposing the project to potential public opposition. New construction almost always involves the risk of encountering costly delays and plan modifications throughout the approval process.

Adaptive use projects also have an advantage of timing because the construction period is usually shorter than that for new construction. While tricky design and engineering is often required to fit a new use to an existing building, much of the structure and infrastructure can be reused, saving time and money. Moreover, adaptive use rarely entails excavation and new foundations, both big risks in new development.

The Trump International Hotel & Tower's luxury residential and hotel condominiums are being created from the shell of a former office tower. The developers took advantage of the existing building's favorable height and setback zoning variance.

The Advantage of Price

One of the most compelling competitive advantages of redeveloping existing buildings can be the ability to deliver a less expensive product. Although the individual nature of adaptive use makes it impossible to generalize about price differentials between reuse and new construction, cost benefits weigh heavily in the feasibility of most market-based adaptive use projects. The economic fundamentals that support many adaptive use projects can be illustrated by an oversimplified but realistic example: Option A is to buy land for $20.00 per square foot and construct a new, high-quality office building for $100 per square foot—for total development costs of $120 per square foot. Option B is to purchase a deteriorated but sound older industrial building for $40.00 per square foot and convert it to office space at an estimated $40.00 per square foot —for total redevelopment costs of $80.00 per square foot. Whereas the reuse project will probably command less rent than the new Class A building (how much less will depend on the local market and the older building's location and amenities), the savings of $40.00 per square foot still makes this development opportunity profitable, providing there is sufficient demand in the local market.

Favorable Zoning

Zoning and building code ordinances can help or hinder the feasibility of a potential adaptive use project, depending on the circumstances. Local building codes can sometimes impose expensive building standards that kill the economic feasibility of a potential adaptive use project. In other situations, local ordinances can provide a tremendous advantage for adapting an existing building rather than constructing a new one on the same site. If prevailing zoning allows a proposed new use "by right," reusing the existing building is almost always quicker and cheaper than new construction and avoids the risks inherent in obtaining public approval.

Zoning ordinances can also present opportunities, such as when an existing building has been "grandfathered" under more favorable zoning provisions. The Trump International

Figure 1-10. Blue Hen Corporate Center

Dover, Delaware

A vacant 90,000-square-foot department store at one end of an underused mall was converted into up-to-date office space as the first phase of the mall's comprehensive conversion to a corporate office center.

Phillip H. Ennis Photography

The four-month conversion gave AEtna Health Plans bright, spacious offices in a prime location. From the standpoints of cost, space, and time, the firm concluded that conversion of the vacant department store would be its best alternative in the Dover market.

The conversion of Blue Hen Mall to Blue Hen Corporate Center was driven by the changing market in the Dover, Delaware, area that resulted in excess retail space. In the 1980s, a new regional mall built approximately three miles north of Blue Hen drew most of Dover's primary retail trade, including Blue Hen's two major anchor tenants.

AEtna Health Plans, meanwhile, began looking for office space in the Dover area, which offered little Class A space. To meet its rapidly growing

Exterior architectural elements and signage such as this entrance detail create a strong corporate identity for office tenants and clearly establish the former mall as a corporate center.

operations, AEtna needed to occupy new space within six months. Blue Realty Corporation, owner/developer of Blue Hen Mall, posed a nontraditional solution to AEtna's space needs: convert one of two structurally sound but vacant anchor department stores at the underutilized mall. AEtna's evaluation of the proposal determined that the conversion would provide excellent space at a better price-for-value ratio than build-to-suit space and other alternatives. Consequently, AEtna leased 68,000 square feet of a 90,000-square-foot, one-story building, with an exclusive option to lease the remaining space for expansion.

AEtna's goals were met: the renovation took only four months, and development costs were substantially lower than for a new office building, allowing AEtna to obtain significantly better office space than other options at a more competitive rental rate. And as a bonus, AEtna's office has built-in expansion space.

AEtna's move attracted other office tenants to the mall, now known as Blue Hen Corporate Center. Blue Hen's other vacated anchor department store, totaling 80,000 square feet, was leased to NationsBank and converted to cor-

porate office space. On the retail side, Blue Realty has experienced a surge in interest from service retailers like fast-food outlets and card shops—a direct result of the influx of approximately 1,500 new office employees.

Given the vast amount of excess mall space around the country, the transformation of Blue Hen Mall into a corporate and retail center demonstrates that underused retail facilities, when viewed with a creative eye, can provide excellent, low-cost office space. Blue Realty owns approximately 30 acres of undeveloped land around the corporate center and hopes to attract other major insurance or financial service companies interested in relocating to the Dover market. (The state and county have helped by creating tax relief and training incentives for relocating companies.) Blue Realty's ultimate goal is to have a corporate campus with a strong retail component.▼

For more information about Blue Hen Corporate Center, see Scott H. Gamber, "The Metamorphosis of Blue Hen Mall," *Urban Land*, September 1995, pp. 66–67, and "Blue Hen Corporate Center," *Architectural Record*, October 1995, pp. 106–7.

The old industrial and commercial districts that can be found in most cities and towns across the country are replete with abandoned and marginally used warehouses and factories. Despite dilapidated, weather-beaten appearances, these buildings are often structurally sound and have good "bones" that, when allowed to show through, can create desirable spaces for a variety of new uses. Underneath grime and latter-day additions, many older industrial buildings have simple, boxy shapes, high ceilings, an abundance of large windows, wood columns and beams, brick walls, and concrete or wood floors, all with the patina of age that cannot be reproduced. Loft conversions like Magnolia Station in Dallas, a 1911 petroleum products distribution center converted to apartments, are highly marketable (building exterior and interior unit above). Customized, moderately priced office space, such as these offices in a former auto repair shop, can be created from small industrial buildings (right).

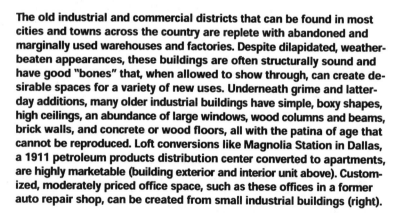

New York City's current zoning, a newly constructed building on this same site could not exceed an FAR of 15.0 and would probably be restricted to a maximum height of 29 stories. TIHT, in contrast, is equivalent to 52 stories. By reusing the office tower's steel frame and completely redeveloping the building's exterior and interior, the developers of TIHT were able to use the existing building's nonconforming height and setback standards, which would never be approved today.

The Marketing Value of Older Buildings

Older buildings can provide certain elements that most new buildings cannot afford to duplicate—high ceilings, well-proportioned layouts, old brick walls, the patina of old wood floors and metalwork—which can be used to advantage in marketing a new project. Behind the plaster walls and false ceilings of many older structures lie brick walls, wooden ceilings, and many other building materials that were considered "unfinished" in their day but now hold great appeal for many people. In reused buildings, these desirable elements are often simply left exposed, providing a double bonus: lower costs and greater marketing appeal.

Hotel & Tower (TIHT), for example, a luxury hotel and condominium building, is being recast from a functionally obsolete high-rise office tower on Manhattan's Columbus Circle (see the case study in Part 2). The former Gulf & Western Building was granted a zoning variance when it was built in 1968 that allowed a floor/area ratio (FAR) of 17.18. Under

Sometimes hidden treasures are discovered only during construction. Sterling Realty Organization made such a fortuitous discovery when it converted a 25,000-square-foot bowling alley that it had owned for decades to a Bookstop bookstore in Bellevue, Washington. The bowling alley's curved ceiling had long been covered over with low acoustical tile to dampen the noise from the bowling lanes. The development team was about to cover the low ceiling with new material when an architect suggested looking behind the tiles. The project team found the original curved cedar ceiling in beautiful condition. The team left the ceiling exposed and layered in new mechanical systems and piping painted a complementary forest green, all far less expensive than had been originally anticipated.

Albert Friedman, president of J.A. Friedman & Associates, understands the historic appeal and marketing value of older buildings. Over a 20-year period, Friedman's Chicago-based development company has acquired and rehabilitated for new uses 35 older commercial properties—small manufacturing buildings, offices, stores, hotels, rooming houses, and taverns—in a once seedy nine-block area in Chicago's River North area close to the central business district. From the beginning, Friedman's strategy has been to acquire only buildings with distinctive architectural and historical characteristics, buildings that have a place within the history of the community, and rehabilitate them for street-level retail uses and above-ground-floor office space. Each building has its own character and identity, which the company carefully accentuates in its marketing brochure. Friedman promotes the entire nine-block area, now called Courthouse District, offering prospective tenants a diverse array of office space plus an unusually large variety of restaurants and retail amenities. The district includes small brownstone buildings, larger, more formal buildings with a doorman, and buildings with particularly nice views or tight security, and every building has a retail component on the ground floor.

Effective marketing is an important part of any real estate development project, but it is even more important when the project is aimed at a selected niche. It can make the difference in prospective tenants' willingness to pay an extra 50 cents or a dollar per square foot, Friedman says, which is enough to make the economics work for some adaptive use projects. Friedman likens his niche office market to the classic car buff—someone who appreciates the car's design, workmanship, and materials and also has a certain nostalgia for the era in which the car was manufactured. Office tenants in Friedman's Courthouse District are attracted to the affordability and charm of the neighborhood and prefer the renovated older

The distinctive ambience of space adapted from older buildings also appeals to restaurants, clubs, and other retailers. Hart Brewery & Pub (top) occupies a converted 1913 brick and timber warehouse in downtown Seattle. The old but sound industrial building needed minimal structural work, exterior restoration, and environmental remediation, but extensive new interior construction was required to accommodate the new use (bottom).

Figure 1-11. The Hudson

Calgary, Alberta, Canada

The Hudson's exterior remained the same after conversion from a 1912 warehouse to loft condominiums—the first project of its kind in Calgary—in accordance with strict requirements for historic preservation.

The conversion of a 1912 warehouse to residential lofts was a bold undertaking for APEX Land Corporation. At the time the development company initiated the project, known today as The Hudson, Calgary had no history of loft condominiums. Despite the risks, APEX managed to secure private equity and debt capital to finance the $3 million development costs. The city recognized the project's potential to spur downtown revitalization and made an exceptional effort to help APEX obtain the necessary approvals, including rezoning, within a brief two-month period.

The five-story structure of solid brick exterior walls, vertical lines, and symmetrical windows was originally built for the Hudson Bay Company, and it remained well preserved over the years until its rehabilitation in 1994. From a gross building area of 42,400 square feet, APEX created 31 residential loft units of approximately 900 to 1,000 square feet, with some larger units on the top two floors. A new two-level parking garage was constructed next to the building, providing 56 parking spaces.

Soaring 11- to 15-foot ceilings, red brick walls, and exposed beams, pillars, and posts characterize the interior of the building. Red brick and sandstone window sills and headers characterize the exterior.

The building is supported by massive Douglas fir timber beams and columns. All the timber beams and columns, laminated floor joists, and brick walls were exposed by sandblasting the entire interior. The original freight elevator was kept intact and is used by residents.

To satisfy Calgary's building code requirements, three major issues had to be resolved: 1) ensuring fire separation in the timber structure; 2) minimizing the transmission of sound from floor to floor; and 3) providing adequate windows for each suite. To address fire separation, quick-release fire sprinklers were placed at each wood column, and the rear wooden stairway was upgraded to new metal stairs. Sound transmission was reduced by installing double-insulated walls between units and a staggered steel wall along both sides of the corridor, and by suspending the floors on neoprene strips, creating a floating floor system. Large windows and French doors were added to the sides and rear elevations of the building. The front street elevation could not be altered because of restrictions on historic preservation.

The risk APEX took in "pioneering" the lofts proved to be worth taking, as two-thirds of all units sold within the first four weeks of opening.▼

The open floor layout of the lofts was an untested concept in Calgary. Prospective buyers could attend space planning and interior design seminars to help them visualize and plan their own loft units. Original wood beams and columns were exposed to give a distinctive look to each unit.

buildings to more sterile conventional commercial space.

Friedman clearly has a passion for restoring "the soul of a building" and making its history come alive for its new occupants. Bringing a building back to life is a labor of love, but at the end of the day, it must also be economically feasible if it is to be one's livelihood. With each adaptive use project, tradeoffs must be carefully weighed, and some compromises are inevitable.

Aside from the architectural and historical qualities, Friedman considers a number of factors when evaluating a building's potential for reuse. Not surprisingly, low acquisition price is a prerequisite. Friedman has purchased diamonds in the rough for as low as $10,000 and $15,000, which are today fully occupied with office tenants. The building also must be structurally sound, which can be deceptive based on the appearance. From the outside, a building can look like it is about to collapse yet still have structural integrity. Conversely, owners might have kept up the building's appearances but neglected structural problems for so long that rehabilitation would be extremely costly.

Friedman also keeps his costs as low as possible by achieving economies of scale wherever possible. Many commercial buildings built during the early 1900s were relatively small—100,000 square feet or less. Taken one by one, the soft costs associated with planning, designing, and marketing the project plus construction costs can overburden a project. Friedman often groups two or more buildings to be redeveloped at one time, significantly reducing costs, especially soft costs.

Not only historically and architecturally significant buildings can be appreciated for their

Courthouse District is a nine-block area near downtown Chicago. J.A. Friedman & Associates has acquired and converted its older commercial buildings of historical significance to offices with retail space on the ground floors. The "courthouse" designation is derived from the firm's flagship property, Courthouse Place, the former Cook County Criminal Courts building (above). Friedman converted the 107,000-square-foot building to multitenant office space. Floorplates in the seven-story Courthouse Place average 14,900 square feet.

Friedman promotes the benefits of Courthouse District as a *place*—its blend of affordability, neighborhood charm, and access to public transportation—and highlights the individual history, architectural features, and amenities of each renovated office building. Prospective tenants can choose from several properties, such as the four separate buildings at 441–449 North Clark Street. All of the buildings have operable windows, manned security, tenant-controlled HVAC, available nearby surface parking, and retail space on the ground floors. These buildings house two restaurants, an interior design firm, a specialty goods store, and a dry cleaner.

To keep costs as low as possible, Friedman acquires buildings one by one but often waits to redevelop them until two or more properties can be renovated simultaneously, such as 500 and 508 North Clark Street.

distinctive characteristics. Underneath layers of grime and decay, much of the older stock of industrial facilities and commercial buildings found in most cities was built with a great deal of concern for design and building materials. When cleaned and equipped for modern uses, these buildings have a characteristic appeal for a growing number of prospective commercial and residential tenants.

Pros and Cons of Urban Livability

Despite the urban problems that continue to drive residents and commerce to the suburbs, a renewed interest in urban living and working may be surfacing. In *Emerging Trends in Real Estate: 1996,* Equitable Real Estate Investment Management, Inc., and Real Estate Research Corporation recommend "24-hour cities"—markets with strong residential fundamentals like New York, Chicago, Boston, Washington, D.C., and San Francisco—and diversified suburban markets as the best location for real estate investment. The reason, say the authors, is that after "pushing the suburban envelope to

the limit, people are determined to live a convenient distance from their jobs." Many others have also observed that suburban sprawl, traffic congestion, and unendurably long commutes to and from work have soured the suburban dream for a growing number of people. It is the proximity to work, conveniences, and amenities that are drawing a growing number of people back to the cities.

The future of cities in this country is a subject charged with complex issues and uncertainty. Whether or not it constitutes the rebirth of cities, it is likely that as larger numbers of baby boomers become empty nesters, more middle-class homeowners and renters will consider urban living. And for the foreseeable future, demand for office space in city centers, with their convenience and business advantage, will continue.

The richly diverse and flexible nature of urban environments makes them naturally conducive for adaptive use. Urban centers possess all types of low-cost, underutilized buildings; mixed-use vitality; a wide range of lifestyles, incomes, conveniences, and amenities that support the market demand for less expensive renovated older space; an extensive submarket of architects, engineers, public relations firms, and other development experts who prefer working with the ambience of older space to new construction; existing municipal infrastructure and services; proximity to mass transportation; and access to labor of every skill level.

Yet the very qualities that support adaptive use in urban settings—density, diversity, and transformation—can also constrain opportunities. Because the location of an existing building is fixed, so then are the particular risks and opportunities inherent in the local market surrounding the building. Older buildings are often in mixed-income neighborhoods, where the demand for potential new building uses is unproved. Until an area has been established by successful pioneer redevelopment, it is difficult to convince lenders and potential tenants to take the risk. Other chronic urban ills, such as crime, poor school systems, and higher taxes, are issues for all urban real estate development and can be especially high risk factors when introducing a new building use into a transitional neighborhood.

Figure 1-12. The Second & Pine

Seattle, Washington

The Second & Pine is located two blocks east of Pike Place Market in the center of Seattle's downtown business district. Formerly a seven-story office building dating from 1908, the upper six floors have been converted to 42 rental apartments with retail space on the ground floor. Before its redevelopment, the building was mostly vacant for 20 years and was generally considered an eyesore. The $1.8 million renovation and conversion to residential use would not have been economically feasible without the use of federal low-income housing tax credits. So that the project can receive the credits, one-fifth of the units lease at below-market rents to individuals or households with low incomes.

Looking for opportunities to redevelop undervalued properties on a fee basis, developer John Walker and his partner, Eric Shelter, approached owner Frederick Scheetz with a plan to convert the building to housing. Through consultation with architects and engineers, Walker confirmed that the structure was well suited for conversion to residential use because of its shallow depth, the presence of windows on all four exposures (including a south-facing light court), and solid concrete construction. Scheetz, the owner/manager of 500 residential units near downtown, was committed to downtown's future and readily agreed to proceed.

Walker's fee as a consultant was based on a percentage of total costs. The development contract specified that decisions affecting more than $15,000 required the owner's approval and provided a formula for sharing cost savings. The project was completed in June 1992.

To minimize construction costs, floor plans were kept simple, and each floor has the same configuration for efficient location of utilities. Exterior terra-cotta cladding was cleaned and restored and a new roof system installed. After a false facade built at

Steve Keating

This seven-story former office building in downtown Seattle has been converted to 42 rental apartments with retail space on the ground floor. The building attracts tenants who work downtown and some who do not but desire an urban lifestyle.

Steve Keating

Several units, such as this corner one-bedroom unit on the seventh floor, have spectacular views of Puget Sound and the Olympic Mountains to the west and the Denny Regrade to the north.

Figure 1-12 *(continued).*

The new residential lobby on Pine Street incorporates carved oak paneling salvaged from the historic Burke Building constructed in 1891 and demolished in 1966 to make way for Seattle's downtown federal office building.

street level had been removed, the existing storefronts were restored to their original appearance. The building had been overdesigned originally to permit the addition of extra stories, and few seismic upgrades were required for the conversion.

The interior floors were completely gutted, all new mechanical systems were installed, and all windows were replaced. As a result of the relocation of the existing entrance from Second Avenue to Pine Street and the extremely small size of the existing elevator shaft, it was necessary to install a new elevator. A new steel stair tower was added to satisfy fire safety codes. The big-ticket items for this project were the new windows, marble and oak paneling for the lobby, the new elevator, and the new electrical and plumbing systems.

The Second & Pine reached 95 percent occupancy within four months of opening. The project's major marketing draw is its location within walking distance of the city's business and retail core. The building has attracted tenants who work downtown and those who simply prefer an urban lifestyle.▼

Roundtable participants emphasized that the starting point for economically viable adaptive use development is to establish the availability of adequate local demand for potential new uses—not to look at the structure itself to suggest an opportunity. A fine old building does not necessarily make a good adaptive use project, no matter how well suited the structure itself might be for a particular use.

This unfortunate paradox is the heart of the problem faced by the city of Baltimore. Downtown Baltimore is full of historic but functionally obsolete buildings that have the structural and architectural potential to be converted to attractive, well-priced residential uses. But very little demand exists for housing downtown, and Baltimore is not a strong condominium market. The lack of an inner-city residential base also deters renovation of the older buildings for entertainment and retail uses that require evening business. One Baltimore residential developer searched for opportunities to convert a deeply discounted older downtown building to housing but concluded that the market demand was too thin. Eventually, he looked for opportunities outside Baltimore and found one in Howard County, a rapidly growing county between Baltimore and the Washington, D.C., metropolitan area. The

Downtown Baltimore has a number of fine old commercial buildings that could easily be adapted for elegant loft housing, but the demand for housing downtown is small. A nonprofit arts organization saved the Maryland Art Place building from further decay by converting it to gallery and performance spaces and offices.

developer converted an old schoolhouse to market-rate condominiums that sold for $115,000 to $235,000. The project has generated an attractive return, not because the acquisition or construction costs were especially low but because the market was so strong.

Structural Opportunities And Constraints

By definition, adaptive use requires converting a building to a use for which it was not designed. Most structures can be adapted to many uses; in each case, however, fitting the new use within the existing envelope requires creativity, patience, and flexibility. The first step a project sponsor should take in evaluating the feasibility of adapting an existing building to a new use is to thoroughly analyze the local market potential (see Figure 1-13). Bruce Hoch, founder and principal of Development Concepts Group, recommends identifying a few alternative new uses that could be supported by local demand and then making detailed estimates of the costs to convert the building to each potential use. The highest and best use for the building will emerge by comparing the income and cost potentials of the alternative uses. Once the developer is convinced that a potential use has economic merit, even more detailed analyses of the structure itself should be undertaken to identify the potential risks in design and construction and to fine-tune the cost and timing estimates. It is crucial that the developer commit the time and money upfront to understand the local market demand for a potential new use and the costs of fitting the proposed program to the existing building layout.

Notwithstanding this sound advice, roundtable participants also noted that in the final analysis, adaptive use is as much an art as it is a science. Adapting an existing building at a cost that is justified by its new use is not a cookie-cutter operation and requires creativity at every turn. Inventive architects and engineers experienced with older buildings can recognize and take advantage of design opportunities presented by the existing building as well as devise cost-effective solutions to structural constraints that are certain to materialize.

Paul H. Groh 1994

Eric Owen Moss Architects

The utilitarian architecture and construction materials typical of generations of American warehouse and factory buildings allow architects great freedom to create highly customized, functional work and living environments (increasingly one and the same). Architect Eric Moss took full advantage of the design opportunities presented by the conversion of a nondescript warehouse building in Culver City, California (top), to offices for the Gary Group, a public relations firm. Moss reinterpreted the industrial concrete, brick, and steel materials used in the original structure to an anything but ordinary effect. From a side view (bottom), a leaning front facade of rust-colored concrete block juts out over the flat masonry front. Inside, offices surround a marble fountain and pool. A second level of open studios was added below the vaulted ceiling, now punctuated by skylights.

Figure 1-13. Project Feasibility: Finding a New Use for an Existing Building

Like form following function, development responds to market demand. And market forces create opportunities for real estate development. The same fundamental relationship applies to adaptive use development.

Effective planning for adaptive use might be described as an inverse development plan—or trying to fill the hole in the doughnut. In conventional development, the developer analyzes the regional marketplace for general needs, selects a local submarket based on its strong market fundamentals, and only then undertakes site selection. For adaptive use, both the site and the local market are predetermined. The tough questions to be asked in this process therefore revolve around the local market. How does the overall regional market affect the local market, and how can the existing facility be modified to serve market demand?

Successful conversions can be typified as those that integrate distinctive site and building characteristics with market-based uses. Preservation efforts notwithstanding, planning for the re-use of an existing building must be no less responsive to the market today than was the original builder in his day.

An experienced developer can objectively visualize the means to bring life back to the building without being swayed by sentimental attachment or bias toward one product. In exploring the marketability of alternative uses, the developer should conduct an infallible two-step litmus test:

1. Would market opportunity warrant the construction of a new facility at the existing location if it were an empty site?
2. Can the existing facility be economically modified to accommodate market demand?

Passing grades for both parts of the examination justify further investigation of the potential, but a poor response to either question should terminate the process.

How does a developer evaluate an existing property's potential? Obviously, all adaptive use projects require individual solutions, although a common framework or methodology underlies all adaptive use feasibility analyses, regardless of the existing building type or the potential new uses. In simple terms, the process should encompass three key areas: market support and economic evaluation; site and locational considerations; and structural considerations. The following checklist for adaptive use is drawn from a composite of many feasibility analyses. It cannot be viewed as the final word but simply as a narrative description of a complex process.

Phase One: Starting Out

Recognition
▼ Look with the mind's eye.
▼ Is there something here that others have missed?
▼ Is this a jewel in the dust? Why did the current use fail?

Creativity and Experience
▼ What does gut instinct say?
▼ What preliminary uses come to mind?
▼ Avoid totally unfamiliar uses unless you can afford to take the risk.

Looking for Opportunity
▼ Location, location, location, but what is the market?
▼ Is this the right time for this project?
▼ What does the present owner need? The new users?

Ideas and Uses
▼ Start a playbook of possibilities for conversion.
▼ Are the uses achievable? Permittable? Financeable?
▼ Make a rough guess of redevelopment costs per use.
▼ Generate a "back-of-the-envelope" pro forma per use.

Proof of Potential (go or no-go evaluation of possible uses)
▼ Are there significant municipal restrictions or requirements on uses?
▼ Do revised cost estimates exceed initial pro forma objectives for uses?
▼ Does the building or site have significant environmental problems?
▼ Is there large-scale competition in the market area for the same uses?
▼ How much certainty exists about the income potential of the uses?
▼ Do pro formas rely on future appreciation for profits?
▼ Do uses require more than two years to break even?

First Intersection
▼ Eliminate red lights ("yes" to any questions under Proof of Potential).
▼ Are there enough surviving playbook candidates for further study?
▼ Decision: Go forward or walk away?

Phase Two: Gathering Momentum

Analyzing Market Demand
▼ Recognize regional market trends. Growth? Stagnation? Decline?
▼ What is the regional impact on the local market? Future projections?
▼ What are consumers' spending habits by category?
▼ What are typical rent/sale prices for playbook uses?
▼ What are absorption/vacancy characteristics per use?
▼ Where and how much competition exists for proposed uses?
▼ How would uses affect/be affected by local competition?

Locality and Neighborhood
▼ How much of a threat is crime in the local area? Projections?
▼ Are population dynamics shifting?
▼ Are economic transitions occurring in the area?
▼ What is the character of adjacent properties?

Figure 1-13 *(continued).*

▼ Would you be a pioneer in the local area? If yes, don't immediately reject it but consider the tradeoffs between taking more risks and the potential to improve the neighborhood and reap a higher return.

Transportation and Access

▼ How accessible is the site? Vehicular? Mass transit? Walking?

▼ Does heavy truck or rail service exist?

▼ What is the size and location of the nearest airport?

▼ Can the site support enough parking?

Quality and Availability of Labor

▼ What is the makeup of the local labor market? Excesses? Shortages?

▼ What are the market area's demographics? Age levels? Median income?

▼ What skill levels are available in the market area? What are wages?

▼ Are any incentives offered? What kind? How much?

▼ Would the local labor market be advantageous for the potential uses?

Educational Amenities

▼ Where are and what is the quality of nearby schools and libraries?

▼ What is the average local educational attainment? High school? College? Postgraduate?

▼ What is the mix of private and public schools?

▼ Any local colleges?

▼ Do schools matter to your market?

Support Services

▼ Are custodial and maintenance firms located nearby?

▼ Are local suppliers available for potential users?

▼ Availability and diversity of restaurants? Local shopping? Hotels/motels?

Infrastructure

▼ Who provides local power? What type of power? Costs?

▼ What are city sewer and water capacities? Costs?

▼ Any special infrastructure for potential uses?

Second Intersection

▼ Eliminate obvious misfits from the playbook.

▼ Are at least two choices left?

▼ Decision: Keep going or turn away?

Phase Three: Rounding the Final Curve

Site Research

▼ Assemble the design team (architect, engineers, consultants).

▼ Research local building codes and ordinances.

▼ Evaluate zoning for extra height, volume, and FAR.

▼ Is the site suitable for more construction?

▼ Is there developable acreage off-site? Cost?

▼ What is the general condition of building(s) on site?

▼ What is the cost of demolition and waste removal?

▼ Would there be foundation and excavation costs? Rocks? Blasting?

▼ Can temporary parking, power, and lighting be accommodated?

▼ What are accommodations for fencing, gates, trade unions? OSHA?

The Facilities Survey

▼ What is the existing building configuration? Framing system?

▼ What are present floor-to-floor heights?

▼ How big are the structural bays (interior columns)?

▼ How much floor loading capacity is there?

▼ What are the facade materials and their condition?

▼ What is the condition and position of elevators, stairs, etc.?

▼ How much accommodation is required to comply with the Americans with Disabilities Act?

▼ What is the type and condition of existing building systems, such as HVAC, plumbing, electrical, life safety?

▼ Are any energy management measures in place?

▼ How is solid waste disposed of now? In the future?

Environmental Questions

▼ What are the historical uses and operations?

▼ What are the local regulatory requirements?

▼ Any downstream effects from on- or off-site operations?

▼ Is there asbestos to be removed?

▼ Any lead-based paint to be removed?

▼ Any underground tanks to be removed?

▼ Any oil-soaked materials to be treated?

▼ Any abandoned material to be removed?

▼ What is the cost of removing hazardous materials?

Making Alterations to Fit the New Use(s)

▼ What are the building's architectural strengths? Can they be saved?

▼ Are there any historic preservation restrictions? Opportunities for tax credits?

▼ What changes are necessary to floor plans?

▼ Can the structure be modified for the proposed uses?

▼ How much demolition? How much new construction?

▼ Do removed items have salvage value?

▼ How are storm runoff and snow removal accommodated?

▼ What are temporary lighting and heating costs?

Figure 1-13 (continued).

▼ How much for architectural fees? How much time?

▼ What is the estimated total cost of conversion per square foot?

Approvals and Permits

▼ Which agencies have authority? What permit types? Costs?

▼ How long will the approval process take?

▼ Are there off-site development requirements or contributions?

▼ How much is the site plan application fee?

▼ What are state, county, and municipal application fees?

▼ Will performance and surety bonds be required?

▼ Will there be sanitary sewer connection fees?

▼ Will there be utility service connection fees?

Financing Picture

▼ Are prospective tenants or users creditworthy?

▼ Are conventional borrowing methods available? Nonrecourse? Guarantees?

▼ Is there a need for equity participation? How much? Investors?

▼ Is the building suitable for rehabilitation tax credit? Low-income tax credits?

▼ Are grants available from the National Historic Trust and other groups?

▼ Is assistance available from local economic development agencies?

▼ Are flips, sale-leaseback arrangements, or tax-free exchange options available?

▼ Any tax abatements or other public incentives available?

▼ How certain are investment returns?

Third Intersection

▼ Do expected returns justify development costs for uses?

Choose a winner and one back-up candidate.▼

Source: Bruce M. Hoch, founder and principal of Development Concepts Group, a firm offering a wide variety of specialty services to corporations, urban agencies, and private developers in determining realistic opportunities for disposition or adaptive use of underutilized commercial and industrial facilities.

Particular types of buildings can offer structural advantages for certain new uses. Warehouses, for example, often have good parking available, which is beneficial for most new uses, especially offices and retail space. The structural integrity of older industrial facilities is normally extremely solid and can support unconventional design and engineering approaches that might be necessary to fit the new use. For example, the 1950s-built AT&T office and warehouse building that Price Enterprises converted to a retail power center was extraordinarily strong—strong enough in fact to house a bomb shelter on the second floor, which, owing to its proximity to the Pentagon, must have been considered a reasonable precaution in those days—enabling engineers to

The small floorplates, ample windows, and high ceilings of many older downtown commercial buildings make them well suited for conversion to office space offering old world charm, modern office amenities, affordable rents, and convenient access to the central business district. The Pilcher Building in Nashville, Tennessee, is a multitenant office building in what was originally a grain trading building. The Pilcher is located in Nashville's old commercial district, which today is in transition from warehousing and junk shops to offices, restaurants, and service businesses. Like many adaptive use renovations, the Pilcher's exterior needed only repair and cleaning; the big-ticket cost items were related to bringing the interior space up to modern standards for comfort, such as the installation of new mechanical systems. A four-story light well was created in the Pilcher to bring natural light into the center of the building.

Figure 1-14. Walt Disney Imagineering

Glendale, California

Walt Disney Imagineering used a derelict warehouse (above) to create an open, stimulating office environment for its theme park designers (right).

Walt Disney Imagineering (WDI), based in Glendale, California, designs and constructs magical environments and attractions for Disney theme parks. WDI's conversion of a simple but cavernous old warehouse at 521 Rodier Drive into office space for its theme park design group took a similar approach. A series of project team "villages" was organized along the building's central spine. The focal point of each village is a large open space for design models. Surrounding work stations were built with low walls so designers can refer to their

models while working. A new mezzanine, which increased the building's usable space to 70,000 square feet, is used for conference rooms. Soft, uniform indirect light was created by installing low-cost shop light fixtures upside down so that light is reflected from canvas banners. Windows and skylights were added in the model areas as sources of natural light. Through the creative use of inexpensive construction materials, conver-

sion of the warehouse was completed for $35.00 per square foot.

When WDI needed a central location to serve as the primary information resource for the design and creation of Disney theme parks, it once again looked for an existing building to adapt to meet its needs. It found what it was looking for in a run-down, graffiti-ridden factory building at 1245 Flower Street. The 30,000-square-foot building's exterior required a substantial amount of cleaning and repair work, but the project's interior required even more. WDI wanted to create a one-of-a-kind environment, in effect a one-stop intellectual candy store of information and ideas. Comfort, humidity control, and security for the valuable materials housed in the building were paramount.

The WDI Resource Center is built around an open space with an interconnecting series of resources—books, magazines, a photography studio, slides, video, artwork, interior design services, and more. The design is deliberately provocative, with floating ceilings, abstract geometrical shapes, and warm colors. To create additional space without compromising the open plan, a mezzanine was inserted over the ground floor.▼

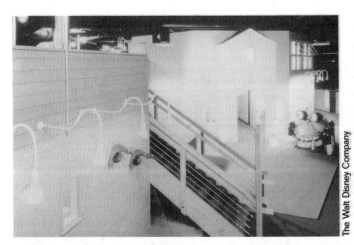

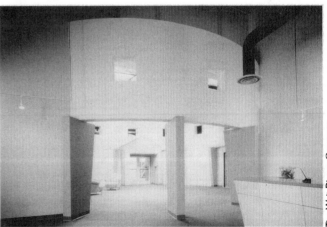

Underneath the grime and graffiti, the basic, angular design of an old factory building provided an ideal framework for the creation of the Walt Disney Imagineering Resource Center.

The Little Building, a 1917-vintage, 12-story office building facing Boston Common, proved to be ideal for conversion to a 750-student residence hall for Emerson College.

Miller Dyer Spears, Inc., Architects & Planners

View from a suite in the dorm across a "finger" to a single room.

construct a parking deck over the tomb-like concrete structure.

It is becoming much more common for a user needing additional space to evaluate both new construction and adaptive use alternatives to determine which option best meets requirements of timing, cost, and space. Users can often find existing structures with layouts, me-

chanical systems, parking, and other building features that are highly complementary of their needs, even though the building was originally designed for a completely different use.

The floorplates of the small professional building in Boston that Emerson College turned into student dormitories were ideally suited for its new use. The many small windowed

Typical residential floor plan. The building's "fingers" and small windowed offices lining the perimeter and the central corridors of the former office building accommodated an efficient layout for the new use as a dormitory.

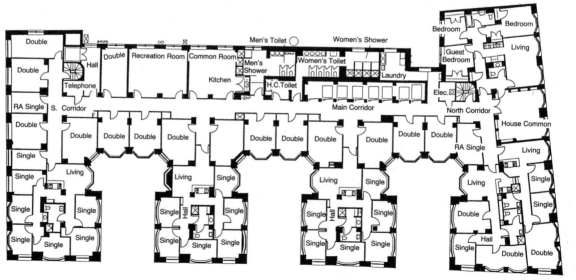

Miller Dyer Spears, Inc., Architects & Planners

Figure 1-15. From Auto Repair Shop to Office Building

Old Pasadena, California

The high ceiling of this distressed auto repair shop presented an opportunity to obtain more usable floor area for office space.

Additional floor space was created by constructing new offices that "float" over the open ground floor. Greenhouse windows and skylights enhance feelings of openness and comfort within the structure.

When the architectural firm Togawa & Smith, Inc., sought new office space, it readily took to the challenge of designing and renovating old space rather than leasing new space. A neglected and deteriorated 6,300-square-foot auto repair shop at 44 West Green Street in Old Pasadena, California, became the focus. The firm now occupies approximately 5,000 square feet of the multilevel office building and leases the remaining 1,300 square feet. Since its completion in 1993, the project has been the impetus for further rejuvenation of the community.

Although toxic waste had to be removed and the building needed seis-mic upgrading, the development team was able to meet the relatively modest development budget of $30.00 per square foot by employing creative design rather than expensive building materials.

To take advantage of existing high ceilings, designers introduced a series of levels that increased the building's usable floor area for private upper-level offices. Sandblasted trusses, exposed foil insulation, white back-lit canvases, angular partition elements, greenhouse windows, and existing skylights enhance the perception of openness and comfort in the interior space.▼

offices that ringed the perimeter of the building and the central corridors allowed the architects to create an exceptionally efficient layout. Another bonus for the new use was the unusual number of elevators in the existing building that required only minimal upgrading. A new retail arcade on the ground level required little reconfiguration from the original office space. The most significant structural challenge for the design and engineering team was fitting the specifications within lower-than-ideal floor-to-ceiling heights.

The case studies in Part 2 give many examples of creative design and engineering solutions found by adaptive use project teams. Architects for Trump International Hotel & Tower, the conversion of a high-rise office building to a hotel and residential condominium, for example, abandoned several unneeded existing elevator shafts, yielding more usable area on the most desirable side of the project (see the case study in Part 2). In the same project, the concrete walls that were added to stiffen the high-rise structure were strategically located to add soundproofing between the condominium units. Another project, the Lake Union Steam Plant, integrated reproductions of the original smokestacks into the design for biotech laboratories and office space by using four of the six stacks for ventilating laboratories; the two remaining stacks can be used for future expansion of the laboratories (see the case study in Part 2). Replicating the smokestacks satisfied community concerns that had posed a serious roadblock for the project in its early stages and also provided an effective means of ventilation.

The Challenge of Financing

Securing project financing is often one of the steepest hurdles facing a project sponsor in a potential adaptive use project. Roundtable participants believe that in some markets, the demand for less expensive, nontraditional space —precisely the characteristics that give adap-

Developer Winter Properties believed an unmet demand existed for housing near downtown Atlanta. Winter hoped to satisfy part of that demand by converting the Carriage Works, an abandoned early 1900s manufacturing building in a once thriving but long since abandoned commercial district near modern Atlanta's CBD, to loft housing (see the case study in Part 2). Unable to allay lenders' concerns about the location and the untested market for loft housing, Winter proceeded to renovate the property, investing equity resources and hoping it could subsequently obtain financing. After a major arts center moved in across the street, helping to attract tenants, Winter was able to secure a bank loan to complete the project, but only if the building were converted to office space.

tive use a competitive edge over conventional development—actually far outpaces the supply of such space. This unmet demand is largely the result of the difficulty that project sponsors have in obtaining financing for market-rate reuse projects.

Conventional sources of debt financing have historically assigned a high level of risk to the structural and market uncertainties associated with redeveloping existing buildings, and many have shied away entirely from financing adaptive use. Awareness is growing among lenders, though, that a strong market potential exists for adaptive use, especially for residential uses in urban centers. Some commercial banks, such as First Interstate Bank of Denver, have developed expertise in adaptive use development and expect this niche to expand as cities like Denver continue to see increasing demand for downtown housing and as businesses continue to seek less expensive office space. Still, even banks that have underwritten sizable portfolios of adaptive use projects generally require high equity contributions and personal guarantees or cross-collateralization of other existing projects. Very little nonrecourse lending is available for adaptive use development regardless of how strong the particular market fundamentals are.

Roundtable participants representing both lenders and borrowers report that lenders look for solid answers to the following types of questions in a loan application for a market-rate adaptive use project:

▼ Has the developer demonstrated that market demand is sufficient for the potential use? Credible market research showing supply and demand fundamentals of the market area is essential, but other market conditions can also help make the case that the market area can support the proposed new use. What types of supporting amenities are available in the area, such as transportation, shopping, entertainment, security, schools, and labor supply, that would be attractive to the target market? What amenities are included in the proposed project that are particularly responsive to the target market? How is the design and location of the project suitable for the local market?

▼ What are the project's risk variables? What is the estimated probability of their occur-

Figure 1-16. Audubon House

New York, New York

The design and redevelopment of Audubon House successfully confronts many of the environmental problems linked to conventional office buildings: excessive consumption of resources, depletion of natural resources, and poor-quality indoor air.

When the National Audubon Society outgrew its high-rise office space and needed to relocate its national headquarters, the organization decided that, rather than leasing new office space, it would purchase an existing building and renovate it to meet its needs. After researching many potential sites, Audubon purchased 700 Broadway, a century-old, eight-story department store building in lower Manhattan that had been largely vacant for over ten years.

Audubon's goal was to demonstrate that an existing building designed for another purpose could be economically transformed into an environmentally sound, energy-efficient, aesthetically pleasing office building. The goal was more than satisfactorily met. Completed in 1992, Audubon House is considered one of the most environ-

mentally advanced buildings ever designed. Based on 1994 and 1995 operating costs, the energy-saving features installed have reduced utility costs by more than $100,000 a year. The building uses approximately 60 percent less energy than a comparable code-compliant office building in Manhattan.

Audubon House is a model of how sustainable use of resources, efficient use of energy, and air quality can be achieved cost effectively. Not including an unforeseen cost dictated by a New York code that required Audubon to repair and strengthen the vaulting under the sidewalk to support a fully loaded fire truck, the project's cost of $122 per square foot is well within the New York City market rate. The project's fully loaded cost was $142 per square foot.

All major design, engineering, and purchase decisions were tested against three criteria. Is it environmentally safe? Is it cost-effective? Can it be achieved through the use of off-the-shelf prod-

Conversion of the Audubon House meets high standards for aesthetic appeal, habitability, building performance, and cost.

The design strategically incorporates skylights, large floor-to-ceiling windows, and specially designed glass partitions throughout the office interior to allow maximum penetration of natural light.

ucts readily available to everyone? The development team used computer modeling software DOE-2, developed by the U.S. Department of Energy, to analyze the interplay between fundamental building components and calculate the financial savings associated with individual energy-saving devices as well as overall energy efficiency. Task-ambient and natural lighting, a comprehensive upgrading of the building's insulation system (roof, walls, and windows), and an innovative HVAC system are some of the energy-saving strategies the team used.

Renovation also demonstrated a concern for the environment through its dedicated use of recycled materials. Not only was the existing structure itself being "recycled" through its renovation, but all of the construction materials removed from the original building during construction that could be recycled were. Any new materials used in construction were selected based on their recycled contents. And the design of the new building incorporates recycling chutes and a recycling center at the subbasement so that office workers can recycle products during their daily work.▼

rence? Are cost and revenue assumptions used in the financial pro forma realistic?

▼ Is the design layout flexible enough for alternative uses if the proposed use fails? What other uses might be supported in the market area?

▼ Is permanent financing available for the project? Although a commitment is not necessarily required, a construction lender does not want to be the only possible player.

▼ Does the project have an exit strategy? That is, what could take the project sponsor out of the debt liability? It could be presales in the case of for-sale residential units or other conditions that could enable another investor to acquire the property.

▼ Perhaps the most important question: What is the developer's track record? Does the developer have experience with adaptive use development or has he or she hired consultants with the appropriate expertise and experience? Most lenders assign a premium to local experience, at least for the project team as a whole.

Financing for adaptive use development is still largely based on equity. Projects are typically funded through a combination of the project sponsor's out-of-pocket financial resources, investment equity, some debt financing, and a little help from public incentives. Public incentives still play a role in the feasibility of adaptive use development although at much-diminished levels from a decade or even five years ago (see Figure 1-17). The Denver Dry Goods Building (see the case study in Part 2), an extraordinary multiple-use, multiphase reuse project, used the full gamut of financing opportunities for adaptive use development. Twenty-three separate sources were used to fund the conversion of the stately old department store into affordable and market-rate housing, retail space, and offices, including equity investments and loans from public agencies and private nonprofit organizations, the developer's equity, private bank loans, pension funds, state bond issues, tax increment bonds, federal and state grants, and the sale of low-income housing and rehabilitation tax credits. The Denver Dry Goods Building is by no means a typical reuse project, but it does illustrate the cooperative efforts and dogged perseverance that often characterize successful adaptive use development.

A crumbling 70-year-old tire and rubber factory complex (top) has been totally transformed into the new 390,000-square-foot corporate headquarters for Indiana Farm Bureau Insurance in Indianapolis (bottom). The first phase of the project involved the demolition of dozens of smaller structures surrounding the main plant and cleaning up extensive amounts of asbestos, petroleum, and PCBs throughout the nine-acre site. The environmental cleanup and site demolition alone took 18 months and $2 million to complete. The existing structure, however, presented numerous advantages for the new use. The former tire plant's 16-foot floor-to-floor heights, for example, allowed dropped ceilings for mechanical installations and raised flooring for electrical and communications systems while retaining 10-foot ceiling heights in the office areas. In addition to satisfying the owner's office space requirements, the insurance company leases over 100,000 square feet of office space to outside tenants. Despite the costly cleanup, the renovation was completed for about the same price as a new office building of comparable high quality. The owners felt that the ample space for parking and future expansion and the demonstrated investment in the city were added benefits of reuse.

Environmental Concerns

Some degree of environmental remediation is almost always required when reusing buildings built before the mid-1970s. The most frequently encountered contaminants that must be removed from nonmanufacturing facilities are asbestos in tile and pipe coating, lead-based paint, and PCBs (polychlorinated biphenyls). A common misunderstanding about adaptive use development is that it involves a high risk

Figure 1-17. Public Incentives for Adaptive Use

In the 1970s and 1980s, well-funded federal programs supported a number of commercial, industrial, and residential adaptive use projects that helped achieve public objectives, such as revitalization of neighborhoods, creation of jobs, and preservation of historic buildings. Over the last five to ten years, however, the most instrumental federal subsidies and grants, such as Urban Development Action Grants (UDAGs), have been eliminated or substantially reduced. As the level of federal assistance has declined, state and local governments have increased incentive programs designed to encourage development that furthers goals of the public sector. In addition to more emphasis on state and local sources, the type of public sector programs available has shifted away from direct subsidies toward noncash financial incentives, such as income tax credits, tax abatements, and assistance with project financing. Today, public incentives can still boost a project's economic feasibility, but they cannot (and should not) mask otherwise poor market fundamentals in any real estate development. The following discussion highlights some of the most useful public sector incentives that can be applicable to adaptive use development.

Federal Programs

A variety of resources are still available through the federal government that can assist adaptive use development. Although few programs specifically address adaptive use, many of the programs targeted for community revitalization, historic preservation, and affordable housing are applicable. The scope of assistance varies, but it includes tax credits, direct loans, formula grants, project grants, and advisory services. The most significant federal programs are briefly described here.

Rehabilitation Tax Credit. Despite modifications made by the Tax Reform Act of 1986 sharply reducing the pro-

gram's benefits, the rehabilitation tax credit is still the most important federal program encouraging private investment in historic rehabilitation. The program provides a federal income tax credit equivalent to 20 percent of the qualified construction costs incurred in rehabilitating income-producing properties listed on the National Register of Historic Places and 10 percent of the qualified renovation costs for buildings built before 1936 but not certified historic.

Over the past decade, between 40 and 57 percent of projects that qualified annually for the tax credit have included housing, predominately multifamily housing. That figure was 53 percent in 1994, with mixed-use properties (including hotel/tourist attractions) following at 28 percent, commercial uses accounting for 11 percent, and office uses accounting for 8 percent of approved projects.

Use of the rehabilitation tax credit does not preclude using other federal, state, and local financial incentives. According to the U.S. Department of the Interior's *Tax Incentives for Rehabilitating Historic Buildings: Fiscal Year 1994 Analysis,* nearly half the projects that qualified for the tax credit in FY 1994 did so. Those projects used the following additional incentives: local property tax abatement (29 percent), low-interest loans (21 percent), the low-income housing tax credit (17 percent), various Housing and Urban Development (HUD) programs (11 percent), grant programs (4 percent), and historic preservation easements (2 percent). The total adds to more than 50 percent, as many projects used multiple sources of subsidy.

One important feature of the tax credit program is that the building owner can sell the credit itself to investors seeking the tax advantage, thus providing an additional source of equity capital. Moreover, the value of the tax credit can be locked in at the beginning of the development process, making it possible to attract

investor equity to help finance construction costs.

A project sponsor interested in applying for the federal rehabilitation tax credit should contact the appropriate state historic preservation officer for information about the procedure for certification and assistance in submitting the necessary forms. The historic preservation officer initiates the request for a project to become certified as eligible for the tax incentives and forwards the application to the National Park Service, part of the U.S. Department of the Interior, the certifying agency. The Internal Revenue Service is responsible for determining which rehabilitation expenditures qualify for the tax credit and for all procedures and legal matters concerning the tax consequences of the certificates.

Low-Income Housing Tax Credit. Of all the public incentives designed to support redevelopment, the low-income housing tax credit (LIHTC) can have the greatest impact on a project's economic feasibility. Congress established the LIHTC in the Tax Reform Act of 1986 to encourage private sector production of low- to moderate-income housing. Administered by HUD, the tax credit represents a shift away from previous rent subsidy and loan guarantee programs. The LIHTC is often used in conjunction with the rehabilitation tax credit.[1]

The LIHTC offers a dollar-for-dollar credit against the federal tax on non-passive income, based on the amount of money invested in qualifying units in mixed-income or low-income rental housing developments. The program offers investors one of two levels of benefit. Over a ten-year period, it returns either 70 percent or 30 percent of the present value costs of the investments in qualifying units. The size of the credit is fixed at the time the property is placed in service and is based on an average of federal interest rates. For properties placed in service in 1987, for example, the per-

Figure 1-17 *(continued)*.

centages of the credit were fixed at 9 percent for expenditures in new buildings and 4 percent on expenditures in existing buildings or buildings constructed with federally subsidized financing, including mortgage revenue bond financing.

For a property to qualify for the credit, one of two requirements for setasides must be met. At least 20 percent of the units must be set aside for families earning 50 percent or less of median income in the area, or at least 40 percent of the units must be reserved for families earning between 50 and 80 percent of median income in the area. Owners must agree to rent units at a restricted sum for 30 years. A process is available, however, that allows properties to phase out controls after 15 years.

Like the rehabilitation tax credit, the LIHTC serves as a vehicle to raise equity. An owner/developer can often attract enough equity capital by selling the low-income housing tax credits to investors to make a substantial difference in the project's feasibility. To obtain a low-income housing tax credit, an owner must file IRS Form 8609 with a state or local allocating agency to receive a share of the state's available credits. The state allocating agency

may accept or reject the application at its discretion.

Grants. HUD administers most federal grants applicable to adaptive use development. Two grant programs in particular can benefit adaptive use projects:

▼ *Community Development Block Grants (CDBGs).* Since their authorization in 1974, CDBGs have provided a flexible source of funding for community and economic development. HUD gives CDBGs to qualified cities and counties on the basis of entitlement; smaller cities and towns receive project-specific funds through state governments on a competitive basis. Money may be used for a wide range of projects that stimulate neighborhood revitalization and community development.

▼ *Home Investment Partnership Act (HOME).* This program was created to encourage investment in affordable rental housing, primarily through the rehabilitation of existing structures, by offering private parties or agencies in participating jurisdictions funds in the form of equity investments and interest-bearing or non-interest-bearing loans.[2]

State and Local Incentives

The number and variety of incentive programs available from states and local jurisdictions that can support adaptive use differ widely. Local jurisdictions often administer state-enacted incentive programs as well as provide separate, locally enacted incentives. Municipalities often use property tax exemptions and abatements to encourage redevelopment related to revitalization and historic preservation as well as financing vehicles like tax increment financing and the issuance of tax-exempt bonds. Tax increment financing can finance urban revitalization through a municipal bond issue that will be serviced from anticipated additional tax revenues generated from the redevelopment project. Tax-exempt revenue bonds issued by a state or local government are free from income tax and are secured by the income from specific projects, including real estate redevelopment, as opposed to claims against tax and other general revenues, as are revenue bonds.

The following incentive programs offered by the state of Maryland, for example, can be applied to adaptive

The legendary Denver Tearoom in the Denver Dry Goods Building (left) was converted to residential units. Asbestos in the ceiling of the tearoom had to be painstakingly removed through the floor above to protect the space's historic elements (right).

Figure 1-17 *(continued).*

use projects to encourage the preservation of historic structures and the revitalization of older urban neighborhoods. They are representative of the types of incentives available in many other states:

▼ The *Neighborhood Business Development Program (NBDP)* is a recently enacted program tailored after the defunct federal UDAG program. NBDP provides grants and loans to small businesses in neighborhoods designated by Maryland's Secretary of Housing and Community Development as revitalization areas. It offers gap financing that can be combined with other public and private resources to help finance the acquisition and construction costs of a rehabilitation project. Up to 50 percent of the project cost ($25,000 to $500,000) can be financed through NBDP.

▼ The *Historic Preservation Loan Program* provides long-term financing to nonprofit and for-profit entities for the acquisition and rehabilitation of properties listed on the Maryland Register of Historic Properties. Individuals and businesses must demonstrate that they sought as much financing as possible through the private sector.

▼ The *Historic Preservation Grant Program* awards grants to nonprofit and for-profit entities for the acquisition, rehabilitation, or restoration of any property listed on the Maryland Register of Historic Properties. This program and the Historic Preservation Loan Program require recipients to convey a perpetual easement to the Maryland Historical Trust before receiving any funds.

▼ The *Local 10 Percent Rehabilitation Property Tax Credit* is available to owners who have rehabilitated certified historic buildings for income-producing uses. In addition, Maryland's *Local Property Tax Freeze*, recently passed by the General Assembly, limits property taxes to as low as the prerehabilitation level for up to ten years for rehabilitation projects that meet local preservation standards.

▼ The *Maryland Rehabilitation Tax Subtraction* provides a deduction on state income taxes for 100 percent of the rehabilitation costs of historic owner-occupied residential properties.▼

[1]For information about how the two federal tax credits can be combined to raise project financing, see National Park Service, *Affordable Housing through Historic Preservation: A Case Study Guide to Combining the Tax Credits* and *Tax Credits and the Secretary of the Interior's Standards for Historic Rehabilitation* (Washington, D.C.: U.S. Dept. of the Interior). Contact the Superintendent of Documents Order Desk at 202-512-1800 to obtain copies.

[2]Parties interested in obtaining federal grants should contact the appropriate HUD field office for additional information.

Sources:

Hobart, Susan, and Robert Schwarz. "Housing Credits: A Leading Financial Tool." *Urban Land*, November 1995, pp. 37–42.

Legg Mason Realty Group, Inc. "Historic Tax Credit Feasibility Assessment: Baltimore City, Maryland." BRR 2884. September 1, 1995.

Maryland Historical Trust, Office of Preservation Services. "Summary of Direct and Indirect Financial Assistance Programs." 1993. Call the Dept. of Housing and Community Development at 410-514-7600 to obtain a copy.

Miles, Mike E., Richard L. Haney, Jr., and Gayle Berens. *Real Estate Development: Principles and Process.* 2d ed. Washington, D.C.: ULI–the Urban Land Institute, 1996, pp. 299–301, 318.

Pencek, Bill. "Cash in Your Pocket? Tax Incentives for Historic Property Rehabilitation." *The Phoenix*, Fall 1994, pp. 1–3.

of discovering unanticipated environmental contamination at some point during construction, which could ruin the project's financial return. In fact, most of the exposure to environmental risk will have been estimated during the predevelopment due diligence process. At the very least, lenders will require a Phase I environmental investigation, which examines the historical uses and operations of the site and indicates the likelihood of buried hazardous wastes and contaminated water or soil. (Figure 1-18 discusses sophisticated environmental databases that can assist a developer in screening a prospective project for environmental risks.) Even if it is not required by a lender, a prudent project sponsor will also hire an environmental

engineer to conduct an environmental survey of the facilities to determine the extent of contamination in the structure itself and the estimated cost of removal. If the Phase I study indicates a high probability of specific contamination on the site—suspected buried tanks or previous spills, for example—a detailed Phase II investigation of the site's soil and water is warranted. Phase II tests are more expensive than those for Phase I and are usually needed only for industrial properties, but they are well worth the expense to further eliminate the risk of unanticipated environmental expenditures. Phase III testing is done on extremely high-risk sites, such as former military bases and some manufacturing facilities.

Figure 1-18. Environmental Due Diligence Made Easy

Most knowledgeable developers and lenders routinely perform a "due diligence test" before closing on a real estate deal. Such a test, known as a Phase I audit, typically involves a review of government records for signs of likely chemical contamination (such as the presence of leaking underground gasoline storage tanks), a site visit, and interviews with current owners or operators. A quicker, less rigorous process for gathering information, called a transaction screen, is often conducted for smaller properties where contamination is unlikely. The transaction screen consists primarily of a review of government records.

The review of government records for a Phase I audit or a transaction screen has been made simple, quick, and relatively inexpensive by the advent of sophisticated environmental databases that can provide the exact location and profile of all known U.S. sites contaminated with hazardous wastes; facilities that generate, store, treat, or dispose of hazardous wastes; underground storage tanks (leaking or not); and garbage dumps. On-line access to these databases allows users to screen one or a portfolio of properties from their desks.

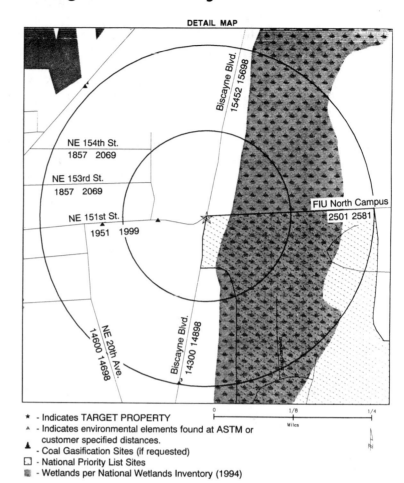

DETAIL MAP

- ★ - Indicates TARGET PROPERTY
- ▲ - Indicates environmental elements found at ASTM or customer specified distances.
- ▲ - Coal Gasification Sites (if requested)
- ☐ - National Priority List Sites
- ▦ - Wetlands per National Wetlands Inventory (1994)

Sophisticated environmental databases can provide maps showing the location of wetlands, contaminated sites, and other factors on and around any specified property.

While due diligence investigations can never entirely eliminate the risk of unexpected environmental remediation, most of the costs are known during predevelopment and can be factored into the costs for the project. If environmental costs are significant enough to make the project uneconomical, the project clearly is one to walk away from.

Successful Strategies And Lessons Learned

Despite the dissimilarity of individual adaptive use projects, a number of common factors emerged as roundtable participants discussed the specific factors and approaches that contributed to the success of specific projects.

Find a Niche

Like developers of conventional forms of real estate, developers who become active in adaptive use tend to acquire expertise in particular niches. The direction that an individual or company takes can stem from prior experience; for example, a developer of new residential products might branch out to include adapting existing buildings to residential uses. Albert Friedman's affinity for older buildings led to redeveloping them. He had had no real estate experience at all when he inherited an aging

Figure 1-18 *(continued)*.

Operated by private companies, the databases contain information compiled primarily from state and federal government sources, particularly the Environmental Protection Agency. In addition, the Sanborn Map Company in Pelham, New York, since the 1870s has produced maps that insurance companies use to locate properties that store or produce hazardous (flammable) materials. Sanborn maps show previous uses of the property, including the location of fuel or chemical storage tanks and where potentially toxic substances were stored.

Given only an address, the firms that operate these databases can provide a report of environmental risk that identifies potential environmental threats on the property and in the general vicinity. They typically provide a report listing all potential problem areas and a map showing the location of contaminated sites, underground storage tanks, and so forth within a one-mile radius of the property. The maps are designed to meet the American Society for Testing and Materials (ASTM) standard for the records search of a Phase I audit and the transaction screen.[1]

The three biggest players in this emerging and very competitive market are Environmental Data Resources, Inc. (EDR), Environmental Risk Information & Imaging Services (ERIIS), and VISTA Information Solutions, Inc.

Environmental Data Resources (3530 Post Road, Southport, Connecticut 06490, 800-352-0050) boasts delivery of maps and reports in only two to three days for a cost of $195. It provides three 8.5- by 11-inch color maps at increasingly larger scales: a two-mile-radius map, a one-mile-radius map, and a one-quarter-mile-radius map. EDR is affiliated with Dun & Bradstreet, which provides on-line access that allows users to obtain instantaneously a list of suspect sites located within a one-mile radius of the target site. For sites in California, EDR's maps also can plot the location of earthquake faults.

Environmental Risk Information & Imaging Services (1421 Prince Street, Suite 330, Alexandria, Virginia 22314, 800-989-0402) provides a radius map and a report in three to four days for $230. It provides a single 11- by 17-inch color map. Twenty-four-hour rush delivery is available for an extra $99.00. The firm offers on-line access through a company called Claritas, also based in Alexandria, Virginia. ERIIS has Sanborn fire maps on microfilm, which it can deliver on disk or as hard copy.

VISTA Information Solutions (5060 Shoreham Place, Suite 300, San Diego, California 92122, 800-767-0403) provides radius maps and a report in two days for $175, with 24-hour rush service available for an extra $50.00. It provides three 8.5- by 11-inch color maps: a one-mile-radius map, a one-quarter-mile-radius map, and a street map. An enhanced report, supported by VISTA staff who review "suspected" risks not mapped by the automated process, is available for $195. The firm offers on-line access, through which a digital map can be downloaded onto the user's computer.

All three firms can provide environmental profiles of individual companies or facilities, examining, for example, companywide violations of environmental regulations.▼

[1]See Carol R. Boman, "Environmental Due Diligence: A Commentary on the ASTM Standard Practice," *Urban Land,* September 1993, pp. 13–14.
Source: David Salvesen, "Due Diligence Screens Made Easy," *Urban Land,* June 1994, pp. 8–9. Salvesen is an environmental writer and consultant based in Kensington, Maryland.

building 20 years ago and decided to rehabilitate it. Although that project failed financially, he had discovered a business opportunity that combined his love of history and architecture and his marketing skills. Twenty years ago, Jonathan Rose was a young man living in New York City at a time when SoHo was just beginning to attract the attention of small developers; he saw an opportunity to provide higher-quality loft space than was being developed at the time. He has since planned and developed many affordable housing and mixed-use projects involving both adaptive use and new construction.

Understanding the profile of the target market is essential in all real estate development. Because adaptive use development relies on attracting a smaller, nontraditional, cost-conscious market, the project sponsor must be extremely sensitive to the nuances of the users' needs and priorities to deliver the right product at the right price. Successful adaptive use developers seem to have an almost intuitive understanding of the subtle style preferences and space requirements of the special niche to which they appeal, as well as how much this market is willing to pay to obtain them.

Resourceful developers can find a niche in the market by seeing a way to reuse existing structures to satisfy the space needs of a specific market segment in a way that is more beneficial to the users than other alternatives.

When industry began to move away from San Francisco's south of market area (the area known as SOMA), scores of warehouse and factory buildings built in the first half of the century to support a thriving commerce of fruit and produce were left vacant or underused for ten to 20 years. When zoning for the SOMA district was changed to allow the use of live/work space, McKenzie, Rose & Holliday Development Company grasped the opportunity to convert abandoned industrial buildings in the area to live/work loft condominiums. The developer has completed several well-received loft conversions in the SOMA district, including ClockTower Lofts (top), a three-building former lithograph plant renovated into 127 live/work loft units ranging from 600 to 5,000 square feet; 355 Bryant Street Lofts (above left), 44 live/work lofts created from a 1916 distribution warehouse; and 601 Fourth Street Lofts (above right), 85 live/work lofts constructed in a 1915 three-story concrete warehouse. Load-bearing exterior walls with internal column and beam structural systems paired with generous ceiling heights made these buildings particularly well suited to the emerging lifestyle of home offices and electronic commutes.

Roundtable participant James Martell discussed the strategy taken by The Prime Group to create a niche for the adaptive use of renovated surplus steel manufacturing plants.

Like most U.S. industries during the late 1980s, the steel industry was reengineering its operations. Steel companies downsized, divested non–value added business operations and assets, and outsourced certain business operations. The Prime Group, Inc., a nationwide commercial, industrial, and residential developer, believed that a new demand for manufacturing space had been created by the steel industry's outsourcing of certain manufacturing processes. Moreover, the company believed that some of the surplus plants that had recently been put on the market by steel companies could be redeveloped and reused for different industrial processes at less than the replacement cost of new facilities. The existing plants often had other tangible benefits for potential users, such as proximity to an available skilled labor supply and transportation links. Prime also believed that the potential to create jobs and environmental benefits would be likely to generate community support for redeveloping the vacant plants. With its in-house expertise and experience with large-scale development, Prime felt especially well positioned to meet the demand for modernized plant space at better than new development prices and began looking for suitable surplus properties in northwest Indiana and southeast Chicago.

In 1990, in a joint venture with a major life insurance company, The Prime Group began negotiations to purchase a 1 million-square-foot, 130-acre former U.S. Steel Company plant. The plant had been designed for a number of manufacturing processes, none of which were well suited for the current owner's steel service center operations. The seller had decided to shut down the operations at the facility and build a new 450,000-square-foot plant for its own use. During the due diligence process, Prime realized it could provide the seller with state-of-the-art space for its service center operations within the existing plant and lease the space to the seller at a rate significantly below comparable new build-to-suit space. One reason was that the cost of a new facility would be high, in part because of the tremendously

strong structure and foundation required for the operation, both qualities that the existing structure possessed. After much discussion and creative thought, Prime was able to convince the seller to agree to a sale and leaseback agreement that included a $10 million purchase price ($4 million above the initially negotiated $6 million) plus $1.5 million in additional tenant improvements. The seller agreed to invest the additional $4 million in the renovation of the plant and new equipment and entered into a 15-year lease.

Before acquiring the surplus plant, Prime had been strongly convinced that a market existed for redeveloped manufacturing space. The company's greatest challenge was how to finance the project, especially given the shaky economic outlook prevailing in the area at the time. A solution emerged when the city agreed to support the project through its capacity to issue bonds. Tax-exempt industrial revenue bonds replaced Prime's short-term acquisition and redevelopment financing. The project also qualified as an Enterprise Zone, eliminating approximately $200,000 in local transfer fees and costs.

Prime redeveloped and subdivided the remaining 500,000 square feet of space for assorted manufacturing processes. Within 12 months from closing on the bonds, the project was fully leased to a dozen tenants at below-market rates. The Enterprise Center, as the project is now called, is a large-scale example of what can also work on a smaller scale: reusing an existing structure to provide specialized space at below-market rates.

Design a Mix of Uses

One of the greatest risks any market-rate real estate project faces is attracting insufficient demand. This statement is especially true for adaptive use projects, which are often targeted to smaller niche markets where demand is unproved. One strategy to minimize market risk for an adaptive use project is to incorporate a mix of uses. For this reason, redeveloped buildings often have a retail component on the ground floor, with commercial or residential uses above. Retail uses can be exceptionally well suited for renovated older buildings,

A view of the redeveloped historic block of Peabody Place across from the new office tower under construction.

An existing narrow street that bisects the block of historic buildings was upgraded into a European-style shopping street called Gayoso Lane.

The Gayoso House courtyard.

as a retail amenity complements both working and living environments. Retailers often like the ambience and one-of-a-kind image that older buildings can create for them. In turn, having stores, restaurants, and service establishments adds vitality to the vicinity and helps attract other residents and commercial tenants.

Although mixed uses make sense programmatically, many lenders view mixed-use development as higher-risk ventures and will not finance such projects. Some smaller lenders, though, are comfortable with mixed-use adaptive use projects, especially when they include a retail component to help carry the debt service for the building. As Jonathan Rose suggests, this dilemma can be overcome in larger adaptive use projects by forming separate ventures and financing packages for different uses (see Figure 1-19).

This approach proved to be the saving grace for the Denver Dry Goods Building, a 100-year-old department store in downtown Denver, Colorado (see the case study in Part 2). The building was vacant when the Denver Urban Renewal Authority (DURA) purchased the build-

Peabody Place is an eight-block urban mixed-use project being developed in downtown Memphis, Tennessee, by Belz Enterprises. The project includes 1.7 million square feet of hotel, office, residential, and retail space in both newly constructed and reused buildings. At the heart of the project is the historic block of Peabody Place, 500,000 square feet of mixed-use space in four contiguous historic buildings. The largest one, Pembroke Square, a former department store, contains 45 residential apartments, 110,000 square feet of office space, and 60,000 square feet of specialty shops and restaurants. Gayoso House is a reuse of a historic 200,000-square-foot hotel for rental apartments and ground-floor commercial space, and 50 Peabody Place, originally a furniture store and warehouse, now has 60,000 square feet of multitenant office and retail space. The renovation and reuse of The Majestic Theatre for a 9,000-square-foot restaurant and brewery was to be completed in late 1996. Other elements of Peabody Place include the renowned Peabody Hotel, a 250,000-square-foot corporate office building (new construction), a 154,000-square-foot multitenant office tower (under construction), and a 300,000-square-foot retail entertainment center (construction planned to begin in 1997). Total project development costs are estimated at approximately $45 million. The four adaptive use buildings were redeveloped for $39.5 million ($79.00 per square foot).

Figure 1-19. Jonathan Rose: Insights and Lessons Learned about Adaptive Use Development

ULI member Jonathan F.P. Rose is president of the Affordable Housing Construction Corporation, a real estate development and consulting firm that plans and develops affordable housing and mixed-use projects with municipalities and nonprofit organizations. Among many other adaptive use and new construction projects, Rose renovated the Denver Dry Goods Building in downtown Denver for affordable and market-rate housing, offices, and retail space. He responded to the following questions from ULI.

How did you get started with adaptive use development?

I entered the real estate business in 1976 in New York City at a time of unprecedented high interest rates, rampant inflation, and the flight of great numbers of manufacturing businesses from the city. Their leaving produced an increase in vacant space in old loft buildings, and as a result, the buildings in neighborhoods surrounding Greenwich Village, particularly SoHo, dramatically declined in value. At the same time, New York City had increasingly become a center for music and art. Young musicians and artists flocked to the city and often moved into old lofts in the factory buildings using illegally built kitchens and bathrooms. To stimulate renovating older buildings into apartments, New York City passed the J-51 Tax Abatement Law, which effectively eliminated real estate taxes in adapted buildings for 13 years. With little new construction in the city, lenders begin making loans for renovations of buildings that fell under the J-51 program. The confluence of these events inspired young developers to begin buying inexpensive loft buildings and converting them on a shoestring to live/work co-ops or condominiums.

Affordable Housing Construction Corporation

Jonathan Rose became enamored with renovating older structures for new uses in the late 1970s, when he converted the American Thread Company Building in TriBeCa to upscale live/work loft condominiums—a new housing concept at the time.

It became clear to me that a market existed for higher-quality loft spaces than were being developed. I had also been reflecting on the changes in manufacturing processes I saw happening all around me—a shift from physical work to intellectual work. I began to look for a project to develop and eventually settled on the American Thread Company Building—a magnificent structure zoned for residential, retail, and commercial uses. I divided the U-shaped 11-story building into 52 live/work loft units that were finished to a very high standard with amenities that would appeal to the downtown market. I believed that the artistic/intellectual worker market for my condominium units needed different support systems from the previous manufacturing tenants, so I enhanced the project by installing desktop computers in every unit and a common Xerox machine. This was three years before the introduction of personal

computers, so the idea of an apartment with a computer and access to data around the world was then quite unusual. This strategy worked: we were able to sell out at prices about 30 percent higher than competitive units.

What types of market-rate adaptive use projects can be attractive for developers?

Over the last 15 years, in almost every city in this country, developers have succeeded in creating market-rate residential rental and condominium projects and in converting older buildings to office space. More recently, developers have combined the rehabilitation tax credit with the low-income housing tax credit to create affordable rental apartments. And the population base created by the market-rate apartments has opened up some very attractive opportunities for retail projects.

What are some of the hard lessons you have learned about adaptive use development through experience?

1. The existing building should be carefully inspected for potential structural problems. Even after the most rigorous scrutiny, adaptive use can cost more than anticipated because of hidden structural conditions. For example, rusted steel in an older building is not readily apparent. Sections of wooden beams may be rotten or have been cut and patched in ways that ruin their structural strength. Include at least a 10 percent contingency allowance for hard construction costs and a 5 percent factor for soft costs.
2. It is essential to think rigorously through the design and anticipate the needs of the new architectural program. It is far easier and cheaper,

Figure 1-19 (continued).

for instance, to design space in the electric meter room and chases to accommodate future power and communication needs at the outset of the project rather than having to add them later. Adaptive use development does not allow much margin for redesign.

3. Know your market! Explore alternative plans. For example, one might do better developing fewer, larger units with a lot of character rather than cramming in lots of smaller, less attractive units.

What kinds of expertise should be brought to the development team?

The categories of expertise needed for redevelopment are really no different from the expertise needed for any other kind of development, but all participants should have had previous experience with the type of product being redeveloped. For smaller projects, the project team should include an architect familiar with adaptive use and structural and mechanical engineers. It is essential to involve a contractor up front. One might also add an expert on the local building code who would know where the code allows some flexibility. For a project that qualifies for rehabilitation tax credits, an attorney familiar with structuring tax credit partnerships should be added to the team. And be sure to use an architect or consultant familiar with

the process. As in other types of real estate development, the developer is responsible for coordinating the work of the project team, making final decisions about the program, securing the financing, and managing sales or leasing of the finished product.

What steps should a developer go through to determine what the new use should be?

The first step is to examine the physical attributes of the existing building to discover its inherent design opportunities and constraints. It is important to take advantage of the physical attributes of a building rather than try to fight them. For example, larger loft buildings located in the middle of a block have very little interior light and can be difficult to convert into housing. Old hotels are usually U- or H-shaped and have narrow floorplates, making them more difficult to adapt to office or institutional uses, but they are well suited to housing with single-loaded corridors. The ground floors of old industrial buildings are often set at loading dock height above the street rather than at street level, which creates difficulties for new retail space. It is often easier to cut away parts of a building to obtain the shape one wants than to add new structures. I once examined a large building that had been combined from several smaller buildings. The walls between the older build-

ings formed thick party walls that were hard to penetrate. The proposed plan suggested cutting holes in the walls to interconnect the corridors of the buildings at great cost. It made much more sense to leave the walls untouched and to develop each building in phases, thereby reducing the financial risk of the overall project and reducing the cost of complying with the fire code.

Once the advantages and limitations of the building are understood, the developer compares the expected total development cost of various alternatives to determine the most natural and financeable alternatives.

What is your experience with unexpected obstacles and delays in adaptive use development?

Because the structure already exists, the redevelopment can be completed much more quickly than new construction. If the new use conforms with provisions of the prevailing zoning, the public approval process can also take less time and involve fewer risks than conventional development. Municipalities are usually anxious to capitalize on their existing infrastructure and are pleased with the prospect of rehabilitation and revitalization. Many cities offer tax abatement programs and financing support, and are introducing more flexible building codes to encourage the reuse of existing buildings.

---

ing in 1988. Over the next two years, DURA considered several proposals to redevelop the 350,000-square-foot building, including a retail mall, a hotel, an aquarium, movie theaters, and upscale housing, but none could obtain leasing or financing commitments. The strategy that ultimately worked was to break the building down into smaller, more manageable and more financeable packages of development. These smaller pieces could be individually

planned for housing, retail space, and offices and then variously packaged for financing and construction.

Share the Risks

A project sponsor can contain some of the potential economic risks of an adaptive use project during predevelopment by identifying the major risk factors and allocating portions

Figure 1-19 *(continued).*

What are some of the peculiarities in obtaining financing for adaptive use development?

The ability to secure financing depends on the product. Although it is difficult to obtain financing for mixed-use real estate development, mixed-use development programmatically makes sense for the redevelopment of larger buildings, especially those in urban centers. Older buildings in downtowns are often very well suited for retail space on the ground floor and offices and/or housing on the upper floors. Unfortunately, there are no existing national nonrecourse lending programs for this kind of development. One option is to "condominimize" each use element and obtain separate financing for each. Purely residential rental projects should be designed to qualify for FHA or Fannie Mae (FNMA) credit programs.

Financing assistance from the public sector is often available when the project features affordable housing or generates an appreciable amount of new employment. In such cases, a municipality might help finance the project through low-cost industrial development bonds, home loans, and city or state loan guarantees. If the project meets rent guidelines for affordable housing, there are many conduits to provide equity in exchange for low-income housing tax credits. If the project qualifies for rehabilitation or low-income housing tax credits, limited partners may invest equity in exchange for the tax benefits. Construction financing is available through local banks that are knowledgeable about the market, although banks will most likely require guarantees or evidence of permanent financing before lending funds.

Do you think opportunities for adaptive use will continue to grow?

Over the last 20 years, many older buildings have been renovated for new uses, especially in urban areas. These projects have established that a solid market exists for renovated converted products, and the ability to finance and market the projects has gradually improved.

Adaptive use seems to go in waves. Adventurous developers pioneer in new neighborhoods where buildings are very inexpensive—neighborhoods where they see infrastructure, public space, and an attractive emerging community or quality of life and are willing to take the risk. If they are successful, other developers follow and a new neighborhood of previously ignored inventory becomes available.

At present, there are more opportunities to reuse buildings in urban centers than in suburban areas. Urban buildings tend to be better fenestrated and are more easily subdivided into a variety of uses than suburban buildings. They are often on high-traffic streets that are conducive to retail uses. Suburban buildings tend to be much more specialized and therefore more difficult to convert. For example, there are almost no alternative new uses for a 100,000-square-foot Wal-Mart store, but there are many for an old downtown department store. Furthermore, urban areas tend to have mixed-use zoning, whereas suburban areas have single-use zoning, making it very difficult to introduce new uses into an area when the market changes.

What advice would you give to someone considering an adaptive use project?

Look at every adaptive use project in your local area and figure out its strengths and weaknesses. Talk to many other developers who have worked with existing buildings and pick one whom you could trust as a partner to work with on your first project. Work only with a developer who is willing to put up some equity. Speak with potential lenders and understand their concerns and requirements. Run dozens of pro formas and evaluate many scenarios. For a first project, choose the one with the least risk rather than the highest return.▼

of the risk to various participants. Developers can assign some of the market and financing risks to the users of a project in several ways. A user often contributes equity to the project and, in turn, might have rights with respect to the renovation contracts or management of the building when it becomes operational. Prospective tenants might make upfront commitments for future revenue streams, provide assistance with obtaining zoning and permitting approvals, or in any number of other ways assume some of the risk. A creditworthy tenant's prelease commitment also helps secure financing.

Because of the financing difficulties and special risks involved in adaptive use development, flexibility and collaboration among the players tend to be unusually high; projects are often structured in such a way that several of the participants have a vested interest in the successful completion of the venture.

The first and second floors of the Denver Dry Goods Building are occupied by retail tenants, with office and residential uses on the four upper floors. To make the massive mixed-use adaptive use project more palatable to lenders, separate housing, retail, and office condominium units were bundled into financing and construction packages.

Like MIT Real Estate with its research and development tenants at 640 Memorial Drive in Cambridge and BioLease with BioTransplant, project sponsors sometimes finance tenant buildout. Accepting warrants for equity in tenant companies with potential for growth compensates the developer in part for the risk of a startup company's failure.

Because of the challenges that arise from fitting a proposed building program into an existing layout, the risk is always present of project cost overruns associated with the design and construction of a reuse project. If adequate analyses of the existing structure and local permitting requirements have been made during the due diligence process, many of the potential design and engineering problems can be identified before the project is ever undertaken. It is during this preliminary stage that the project sponsor should evaluate whether the costs of working through the particular structural constraints would be justified by the project's potential income. Easily identifiable potentially costly design problems include low floor-to-floor heights, insufficient floor loading capacity, or unsuitable existing building layouts. Less easily spotted obstacles can exist from the bottom of the building to the top, including poor foundations, hazardous materials, inadequate structural systems, problems with the facade, and faulty roofs, among others.

Once a project is initiated, one of the highest priorities for the project team should be to identify the potentially high-risk design and construction items early in the planning phase of the project and determine where the financial responsibility for the risks will lie. Frank Mead, president of Mead Consulting, Inc., a construction project management firm, suggests that at the onset of the project, the project team should establish detailed design and cost criteria, prepare a conceptual project budget and schedule, estimate the probabilities of cost overruns for high-risk items, and quantify the risk range of these potential costs. Risk can be lessened by selectively raising the contingency for specific line items in the budget.

During planning, the project sponsor generally suggests who will accept responsibility for individual items of risk. For example, the risk of mitigating hazardous materials found during renovation usually lies completely with the owner of the building. The risk of fitting new mechanical systems into the structure often lies completely with the contractor. The risk of overruns related to repairing a facade could be shared by the contractor and the building owner, perhaps with a fixed dollar amount for specific items. Many other allowances and separate cost allocations are possible, depending on how the project team sees its ability to control costs and how much contingency the parties include for each line item.

Another way that project sponsors can manage risk in adaptive use development is to select the types of contracts and bidding methods that will be used with design and engineering consultants and contractors based on the level of risk identified for the project. The classic design-bid-build contract, where architectural and engineering construction documents are bid competitively and awarded to the lowest qualified bidder, is commonly used in moderate-risk conventional development projects. This arrangement can be less attractive in adaptive use development when the design and engineering requirements are not as predictable and a particular need exists for collaboration among the project sponsor, architects, and engineers. Design-build contracts, where one source takes responsibility for the design and construction of a project at a fixed price based on specific performance specifications, can be efficient in relatively low-risk adaptive use projects. But this arrangement can lead to a problem if cost overruns are encountered and the contractor tries to compensate by downgrading the quality of the contract.

Speculative buildings designed for specialized users, such as biotech research and development firms, incur a higher risk than most of scheduling delays and cost overruns. Such buildings are among the least predictable in terms of project costs. They often require expensive building systems, allow very little flexibility for alternative uses, and can be subject to changes in design criteria throughout development. Frank Mead suggests two approaches to project management that can be effective in such circumstances: 1) the program planner, design consultants, and the contractor function as agents or professional consultants to the owner—and the building program, design of the building systems, and construction costs evolve simultaneously; or 2) a program planner assumes responsibility for developing the building program, establishing budgets, and preparing a conceptual design, then hands off the design to a design-production team to prepare final construction documents for a construction manager to implement. Cost plus a fixed fee is appropriate for the construction contract.

Take a Collaborative Approach

Another key to successful adaptive use projects is collaboration from the very beginning among the project's constituents—the property owner, lenders, public officials, neighborhood and special interest groups, and the project team. Local government officials can provide helpful information about requirements of zoning and building codes, tax credits and other incentives that might be available, and neighborhood hot buttons. They generally know what will fly and what will not. Some municipalities charge a preapplication fee to discuss potential development, which can be credited to later fees if the project goes ahead. Landmark buildings or buildings in historic districts might have no preapplication fees. This relatively small cost to obtain very early guidance for a project will be returned many times over by exposing pitfalls that might lie ahead and expediting the permitting process.

Like all real estate development, resistance from neighborhood and special-interest groups is a risk for adaptive use development. Introducing a new use into an area will generally not please everyone, at least not initially. Neighbors raise concerns about the impact of traffic, which elements of the existing building will be changed, the propriety of a proposed new use for a historic building, bringing in mixed-income neighbors or multifamily units to a single-family neighborhood. Yet in most cases, residents and businesses appreciate improvements in their neighborhoods. The best strategy is to approach the interested parties early in the process, listen to their concerns, and respond with solutions and compromises.

Notes

1. Extracted from SIOR and Landauer Real Estate Counselors, *1995 Comparative Statistics of Industrial and Office Real Estate Markets* (Washington, D.C.: Author, 1995).

2. Ibid., p. 22.

3. Donald L. Williams and Sally M. Dwyer, "Recycling Manufacturing Properties, *Urban Land*, January 1995, p. 21.

4. Bruce M. Hoch, "Adaptive Reuse: Opportunities, Challenges," *Corporate Real Estate Executive,* October 1994, pp. 30–31.

5. Janet Smith-Heimer and David Shiver, "Progress in Bay Area Base Conversions," *Urban Land,* December 1994, pp. 38–41.

6. *Base Reuse Report* is a monthly publication containing current news and analysis of the issues surrounding the closure of U.S. military bases and their reuse for civilian purposes. For information, call 916-448-6168.

7. Ellen Kirschner Popper, "Developers Are Bullish on Wall Street," *New York Times,* June 30, 1996.

8. Cecil Baker & Associates, Eugene LeFevre, and Center City District, *Turning On the Lights Upstairs: A Guide for Converting the Upper Floors of Older Commercial Buildings to Residential Use* (Philadelphia: Author, 1996), p. 5. The guide is available from Center City District, 917 Filbert Street, Philadelphia, PA 19107, Phone: 215-440-5500.

9. David Lake, "The Exchange Building: From Offices to Apartments," *Urban Land,* April 1995, pp. 66–67.

10. Much of the following discussion of CCD's demonstration project is from *Turning On the Lights Upstairs,* op. cit.

11. Ibid., p. 10.

12. To order a copy of the guide, call 312-744-3200.

13. Baltimore Heritage, Inc., "Proposal to The Abell Foundation for Class B Office Buildings Study," July 7, 1995.

Part 2

Case Studies

City Lofts

Portland, Oregon

A 70-year-old distribution warehouse in Portland's Pearl District has been refashioned into upscale residential lofts and street-level retail space. City Lofts is Portland's first loft condominium project.

City Lofts is an adaptive use renovation of a light industrial building constructed in 1927 as the headquarters for Eoff Electric Co. and occupied later by Kilham Stationery. Completed in June 1994, the project contains 13 residential loft units (six one-story flats, six two-story townhouses, and one three-story townhouse) and 6,587 square feet of street-level retail space. City Lofts was the first loft condominium project in Portland and the city's

first example of condominium retail space (as opposed to rental) in such a project.

The building occupies one-quarter of a city block in the heart of the Pearl District, one of the fastest-growing residential markets in Portland. A neighborhood close to downtown characterized by old brick warehouses and rutted streets, the Pearl District was named by a gallery owner who noted that much of the neighborhood's beauty is

hidden behind crusty facades, like pearls in oysters. The area did not follow the redevelopment cycle common in cities with thriving residential loft neighborhoods, such as New York and San Francisco, where artists typically act as urban pioneers. In Portland, the urban pioneers were not artists but a few prescient developers who purchased most of the property in the Pearl District. These developers and property owners secured designation as a historic district for a principal section of the Pearl District and created a local improvement district to redevelop the old 13th Avenue railroad tracks with paving and lights. The city of Portland also encouraged the redevelopment of the district when it rezoned the area in 1979 for mixed-use development.

When City Lofts was planned in 1991, four apartment loft projects with a total of almost 250 units had been developed in the Pearl District. Although the market for relatively high-end rentals had been proven, the for-sale market had yet to be tested. In an attempt to broaden the market base for the loft units, the developer, Brandt Development Corporation, decided to deliver nearly half the residential units as shells that condominium owners could finish to suit their individual preferences. Brandt believed that it would be easier to sell the flexible shells (presales being critical for obtaining financing for the project) than fully built-out units. The remaining units were finished with kitchens, bathrooms, and utilities. Selling shell units, though attractive to prospective City Loft buyers, turned out to be the source of numerous problems. Developer Terry Brandt candidly acknowledges that, given the benefit of hindsight, completing the individual units for a more specific market, based on a comprehensive market study, would have been a better strategy than the broad-based approach used.

Financing

As is often the case with adaptive use projects, particularly speculative ones, securing the financing for City Lofts proved to be one of the most challenging aspects of the project. During the early 1990s, conventional bank financing for project construction was generally unavailable unless a development had been presold. The different uses also made it difficult to finance City

Lofts, as lenders had difficulty deciding whether to categorize the project as commercial or residential. Had the units been planned as rental apartments instead of for-sale condominiums, lenders might have had an easier time characterizing it as a commercial project. And lenders were squeamish about the location. Although the Pearl District is now considered part of downtown and one of the city's prime residential markets, before City Lofts the market was regarded as frontier territory. After exhausting traditional lending sources, Brandt was able to raise $1.65 million from a group of private investors, who formed City Lofts Investors, Inc.

Brandt began marketing the lofts six months before construction began, eventually preselling six two-level townhouse units and collecting from $5,000 to $10,000 in nonrefundable earnest money per unit. (The money was later applied to the purchase price of the reserved units.) These units were sold as shells, with the expectation that buyers would hire their own contractors and architects to com-

plete their unit's main living components. The base purchase price for these units included a $15,000 allowance that covered the costs of completing a basic kitchen and bathroom. The costs for finishing the shells ranged from $100,000 to $600,000 per unit beyond the initial purchase price. The project's architects, Vallaster & Corl, which also designed several of the buildouts, note that each client had a different idea of what a loft should be in terms of materials and expression.

U.S. Bank agreed to make condominium home loans, provided the developer met specific requirements of the Federal National Mortgage Association (Fannie Mae). First, the bank would close on an individual loan only after 70 percent of the units (in this case ten) had been presold. Second, the project had to be 100 percent completed before the bank would close on an individual loan. Although the developer fell short of preselling the requisite ten units (six units were presold), U.S. Bank helped by warehousing the loans for a period before reselling them to Fannie Mae.

The requirement for 100 percent completion was more difficult to meet. Once construction was finished on the main structure, buyers were given 60 days to finish building out their shells. As it turned out, 60 days was not enough time. Because one owner's inability to complete construction could jeopardize the loan closings for all the other units, Brandt found itself in the awkward position of having to pressure individual purchasers to complete construction. In the end, the developer continued preselling the units until it completed basic kitchens and baths on the unsold units and could satisfy Fannie Mae's requirement. Fannie Mae also allowed broad interpretation of the

Originally, the building was the headquarters for Eoff Electric Co. and later Kilham Stationery. The original sign on the north side of the building was preserved.

word "habitable" in the definition of 100 percent completion.

Design

Like most adaptive use conversions, the redevelopment of City Lofts required a creative and flexible approach to solving problems. The overarching goal of design was to preserve the building's industrial character. Features that potential loft buyers had identified in a preliminary market survey as desirable—high ceilings with exposed old timbers, wood floors, brick walls, and industrial steel sash windows—set the tone for the renovation.

The primary structural change to the existing building was the addition of the fourth story to accommodate two- and three-level townhouses, which triggered the city's design review process. The design commission wanted the ground-floor windows on NW 10th Avenue and Glisan Street to be lowered to their original position to enhance the pedestrian environment. The developer complied and lowered all the ground-floor windows approximately three feet to be consistent with the two original windows on NW 10th Avenue.

To retain maximum flexibility for the project's retail space, Brandt submitted three alternative design configurations to the city. All three versions were approved, but the retailer that eventually leased the space (with an option to buy) wanted the main entryway on the south side to be relocated to the east side, requiring a subsequent amendment to the approved design. Similar to other industrial buildings in the neighborhood, the first floor was constructed about three feet above grade to facilitate loading. The developer installed a lift in the retail entryway to make it accessible for the handicapped.

Planners determined the size and number of residential units to be offered based on the number of parking stalls that could be created in the 10,000-square-foot basement pad. Each stall provides at least one space per unit. Portions of some of the larger stalls, which contain as many as four parking spaces, have been turned into storage space. Terry Brandt notes that if the project were built today, he might provide less parking. When City Lofts was first planned, security was a major concern and residents were reluctant to park on the street. Now that more people live in the area, concerns have eased somewhat and residents might be more willing to park and walk a block or two to the building.

The residential entry was separated from the retail space to establish an identifiable residential component for the project as well as to strengthen security. A self-locking front door with keypad access was installed at the main residential entry lobby. Separate locked doors secure the garage. Despite these measures, however, numerous break-ins have occurred. Part of the problem is that the residential entryway is recessed some ten feet from the sidewalk, so that at night, the entryway is dark and intruders are not easily seen from Glisan Street. Although Glisan Street is heavily trafficked, the building directly across the street—an automotive repair shop—closes at 5 P.M. and there are consequently no "eyes on the street" to survey the block. Owners have installed steel grilles on first-floor windows and extra locks on doors. Much of the glass in the entryway has been replaced with high-impact plexiglass. A video surveillance system will also be installed in the lobby and garage.

Renovation

Offering shells rather than completed units for sale created innumerable construction complications that resulted in delays and budget overruns. One problem was that some of the contractors hired by owners to finish individual units had no experience with adaptive use development and badly under-

City Lofts before it was converted to loft condominiums.

Because the demand for loft condominiums in Portland was untested, the developer sold half of the residential units as "shells" that the individual owners would build out, believing that shell units would appeal to a broader customer base. While the shell approach may have had marketing appeal, it created construction complications and time delays.

The interior of this built-out townhouse unit and the shell unit above highlight the industrial design vernacular incorporating wood beam ceilings, exposed brick walls, steel sash windows, and polished cement.

estimated construction time. Because of Fannie Mae's requirement that all the units be completed before U.S. Bank would close on any one loan, unit owners were under the gun to finish their construction on time. In addition, the ineptitude

of the developer's contractor, who was eventually replaced, further stretched out construction time from the planned six months to a year.

The most serious construction issue involved the transmission of

sound between the residential floors and walls. Because the building initially served an industrial function, no attempt had been made to minimize sound transmission. Complicating any solution to the problem was that the very design features that preserved the industrial integrity of the space and that potential homeowners said they most desired —high ceilings, exposed brick walls, wood beam ceilings, and wood floors—amplify noise. The steel I-beams that were installed in City Lofts as seismic bracing exacerbated the problem.

The sound transmission coefficient (STC) rating promised in the condominium documents exceeded the code requirement of 45 (field test). Brandt hired a sound engineer to devise a system for City Lofts that would achieve a 60 to 65 STC laboratory rating. This higher threshold, which is considered exceptional, is extremely costly and difficult to achieve, even with new construction. Because of cost constraints, the comprehensive system the sound engineer recommended was not fully constructed. The primary method to decrease sound transmission in the project was installation of a layer of gypcrete between each floor, but it apparently is not sufficient.

In addition, the strategy of offering shells for sale opened a Pandora's box of difficulties with sound transmission. Some contractors hired to complete the individual units unknowingly wreaked havoc during construction with the noise buffering system that Brandt had installed. Furthermore, where brick walls touched a ceiling, the developer had sealed the area to prevent flanking noise, and many of those seals were undone by the construction on the shells.

One resident, who is currently retrofitting his one-level apartment with additional sound buffering, describes the building as a "giant vibrating drum." He has torn out several demising walls, added more studs, and staggered them as a way to minimize sound vibrations. He has also dropped the ceiling about five inches so he could add some three and one-half inches of fiberglass between the joists and about an inch more of air space for sound insulation. Wall-to-wall carpeting could help mute floor-to-floor noise, but many of the owners invested in expensive hardwood floors, which they are loathe to cover.

In addition to the problems caused by construction inside the units, the developer also had to bear the cost of repairing common stair and hallway finishes damaged by the contractors. At last count, all common doors and hallways had been repaired and repainted four separate times. Although the developer delayed completing these finishes as long as possible, contractors for the unit owners were slow to claim responsibility for damage they may have done to common areas.

Marketing and Leasing

The target market for City Lofts included middle- to upper-income professionals who already lived in the loft district and those who wanted to leave single-family houses and live closer to downtown. In reality, the anticipated market closely resembled the profile of the actual buyers of the lofts. Two loft renters purchased apartments at City Lofts; middle-income professionals and some retired people purchased the remaining units. Professionals and empty nesters, most of whom left single-family houses in Portland's

affluent suburbs, purchased the more expensive units. It took six months to presell the first six units; the remaining units sold within a year following construction.

The main challenge to marketing the retail space was that it was Portland's first example of condominium retail space in a project comprising more than one use. Moreover, the space was unusually large. The economics-driven strategy of marketing the full 6,587 square feet to one purchaser, instead of breaking up the space, called for a large retailer, such as a furniture store or showroom. The space fronts directly onto two busy streets with reasonably high traffic counts. The condominium agreements disallowed restaurants or other retail uses that would emit smells or generate noise late at night.

Several potential retailers turned down the space because it had no on-site parking. It took nearly four years to fill the space, which was ultimately leased in 1995 (with an option to buy) to Roche Bobois Furniture and Interior Design. This French-based company, with more than 20 outlets in the United States, is accustomed to working in dense, urban locations. To compensate for the lack of off-street parking at the Portland store, the retailer generally delivers merchandise directly to customers' homes.

Experience Gained

▼ Because City Lofts was a pioneer project and the demand for loft condominiums unproven, the

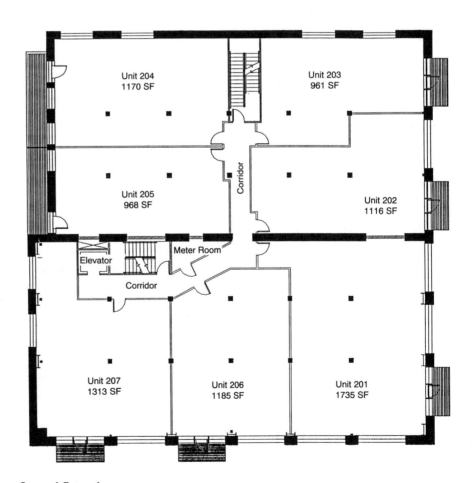

Second-floor plan.

▼ Project Data

Land Use Information

Site Area: 0.23 acre
Total Dwelling Units: 13
Total Retail Units: 1
Gross Density: 56 units per acre
Off-Street Parking Spaces: 13

Land Use Plan

	Square Feet	Percent of Building
Basement	9,750	20.0
Ground-Floor Retail	6,587	13.5
Housing	22,011	45.0
External Terraces	3,650	7.5
Internal Common Areas	6,752	14.0
Total	48,750	100.0

Residential Unit Information

Unit Type	Unit Size (square feet)	Number of Units	Range of Initial Base Sale Prices
1-Story Flats	961–1,735	6	$144,000–180,000
2-Story Townhouses	1,829–2,487	6	$168,500–280,000[1]
3-Story Townhouse	2,456	1	$269,000

Ground-Floor Retail Space

Square Feet	Number of Tenants	Initial Sale Price
6,587	1	$450,000[2]

Redevelopment Cost Information

Acquisition Cost	$720,000

Site Improvement and Construction Costs

Demolition	$ 75,000
Superstructure/seismic upgrade	145,000
HVAC/electrical/plumbing/sprinklers	200,000
Finishes	605,000
Fees/general conditions	130,000
Elevator	45,000
Total	$1,200,000

Soft Costs

Architecture/engineering	$ 78,000
Project management	60,000
Marketing/sales and leasing commissions	60,000
Legal/accounting	35,000
Taxes/insurance	15,000
Title fees (not including unit sales)	7,000
Construction interest and fees	202,000
Appraisal/environmental/survey	25,000
System development fees/water/sewer	25,000
Total	$507,000

Total Redevelopment Cost	**$2,427,000**

Total Redevelopment Cost per Unit	**$153,846[3]**

Developer

Brandt Development Corporation
800 NW 6th, Suite 301
Portland, Oregon 97209
503-227-2777

Architect

Vallaster & Corl
711 SW Alder
Portland, Oregon 97205
503-228-0311

Marketing

R.C. Ford Company
1815 NW Northrup, Suite 100
Portland, Oregon 97209
503-224-7085

Development Schedule

Site Purchased: November 1991
Planning Started: October 1991
Construction Started: June 1992
Sales Started: January 1992
First Closing: October 1993
Sales Completed: June 1994

Notes:
[1] Includes $15,000 allowance for buildout of kitchen and bath.
[2] Original asking price. Unit was subsequently leased at $8.00 per square foot, triple net, with an option to buy.
[3] Excludes cost related to retail space.

---

developer decided to offer shells for owners to finish, believing the ability to design a custom-built house would offer the most flexibility and appeal to the broadest customer base. In hindsight, a more economical approach would have been to undertake a comprehensive predevelopment market study and tailor the units to a more specific market.

- Closer supervision of construction plans and activity in the units by the developer, architect, and loft owners would have eliminated some of the problems. For instance, the way that skylights were installed in some of the units weakened the roof membrane in several spots, subsequently leading to leaks.

- Redevelopment of existing buildings invariably uncovers surprises that can generate unanticipated costs. To allow for the unexpected, higher contingency factors should be included in the construction budget.

- To avoid unanticipated construction costs associated with sound transmission, a sound engineer should undertake a thorough on-site inspection, detailing all wall-to-wall and ceiling-to-floor sound-related connections and specifying precise methods needed to remedy particular noise "hot spots."

- Because it was difficult to finance City Lofts, the project might not have been adequately capitalized to cover unbudgeted construction costs. Although some of these costs were caused in part by the first contractor's shoddy work, it usually does not pay in the long run to skimp on fundamental systems (in this case sound transmission).

- Based on profits from resales of City Loft units, the initial sale prices could probably have been set at least 20 percent higher. Higher prices would have provided more cushion in the construction budget so that the developer would have had more flexibility to absorb some of the hidden costs without reducing overall profitability.

- The developer paid a significant price for preserving the original industrial materials. It would have been simpler and less expensive to simply cover the wood timbers in the ceilings with plasterboard and sheathe the brick walls with plaster. Certainly, the problems with noise transmission would have been less severe if the developer had selected these alternatives. Despite the arduous construction process and annoying inconveniences, however, residents are generally pleased with their profitable investments.

- Although it took some four years to lease the retail space, the developer eventually secured the ideal tenant—at a higher rate than if it had leased the space immediately. Retailers of the type that was targeted for City Lofts are generally adverse to locating in higher-risk market areas. Although the Pearl District is now viewed as part of downtown, it certainly was not when the space was first marketed.

Lake Union Steam Plant

Seattle, Washington

For nearly a decade after the city closed this landmark power plant, its highest use was as a home for vagrants. After extensive environmental cleanup and a highly complex but efficient adaptive use renovation, the Lake Union Steam Plant is now the headquarters office and laboratory for a biotechnology research company.

The metamorphosis of the Lake Union Steam Plant to modern laboratory and office space for biotechnology research and development reflects the lasting utility and renewable value of many 20th century industrial buildings. Extending over the eastern shore of Lake Union, about one mile from downtown Seattle, the steam plant provided power to the city for more than 70 years. The massive trapezoidal structure, with its seven tower-ing smokestacks and large window bays, has been a prominent landmark on the Seattle waterfront for generations. During its prime, 50-foot-high lit letters towered above the plant, spelling out the name of this publicly owned power plant.

When the old plant was decommissioned in 1984, the city and many in the community hoped to find a new use or a buyer for the property, but the building was to remain vacant and unmaintained for nearly a decade. In June 1994, after first attempting to convert the building into a 109-unit condominium project, the Koll Company completed 14 months of extensive renovations to transform the Seattle Steam Plant into a headquarters and laboratory for ZymoGenetics, a Seattle-based biotech firm.

Site History

Seattle City Light, the city-owned utility, built the steam plant in three stages between 1911 and 1922. An addition to the plant was planned but never built, because a more efficient source of power—hydro-electricity generated from dams and transmitted to the city—became available. Adjacent to the steam plant is a tiny house-like hydro-electric station—a 1,300-square-foot mission-style structure—built before the plant was constructed to generate electricity through tur-bincs using water piped from an upland reservoir. The Hydro House, as it is called today, ceased operations in 1931 but is back in service as a cafeteria for ZymoGenetics's employees.

After 1938, the steam plant was no longer Seattle's primary source of electricity, but its seven pairs of boilers were kept operable until 1980 to provide auxiliary power to the city. The facility was shut down completely in 1984. Over several years following its decommissioning, the city tried unsuccessfully to find a buyer or alternative use for the extensively contaminated and deteriorating historic property, but the plant remained vacant and become a haven for vagrants. In 1988, in an effort to save the structures for future rehabilitation, a group of citizens successfully nominated the Lake Union Steam Plant and the Hydro House for designation as historic landmarks.

Project Feasibility

In 1989, shortly after the steam plant's designation as a historic landmark, Koll Real Estate Group offered another parcel of land to the city in exchange for the steam plant and began planning to redevelop the property into residential condominiums. During 1990 and 1991, Koll took the proposed project through a lengthy public hearing process, including 28 public meetings with the Seattle City Council and numerous other meetings with the Seattle Landmarks Preservation Board.

The developer was successful in obtaining all the necessary approvals, including a ten-year property tax abatement from the state for restoration of a historic landmark. Unfortunately, the timing of the project coincided with a period of severely tight credit, and Koll was unable to obtain nonrecourse construction financing for the condominium scheme, even after taking deposits on 55 of the 109 planned units. The company continued its search for funding for the building's use as a condominium until Koll approached a potential biotech

user that could internally finance an adaptive use renovation.

To make future redevelopment of the steam plant more feasible, the city assumed responsibility for environmental remediation. While negotiating with Koll for the property, the city offered the developer a $1 million discount (its estimate of the cost of cleanup) to take the property in its present condition, assuming that Koll could do the cleanup for less by avoiding the public bidding process required for city contracts. William Justen, Koll's senior project manager for the steam plant property, says the company declined the offer, accurately assessing the cost to be much higher. The city proceeded to remove asbestos, heavy metals, oils, heavy concentrations of PCBs, and over 23 million pounds of piping, boilers, generators, turbines, and other material at a cost of nearly $4 million. Koll eventually spent an additional $170,000 to remove lead paint that was not included in the city's scope of work.

In fall 1991, Koll made a proposal to ZymoGenetics to convert the steam plant into an office and research facility for the biotech firm. ZymoGenetics had considered other options to house its rapidly expanding operations, including moving into other existing properties or building a new facility. The company finally chose to reuse the Lake Union Steam Plant, partly because its parent company (Novo Nordisk, a large Danish pharmaceutical company based in Copenhagen) is strongly committed to the preservation and reuse of historic structures. The steam plant's proximity to the University of Washington and the Fred Hutchinson Cancer Research Center (developed by Koll), with which ZymoGenetics works, also made the location attractive.

With a firm commitment from ZymoGenetics in hand to occupy the building, Koll initiated the $25 million renovation. Obtaining approvals for this radically revised use required taking it before citizens groups that were expecting condominiums. Use by Zymo-

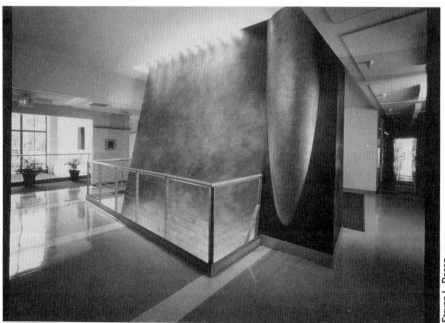

A new central stairway rises through an open shaft, subtly changing shape along the way.

Genetics was eventually approved, but only after Koll agreed to retain some specific characteristics of the building, including reproducing the original smokestacks and the existing window system. During design, it became clear that the research and development use allowed a closer facsimile of the original appearance of the industrial building than the residential use would have permitted.

Physical Configuration

The original steam plant is a massive concrete structure, 300 feet long by 90 feet wide by 50 feet high. The 127,000-square-foot building is a trapezoidal structure with no true parallel walls. Visible from many vantages throughout the city of Seattle, the building has five bays of glass on the north and south ends of the building and 19 glass bays on the lake and street sides of the building. These huge bays give the building a monumental presence indicative of an era when public buildings had great civic importance. Because the building is located over the edge of Lake Union, it is supported on approximately 2,000 12-inch-diameter timber piles. The concrete pile caps extend below the mudline so that the pilings are always embedded in earth, thereby maintaining their structural integrity.

Directly above the lake were the plant's two operating levels: the basement and the main floor located 20 feet above the basement. The floors were cast-in-place concrete beam and slab structures able to carry heavy industrial loads up to 600 pounds per square foot; they were supported by the main columns and a labyrinth of interme-

diate columns. Concrete columns 30 to 36 inches square supported the building shell, and deep lateral spandrel beams interconnected the perimeter columns to provide lateral stiffness. The main floor and the columns below supported seven pairs of boilers, each housed in a steel skeleton and brick shell. These boilers also functioned as support for the original 92-inch-diameter steel smokestacks, which extended 105 feet above the roof. The stacks were laterally supported by guy wires and attached to the top of the concrete columns.

Conversion

The complex conversion of the steam plant began in April 1993 and was completed ahead of schedule in June 1994. The existing building presented many design and engineering challenges but also offered some special opportunities. One important advantage was that the structural work could be sequenced from the top down to allow an early start on the most intensive work—the rooftop mechanical systems and the mechanical system for laboratories on the upper floor. This top-down sequencing saved time on the aggressive schedule set by ZymoGenetics, as it allowed roofing and finish work to proceed much more quickly. Another advantage was a fortuitous discovery of a 1915 University of Washington research paper that provided crucial information on the construction of the steam plant.

Koll's design team began by conducting extensive interviews with the ZymoGenetics staff to outline laboratory and administrative functions, and requirements for laboratory mechanical and gas systems. Extensive surveys of the existing building revealed that the

main structural components were adequate for ZymoGenetics's needs. Daly and Associates, the project architect, and Ratti Swerison Perbix, the structural engineer, were familiar with the existing building, having worked on Koll's plans for condominiums. Moreover, NBBJ, the interior architect, had recently completed a laboratory and pilot plant for ZymoGenetics near the university campus. Koll hired the mechanical, electrical, and plumbing subcontractors on a design-build basis and brought them on board at the beginning of the project. According to the project architect, their quick reviews of cost, constructability, and performance during design saved time and money in the long run. Careful planning from the very beginning was a major factor in the project team's success in meeting ZymoGenetics's requirements for space, budget, and deadline.

The final program indicated a need for 95,000 usable square feet at initial occupancy. ZymoGenetics needed predominantly clear-span laboratory spaces, a well-organized mechanical distribution system that could be easily modified and expanded, and a common service core between laboratories for shared equipment and conference rooms. ZymoGenetics also wanted to emphasize the laboratories and orient them toward the building's exterior to take advantage of views and natural light. The offices would be grouped around the center of the building to encourage informal interaction among scientists, a design that expressed the dynamic nature of the company's work.

The high vertical floor clearance required for the laboratories' mechanical systems emerged as a critical factor in design. Existing constraints on height and bulk limited expansion of the building envelope.

Working within a stringent budget, the designers created the needed vertical space by devising a three-floor scheme. It required constructing two new floors above the existing main floor for laboratories and offices and replacing the heavy main floor 18 inches lower than the original, which provided the extra clearance necessary for the new floors above. The original penthouse on the roof was expanded and a floor inserted to create two additional floors for laboratories and mechanical rooms. Finally, two levels of parking were constructed in the former basement.

Although the existing building greatly exceeded heights permitted by the zoning code, it was grandfathered under the previous zoning ordinance. A zoning variance was required, however, to expand the existing penthouse. The variance was approved on the basis that the expansion of the penthouse was necessary to support replacement smokestacks on the roof, as required by the Seattle Landmarks Preservation Board. The seven old deteriorated stacks were removed with the demolition of the seven pairs of interior boilers that had supported them, so structural support for the replacement stacks was no longer available. The penthouse provided the necessary support and, as a bonus, created 17,000 square feet of office and laboratory space on top of the building.

Structural Concerns

The insertion of the new floor slabs created new structural requirements for the building. Three existing primary structural bays supported the main portion of the building, but designers determined that the heavy

The laboratories have open views of Lake Union and its ever-present fleet of sailboats, emphasizing the labs' importance to the research and development company. Scientists' offices are on the street side of the building.

new floors would overload the existing center bay. Modification of the existing pile caps or other work on the building's foundation was effectively precluded by the presence of toxic waste in the lake under the building. To solve this problem, a new center column line was installed following an existing line of pile caps.

Another structural concern was that the existing main floor needed additional support. New support columns could not be used, because they would interfere with the basement parking garage. The architects considered using a framework of

steel beams and columns but ultimately determined that it would be more cost-effective to replace the existing floor.

Because of the change in use and the amount of demolition involved in the project, the city required a substantial amount of seismic retrofitting, achieved by strengthening and bracing both ends of the building and down the center. (See *Civil Engineering* [September 1994, pp. 44–47] and *Modern Steel Construction* [January 1995, pp. 36–43] for more specific information about the structural design of this project.)

1 Entry Lobby
2 Atrium
3 Offices
4 Mechanical Room
5 Parking

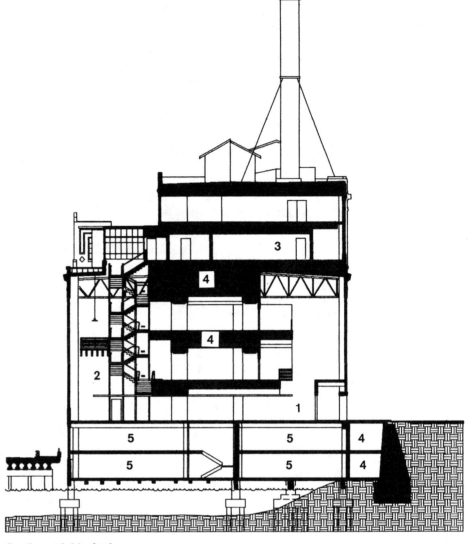

Section at lobby/atrium.

Floor Construction

The second and third floors for offices and laboratories were the first to be installed. The floors were framed with composite steel beams, which were found to be more cost-effective than a post-tensioned concrete slab. Construction of the floors also helped to provide lateral stability during demolition of the main floor, which occurred after the second-floor metal deck was welded.

The penthouse floors were constructed after the second- and third-level floors were in place. The penthouse was the only external structural change to the building. The expansion created two levels of office and laboratory space, the upper of which is now vacant and intended for future expansion. Two hydraulic cranes lifted construction materials to the roof for expansion of the penthouse, an operation that had to be conducted over a weekend to accommodate the closing of a street that serves as a major staging area for commuter buses. More than 400 structural steel members were installed in two days.

Replacement of the main floor slab was the next phase. Demolition of the main floor structure was phased to provide interim structural stability and to retain a way to get between levels. Like the upper floors, the main floor was replaced with a composite steel-frame floor.

The upper parking level in the basement was the final slab to be constructed; it was built between the existing basement slab and the new main floor slab. To maximize floor-to-floor space for mechanical systems in the laboratories, the two parking levels were located as low as possible, with the first level of

parking on the original concrete deck three feet above the lake below. No construction below the building's basement level was permitted because of the presence of contaminated sediments approximately six feet below.

Interior Renovation

ZymoGenetics's administrative offices and main lobby occupy the building's first level. Only one elevator services the building, a con-

First floor.

Laboratory floor.

scious effort to encourage interaction among the scientists on the stairwells and landings, although the elevator shaft is designed for a second elevator should one become necessary in the future. The offices surround two vertical atria, and the laboratories are located at the north and south ends and west side of the building. The atria help to retain a sense of the original steam plant's high-bay configuration. A staircase that changes form as it twists upward 50 feet connects the first level with the laboratories and offices above; it is based on a spiral metal staircase that had to be taken out of the steam plant because of concerns about safety. The new stairway serves dual purposes: it offers faster access than the elevator, and it provides social space for employees, particularly on a wide landing facing the lake known as

"the raft," which is furnished with comfortable seating.

Community Concerns

The steam plant's designation as a historic landmark meant that all modifications to the building had to be approved by the Seattle Landmarks Preservation Board. In addition, a citizens advisory committee provided public comments on the uses and design of the project because it had been a publicly owned building for so long and was now going into private use. The final plans for ZymoGenetics's new building responded to concerns about preserving the building's architectural and historic integrity. The smokestacks proved to be the

most controversial aspect of the project. Some 50 newspaper articles across the country as well as radio and television coverage reported the controversy. Although many in the community wanted the developer to keep the building's seven original smokestacks and original glass windows, the old stacks and window frames were so badly deteriorated that they could not be preserved. Koll's proposal, which was ultimately approved, was to construct six close reproductions of the original stacks, which are supported by the penthouse. The new stacks are 72-inch-diameter steel pipes that extend 55 feet above the penthouse roof. The new stacks are not just for show: four of the stacks are used for ventilating laboratories, and the other two will be used when the building is fully occupied.

▼ Project Data

Land Use Information

Site Area: 56,716 square feet
Site Coverage: 70%
Gross Building Area (GBA):
  Office and Laboratory: 125,000 square feet
  Other: 2,000 square feet
  Total: 127,000 square feet
Percent Usable: 91.3%
Typical Floor Size: 27,000 square feet
Floor/Area Ratio: 2.24
Parking:
  Structured: 172 spaces
  Surface: 17 spaces
  Total: 189 spaces

Land Use Plan

	Acres
Buildings (2)	.64
Parking Structures (basement)	.23
Paved Areas (surface parking/roads)	.10
Landscaped Areas	.23
Other	.10
Total	1.30

Redevelopment Cost Information

Site Acquisition Cost (land and building)	$3,595,000

Site Improvement and Construction Costs

Earthwork	$ 923,000
Sprinklers	227,000
Structure	3,392,000
Demolition	848,000
Exterior renovation	1,965,000
Roofing	387,000
Interior construction	2,967,000
HVAC	3,302,000
Electrical	1,836,000
Plumbing	1,113,000
Plumbing (energy testing)	8,000
Energy rebate	(194,000)
Lead paint abatement	168,000
Washington State sales tax (8.2%)	1,439,000
Other	259,000
Total	$18,640,000

Soft Costs

Architectural/engineering	$1,416,000
Furnishings	134,000
Testing, inspection permits, as-built survey, environmental evaluation	1,024,000
Total	$2,574,000
Total Redevelopment Cost	**$24,809,000**
Site Improvement and Construction Cost per Gross Square Foot	$147

Developer

The Koll Real Estate Group
2033 First Avenue
Suite 1700
Seattle, Washington 90121
206-718-2764

Owner

ZymoGenetics
1201 Eastlake Avenue East
Seattle, Washington 98102
206-442-6600

Architect

Daly and Associates
2025 First Avenue
Seattle, Washington 98121
206-728-8063

Interior Architect (lab/office design)

NBBJ
111 South Jackson Street
Seattle, Washington 98104
206-223-5555

Mechanical Design-Build Contractor

Holaday Park, Inc.
4600 South 134th Place
Seattle, Washington 98168
206-248-9700

Development Schedule

Site Purchased: May 1992
Planning Started: May 1992
Construction Started: April 1993
Project Completed: June 1994

Another public concern was that the industrial look of the exterior windows be preserved. The badly deteriorated, old, small single-pane windows and steel sashes had to be replaced. Koll proposed an aluminum window-wall system that retained the original appearance but incorporated slightly larger panes of energy-efficient glass, which the community accepted.

Access to the building was another source of concern. The nature of ZymoGenetics's business requires extremely tight security. But because it previously had been a public building, the city of Seattle felt that some degree of public access should be available. The Hydro House adjoining the steam plant was part of the solution; it offers an espresso bar and a dining/community room open to both employees and the public. The walls of the Hydro House are lined with an interesting display of historic photos depicting the plant's construction and appearance during its early years. The public can view the main building's lobby and get a sense of its high bays only through a glass-enclosed vestibule in the main entrance of the building. A 400-foot public walkway with a small launch for non-trailered boats also was constructed on the lake side. The president of ZymoGenetics, a former Olympic rower for Great Britain, was very "keen" on this public amenity.

Experienced Gained

▼ The project used a negotiated construction contract and design-build subcontractors for mechanical, electrical, and plumbing work. These individuals were brought in during the design phase of the project so that they could provide valuable input to the design team. In the architect's view, doing so saved money in the long run.

▼ ZymoGenetics's need to have the project completed within two years once it approved plans was very aggressive for such a complex project. Koll was able to meet the tight schedule largely through time saved by the top-down construction sequencing. Having the principal contractors on board during the early planning stage was crucial to the project team's ability to design and execute the strategy.

▼ Early in design, the mechanical engineer used a CAD (computer-aided design) structural drawing to plan the project's complex mechanical requirements, which were made more difficult by the variable structural conditions of the existing building.

Pentagon Centre

Arlington, Virginia

A vacant 445,000-square-foot 1950s office and warehouse structure now houses a retail power center. Shown above is the former office portion of the building before the conversion. The entrance to the new interior mall (below) is at the center of a row of storefront restaurants added to the original building.

Pentagon Centre is a 320,000-leasable-square-foot retail power center in Arlington, Virginia, that was redeveloped from an abandoned warehouse and office building dating from the 1950s. The reasons the project owner/developer chose to reuse this particular building over other alternatives considered, including constructing a new facility

or redeveloping other existing structures, highlight some of the distinct competitive advantages of adaptive use under certain circumstances.

Price Enterprises, Inc. (formerly PriceCostco, Inc., and The Price Company), owner and operator of the Price Club warehouse/grocery club chain, opened Pentagon Centre in two phases in spring and fall

1994. A 155,000-square-foot Price Club membership warehouse anchors the power center. An adjoining 165,000-square-foot interior mall includes four big-box users: Best Buy, Borders Books & Music, Linens 'N Things, and Marshalls. Four food operators totaling 22,500 square feet have storefronts on the street: California Pizza Kitchen, Chevys Mexican Restaurant, Fresh Choice, and Starbucks Coffee. A freestanding 4,000-square-foot tire center is adjacent to Price Club. The project has a total of 1,226 parking spaces: 639 on grade and 587 in a garage created out of the second floor and roof of the office portion of the original building.

Site History

For many years, the site was served by a freight rail line and occupied by a brick-manufacturing yard. Western Electric constructed a regional telephone servicing facility there in 1957 to serve the equipment repair and distribution needs of the mid-Atlantic and New England regions. The facility employed 500 people in its 240,000-square-foot warehouse and connected 205,000-square-foot two-story office building. The warehouse was constructed of steel, and the adjoining offices were built of poured-in-place concrete. Reflecting the Cold War of the 1950s and the site's one-half-mile proximity to the Pentagon, the second-floor employee cafeteria was constructed solidly enough to double as a bomb shelter.

The site was zoned for industrial uses when Arlington County adopted its first zoning ordinance in the 1950s. During master planning for Pentagon City (the section of the county surrounding the site) in the early 1970s, the Western Electric facility was deliberately omitted from the master plan and from subsequent rezonings. The site's grandfathered industrial zoning designation allows higher uses, including office and retail space, by right. The maximum density allowed for the site has continued to be approximately 1.05 million gross square feet of building area, or a 1.5 floor/area ratio.

In 1979, the Washington Metropolitan Area Transit Authority (WMATA) acquired the northwest corner of the property to provide an entrance to a planned subway station. The opening of the subway spurred rapid development, which was supported by the county's policy of concentrating high-density growth at subway stations. The Pentagon City area developed dramatically in the 1980s, with new residential townhouses, apartment buildings, 12-story office buildings, hotels, and an 820,000-square-foot, high-end regional shopping mall directly across the street from the Western Electric site.

The deregulation of the telecommunications industry in the early 1980s eventually eliminated the need for Western Electric's office and warehouse operations. AT&T, the successor to Western Electric, closed the facility in 1989. A private developer put the site under a $70 million contract at that time for a

Much of the former warehouse section of the building (top) was converted into a 155,000-square-foot Price Club grocery/warehouse (below). Designers were able to reuse several of the original loading docks, the cement slab floor, the gypsum roof, and interior steel columns from the old warehouse. The only major structural change made to the existing building was constructing a parking deck on the second floor and roof of the old offices.

new development of 1.5 million gross square feet of office space. Arlington County planners supported this density, which was higher than allowed by right, to reinforce their policy of high-density uses around subway stations. The new development did not pan out, however, and the contract was dropped when the local office market plunged. The next expression of interest came in 1992 from the federal General Services Administration (GSA), which put the site under contract for $52 million with the intent of relocating Navy Headquarters to the site. GSA planned to develop 1 million gross square feet of office space for up to 6,000 workers. Like the earlier contract to purchase the property, the deal fell through, this time because of changes in federal military spending allocations. Price Enterprises started looking at the

property in October 1992 as a potential site for a new Price Club facility and finally acquired it for $40.6 million in September 1993.

Project Feasibility

While Price Club and most of its eventual cotenants at Pentagon Centre had several suburban stores located outside the Washington Beltway, those locations were not adequately serving the dense and affluent inner suburban neighborhoods of Arlington, Alexandria, and northern Fairfax County. Nor were they reaching the employment center of the District of Columbia.

During 1992, Price considered several alternative sites in Arlington County and the District of Columbia to serve as its "downtown" location for the Washington metropolitan market. The company's primary objective was to enter this market as quickly as possible without incurring excessive costs. Several sites that Price looked at in Arlington County, including a vacant Sears building in the Clarendon section of the county, were rejected because of the anticipated opposition from neighbors and uncertainty about achieving the necessary zoning. Price also rejected several sites in the District of Columbia because of high land costs.

The available AT&T property in Arlington, directly across the Potomac River from Washington and easily accessible by major commuter corridors (I-395 and U.S. Route 1) and by subway and bus, appeared to be a prime location for a new Price Club store. The success of the Fashion Centre mall directly across Hayes Street had already established Pentagon City as a major shopping destination for Price's targeted core metropolitan customers.

Price explored a range of options at the Pentagon City site before finally deciding to buy the entire property and reuse the existing industrial building, which was more than twice the space needed for the Price Club facility. First, the company considered leasing space in the AT&T building for a Price Club grocery store; then it explored the possibility of a joint venture with AT&T for a high-density office and retail project. AT&T was unwilling to tie the property up in a long-term lease, preferring instead to preserve the potential office value of the site. When it finally decided to buy the property, Price seriously considered demolishing the existing building and developing a new multilevel Price Club store. Ultimately, it decided to reuse the building, because this option offered the most expedient completion and opening.

The glass, steel, and simple lines of the restaurant storefronts added to the front of the industrial building create an open, contemporary feel.

Development of a high-density mixed-use project would have necessitated obtaining public approvals. As for demolishing the existing building and building a new facility, new construction of any kind would have taken longer than an adaptive use renovation of the existing building, thus delaying the Price Club opening. Because the prevailing industrial zoning allowed retail uses by right, approval for adapting the old office and warehouse building for retail space would be a relatively routine administrative process, and the new store could open within six to nine months.

The favorable zoning designation of the AT&T site would not only allow Price to open a warehouse quickly, but would also eliminate the need to go public early in the process, which could stir up public opposition or competition from other retailers for this "office" site. Price was able to negotiate an acceptable purchase price and put the property under contract. Because the $40.6 million purchase price was significantly lower than earlier contracts, AT&T allowed no permit contingencies and granted a very limited period in which Price had to make a decision. During the due diligence period, the company met with a local attorney and the county economic development and planning departments and concluded that there would be little resistance to the proposed retail use. In fact, the only exposure to the public approval process that Price would eventually undergo would be to request approval for appropriate retail signage for the former industrial facility.

Having determined that an adaptive use strategy would best accomplish its objectives for opening a Price Club facility, Price considered the real estate opportunity presented by the surplus space. The existing 445,000-square-foot structure (240,000 square feet of warehouse space, 205,000 square feet of office space) was considerably larger than the 155,000 square feet required for the Price Club. Given the site's premier retail location, Price decided it would use the remaining space to develop a power center that would include big-box retailers and restaurants. Although Price did not have commitments from tenants before acquiring the site, the company and its leasing agents felt confident that signing tenants would not be difficult.

Physical Constraints

The challenge in configuring the new mall space was to create a functional scheme that would maximize leasable retail space and parking while limiting new construction to keep costs down. The physically constrained site required the big-box tenants to adjust their normal layouts to fit into the available space. Although these tenants prefer exterior primary store entrances, the very limited setbacks and the lack of peripheral parking excluded that option. Instead, each big-box tenant has its main entrance from the central concourse of the interior mall. Tenants initially were concerned about these conditions, but the location's strong retail value outweighed any reservations. Other constraints in the mall portion of the development resulted from existing column locations and low ceiling heights in the concrete structure of the old office building. The concourse could be only 20 feet wide, the minimum allowed by the fire code, and the ceiling heights measured just 13½ feet, far different from the lofty, open designs of most modern shopping malls.

The large existing building footprint and limited setbacks on three sides of the building greatly limited the parking field. To provide adequate parking, a parking deck had to be constructed above the retail stores. In addition to the difficulty of the actual construction, placing the parking deck on top of retail facilities created a number of other problems, such as locating and configuring the mechanical systems without adversely affecting the retail stores or sacrificing valued parking stalls.

The final architectural design respects the palette of materials in and the character of the original building, despite adding entrances, loading docks, parking, and other elements necessary for a retail center. Michael Gick of Morgan Gick and Associates, architect for the project, says the intent was to make the mall inviting from the street and in the public areas with lighting, storefront glass, signage, and canopies, while keeping costs to a minimum.

Conversion

The existing industrial building was exceptionally strong structurally and accommodated some unconventional design approaches that were necessary to fit the new use. The first phase of the project entailed the development of the Price Club facility from part of the existing warehouse and the surface parking lot. Price Club was able to use the original concrete slab floor of the warehouse, which was in good condition. The original gypsum panel–decked roof above the Price Club portion of the project was retained and carefully modified to accommodate the new HVAC (heating, ventilation, air-conditioning) system. Some of the original loading docks were upgraded for Price Club's use, although the spaces were tighter than ideal. The tight site left little room for construction staging. Even the inside of the warehouse was used to stockpile earth and construction debris temporarily while construction of the Price Club and the parking lot was in progress. Price Club's operations suffered somewhat while the next phase of the project was under construction but benefited in the end from being

The site was constrained by the large existing building footprint and limited parking field. To compensate for the tight space, the power center was designed as an "interior" mall. Initially, the four big-box tenants were skeptical about the layout, as the stores have interior entrances from a central court rather than separate exterior entrances and no front-door parking. Nevertheless, these national chains were willing to adjust their profiles because of the premier retail location.

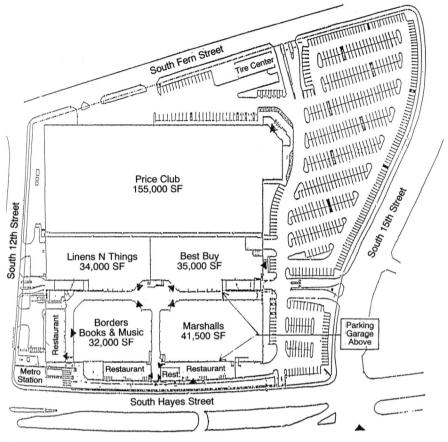

Pentagon Centre site plan.

able to open seven months before the adjoining mall was completed.

During the second phase of construction, the interior mall was created from the remaining portions of the existing warehouse and the office building. Stores for Linens 'N Things and Best Buy, each about 35,000 square feet, were constructed next to Price Club using the remaining portion of the warehouse. Most of the first-floor office space was converted to stores for Borders Books & Music (32,000 square feet) and Marshalls (41,500 square feet). The stores were linked by a 20,000-square-foot interior public concourse that provides access from three exterior entrances to a central court.

A row of restaurant storefronts was added to the front of the original office building, helping to draw patrons into the mall. The main entrance to the mall retains the limestone facing, curved stainless steel canopy, and bowed window framing of the original office facade encased in a new interior atrium entrance.

The most difficult structural challenge was tackled during construction of the mall—converting the second floor and roof of the original office building to a two-level parking deck above the retail stores. Traffic loads and waterproofing were the primary concerns. Fortunately, the original concrete structure could easily bear the weight of vehicles, but the additional weight of the concrete topping strained the load-carrying capacity. The problem of the added weight was resolved by designing a new reinforced concrete topping to work as a composite system with the original roof slab.

A 25- by 575-foot section of the warehouse next to the office building was removed for installation of two-level vehicle ramps and an escalator/elevator core to connect the first-floor tenant spaces to the two levels of parking above. The cast-in-place concrete ramps required their own new structural system, because the concrete load was too high for the existing steel columns of the warehouse. New footings and columns had to be constructed between the existing steel columns of the warehouse structure. To spread the load and provide added stability, the existing steel columns were attached to the ramps, then cut and removed from the ground up to the underside of the new construction. This approach provides the necessary structural support while avoiding a dense row of columns in the retail spaces below the ramps. Traffic-impact barriers were provided by adding new concrete walls and post-tensioned vehicle-impact cable railing around the edges of the middle-level deck. To prevent water from ponding on the parking decks, a new drainage system had to be constructed. Sloped concrete topping directs the water away and creates a suitable surface for vehicular traffic. Cast-in-place concrete guard walls at the roof level of the parking structure provide traffic barriers as well as visual screening and signage.

HVAC units for the Price Club and the two tenants in the warehouse portion of the project are located on the roof directly above the spaces they serve; those for the retail tenants in the former office portion of the project are placed on new concrete structures over the parking ramps, with ductwork running through the middle-level parking deck to connect them with the retail spaces they serve. HVAC units for the restaurants are on the roof of the new addition. Builders took

▼ Project Data

Land Use Information

Site Area: 16.8 acres
Gross Building Area: 350,000 square feet
Gross Leasable Area (GLA): 320,000 square feet
Floor/Area Ratio: 0.48
Number of Levels: 1 (plus 2 levels of parking)
Total Parking Spaces: 1,226
    Surface Spaces: 639
    Structured Spaces: 587

Land Use Plan

	Acres	Percent of Site
Buildings	8.1	48%
Paved Areas (surface parking/roads)	6.2	37
Landscaped Areas	1.0	6
Other	1.5	9
Total	16.8	100%

Retail Tenant Information

Classification	Number of Stores	Approximate Total GLA
Membership Club	1	155,000
Food Service/Restaurants	4	22,500
Clothing and Accessories	1	41,500
Home Furnishings	1	34,000
Home Appliances/Music	1	35,000
Hobby/Special Interest	1	32,000
Total	9	320,000

Major Tenants (over 10,000 square feet)

Tenant	Space Occupied (approximate square feet)
Price Club	155,000
Marshalls	41,500
Best Buy	35,000
Linens 'N Things	34,000
Borders Books & Music	32,000

Average Length of Lease: 15–20 years, with extension options

Typical Lease Provisions: Rents net of taxes, insurance, utilities, and maintenance charges; percentage rents in most major tenant leases

Annual Rents: $19.00–40.00 per square foot (excluding Price Club)

Redevelopment Cost Information

	With Price Club Facility	Excluding Price Club Facility
Site Acquisition Cost	$40,600,000	$18,500,000
Site Improvement Costs (including parking garage)	3,550,000	2,700,000
Construction Costs	13,900,000	10,100,000
Soft Costs	2,800,000	2,425,000
Total Redevelopment Cost	$60,850,000	$33,725,000

Owner/Developer

Price Enterprises, Inc.
4649 Morena Boulevard
San Diego, California 92117
619-581-4530

Development Consultant

K&F Development Company
145 South Fairfax Avenue
Fourth Floor
Los Angeles, California 90036
213-937-8200

Architect

Morgan Gick & Associates
3110 Fairview Park Drive, Suite 110
Falls Church, Virginia 22042
703-876-5600

Property Management

The Price REIT, Inc.
145 South Fairfax Avenue
Fourth Floor
Los Angeles, California 90036
213-937-8200

Development Schedule

Site Purchased: September 1993
Planning Started: April 1993

	Phase I (Price Club)	Phase II (Pentagon Centre)
Approvals Obtained:	October 1993	April 1994
Construction Started:	October 1993	May 1994
Leasing Started:	N/A	Fall 1993
Project Opened:	March 1994	October 1994

care to properly separate fresh air intakes from kitchen and restroom exhausts.

Other less dramatic alterations to the building were necessary. The local building code required the installation of new sprinkler and smoke detector systems. New gas, electric, and water line taps and additional sewer lines also had to be installed. Undocumented or misdocumented utility lines confounded the process of upgrading. The developer had anticipated environmental problems, as investigations had identified the presence of underground storage tanks, asbestos, and PCBs (in light ballasts), although the amount of asbestos found was more extensive than expected. Removing underground tanks was likewise more costly than expected.

The project was completed on time and on budget. Price Club opened on March 1, 1994, less than six months after acquisition. Price Enterprises delivered unfinished tenant space in late July, and the first tenant opened the following October, just 13 months after acquisition. All major tenants opened by December 15, 1994, and the last tenant, a restaurant, opened in March 1995. To stay within budget, many cost-saving adjustments were made midstream, and some elements, such as supplemental landscaping, were deferred until after the mall opened.

Experience Gained

▼ An excellent location can justify the need to make some compromises with the physical space. Big-box, value-oriented tenants were concerned about having interior entrances rather than separate exterior entrances, no parking at their front doors, and limited on-site parking. Nevertheless, tenants report strong sales and expect the project to be an excellent retail site. This Price Club rapidly has become the top sales generator of its seven metropolitan Washington locations. Initial sales reports indicate that both Marshalls and Linens 'N Things were ranking nationally numbers 4 and 5, respectively, in their chains.

▼ On this urban site, managing the parking lots is a major operating problem, as commuters and office workers from nearby buildings "poach" Pentagon Centre's parking spaces. Nevertheless, a limit of two free hours was increased to three when shopping customers complained. Management considers a validation system for shoppers too cumbersome.

▼ Adaptive use projects entail unusual costs. The architect's rule of thumb for adaptive use projects is to use a 15 percent contingency factor for unexpected costs instead of the 5 to 10 percent factor typically used for new construction.

▼ A thorough survey and documentation of existing conditions is critical to minimize surprises. At Pentagon Centre, for example, underground public utilities, a surprise discovered during construction, had to be relocated.

▼ It is even more important in an adaptive use project than a new one to bring key development team members on board early—from initial planning through investigation, design development, and construction. For example, the marketing team should be involved from the beginning because constraints in the building might affect what can be delivered in a lease.

640 Memorial Drive

Cambridge, Massachusetts

Originally one of Henry Ford's first automobile assembly plants, 640 Memorial Drive is now home to emerging biotech tenant companies.

Designed and constructed as Ford Motor Company's first multistory automobile assembly plant, 640 Memorial Drive in Cambridge, Massachusetts, has been "retooled" as a speculative multitenant biotechnology, office, and laboratory facility. Fronting the north shore of the Charles River, the 236,250-square-foot, five-story building is at the corner of a triangle formed by the entry into Cambridge from Boston, with the Massachusetts Institute of Technology (MIT) to the east and Harvard to the north.

The redevelopment of 640 Memorial Drive was spearheaded by the MIT Real Estate Office, a semi-independent division of the university created in 1977 to maximize the institution's return on real estate assets not used for academic purposes. Acting as the owner, developer, sole financier, and prop-

erty manager of the project, MIT plans to use the property's income to assist in the funding of academic-related development initiatives.

Site History

When constructed in 1913, the building was one of a variety of similar facilities built by the Ford Motor Company during the first quarter of this century that were premised upon the then-prevailing vertical manufacturing technology. The facility included corporate support offices and a retail sales showroom. Ford's auto manufacturing was transferred elsewhere in 1926, after the introduction of horizontal manufacturing procedures rendered the older vertical systems obsolete.

From 1926 to 1956, the facility was used for retail-related warehousing and assembly for the defense industry. MIT acquired the building in 1956 and until 1984 leased it to Polaroid, which used it to manufacture components for instant cameras. For a few years, a portion of the facility was used by a video projection company that vacated the building upon termination of its lease. The old assembly plant remained vacant until MIT renovated it and opened its doors again in 1994.

Redevelopment Strategy

MIT's first thought was to use the building for academic-related purposes, but analyses conducted by the MIT Real Estate Office concluded that redeveloping the plant for new commercial uses would yield a much higher return on the university's asset. Although the inventory of properties for which MIT is landlord and manager exceeds 1 million square feet, MIT's Real Estate Office had initiated very little speculative development before 640 Memorial Drive.

When it first began to examine the structure's possibilities for redevelopment, MIT hoped to capitalize on a then-booming real estate market. In 1988, MIT solicited competitive bids from developers for a 45-year ground lease for an undetermined use. The only physical requirement attached to the request for proposal was that a significant portion of the original building architecture be retained. MIT received more than 40 expressions of interest, but by the time the proposal process was close to completion in 1989, the Boston area real estate market had suffered a severe downturn. Some of the competitors had gone out of business, and few of the remainder were still interested. The lack of financing for speculative projects and other ills facing the real estate community effectively eliminated MIT's ability to redevelop the property through a venture with outside interests, as it had once considered.

The options were to mothball the property until the market improved or devise an alternative plan for redevelopment. Leaving the property untouched carried a negative value because of the significant costs for minimal annual maintenance and property taxes (MIT is not exempt from local taxes unless the facility is being used specifically for educational purposes). Another drawback to leaving the property undeveloped was the possibility that the building's potential for producing income could be diminished by the enactment of more restrictive regulatory requirements in the future. The prevailing zoning for the property prescribed few restrictions on use.

Convinced that the old assembly plant could generate commercial income, MIT's Real Estate Office recommended that the facility be redeveloped by the university for commercial tenants. The income from the project could be used to leverage the construction of campus housing and other academic buildings that the university normally must subsidize. But it was not until 1990 that the MIT board gave the go-ahead for the Real Estate Office to begin investing hard dollars in the project's development.

The decision to redevelop the historic structure into a speculative biotech facility was based on several parameters, including the building's physical attributes, its proximity to technological and medical-related activity, and MIT's knowledge of the local real estate and biotech markets.

Despite the depressed real estate market at the time, forecasts for explosive growth in the biotech sector remained strong. Nevertheless, limited financial resources were (and still are) available to emerging biotech companies other than funding for research and development through venture capital firms. MIT recognized that the scarce financing had created a pent-up demand for office and laboratory space near research centers. The university was able to proactively respond to the demand by financing tenant improvements, which in some instances included buildout of lab

The original steel and glass train shed used by the Ford Motor Company has been redeveloped into a daylit lobby and common area.

and manufacturing space costing up to $70.00 per square foot.

MIT financed the buildout for all six of the building's tenants and is amortizing the improvements over the life of the leases. The university also offered "venture leasing" for a startup pharmaceutical firm with high potential for growth (which now occupies 48,000 square feet of space). Under this arrangement, MIT acquired stock warrants in the company (much like a venture capital fund would) as an additional risk premium over and above financing the buildout, which can be exercised in the future should MIT wish to do so.

Underlying MIT's strategy to convert the plant into speculative office and lab space was the belief that sufficient demand existed for the space should any of 640 Memorial's tenants fail. Moreover, because of the university's substantial property portfolio in the immediate vicinity, MIT could likely accommodate tenants that need to expand or to downsize. This added flexibility enhanced 640 Memorial's appeal to potential biotech tenants.

In 1990, MIT began efforts to achieve commitments to prelease 50 percent of the space. Because the existing manufacturing plant was badly deteriorated, MIT relied heavily on architectural renderings, models, and personal contacts to attract tenants. Clearly in MIT's favor was the fact that virtually no competition existed in the Boston/ Cambridge area for a comparable combination of location, building character, rental rates, and financing of tenant improvements. Project architects were able to take advantage of the building's 12- to 18-foot ceiling heights to offer another important amenity to prospective tenants —storage and meeting space on the mezzanine level for a fraction of the base rental rate per square

Blending old and new, 640 Memorial Drive's contemporary entrance reflects the building's high-tech tenant profile.

foot. Marketing was also enhanced by MIT's reputation and capability as the sponsor.

Lifeline Systems was the first tenant to sign, committing to 105,000 square feet. But by late 1991, Lifeline had downsized, leading to a restructured lease for 74,000 square feet. This situation allowed for greater flexibility in accommodating a variety of smaller tenants and proved advantageous for leasing the remainder of the building. Millennium Pharmaceuticals moved in in January 1994, two months before all base building construction was completed, and three other tenants moved in over the next three months.

Physical Configuration

Originally designed by John Graham, the five-story building featured a brick and terra-cotta facade fronting public spaces along the Charles River. The 450- by 75-foot rectangular building is one of the earliest examples of poured-in-place concrete construction. The building's

east, south, and west exteriors exhibit decorative features, such as a terra-cotta cornice line, arched windows with terra-cotta lintels, and a clock tower. The highly ornate front facade is more reminiscent of office buildings from an earlier era than purely industrial buildings. This elaborate exterior design made the former heavy industrial building particularly suitable for office use.

A five-story glass and steel train shed running the entire length of the structure originally dominated the rear of the building. Behind the building, away from the river, was a large area occupied by on-grade parking, lean-to buildings, and storage sheds that had been added to the building over the course of decades.

The original assembly line areas inside the building were constructed with a cast-in-place concrete structural system that featured columns and shear capitals that supported 450-foot-long, 10-inch-thick floor slabs. Glass roll-up doors separated the assembly areas of each floor from the train shed. Two auto-size freight elevators and one four-person elevator served the building.

Exterior Construction

Conversion of the building began in August 1992 and was completed in March 1994. MIT decided early in the project to be as faithful as was economically possible to retention and restoration of the building's decorative facade and other historic characteristics. Although the building was eligible for listing on the National Register of Historic Places, an agreement between MIT and the Cambridge Historic Commission kept the building from being officially listed. MIT pledged to cooperate informally with the commission to address the commission's concerns.

Most of the building's terra-cotta cornice was sound, but the glazing had deteriorated. To lower costs, fiberglass molding fabricated to appear identical to the original terracotta was used to cover the cornice. In other areas, precast concrete was used as an economical way of replacing numerous oddly shaped terra-cotta pieces. In all, some 30 percent of the original terra-cotta was covered or replaced with fiberglass or precast concrete. Deteriorated window structures, originally composed of a grid of small panes, were replaced with new, wider panes more appropriate to the building's current use. The original steel sashes were replaced with less expensive aluminum sashes. Two rows of smaller panes were retained in the upper portion of each window to preserve some of the building's industrial feel.

The original brick skin needed nearly $1 million in structural enhancements, largely to correct problems with evaporation and drainage. While generally in good condition, the outer brick veneer had begun to fall away from the building by as much as one inch. The problem was attributed to a design flaw in the original construction. The interior wall, of low-quality sewer brick, and the outer wall, of high-quality brick, were separated by only one-half inch of air space. In contrast, modern construction standards specify at least two inches of air space to promote evaporation and drainage. In addition, the brick veneer was fastened to the inner withe by small, thin steel ties embedded only one-half inch. Engineers shored up the exterior brick wall while installing new supports and anchors to the brick veneer. Areas of the inner withe that had weakened were braced with steel and concrete beams integrated into existing concrete columns.

The original design of the brick walls also lacked dampproofing measures. Water penetrating the first layer of brick accumulated on metal angles that led the water into the terra-cotta lintels above the windows, eventually causing the metal angles to corrode and the lintels to disintegrate. Engineers removed the terra-cotta lintels, steel angles, and several layers of bricks above the windows and installed new fiberglass lintels with drip edges to direct water away from the building below new steel angles. Lead-coated copper flashing was installed throughout the facade over the new steel angles.

Treatment of the glass and steel train shed at the rear of the property was the most controversial aspect of the project. Designers sought to mix characteristic features of the past with an overall contemporary feel. This continuity between old and new was achieved by using five bays in the central portion of the building's original five-story train shed as a skylit entry atrium. The Cambridge Historic Commission had first asked that the entire shed structure be retained but was willing to compromise later in light of the prohibitively high cost it would entail. The new steel trusses were joined to the existing brown exterior truss columns by gusset plate construction. The new mullions and structural steel were painted white to distinguish the new construction from the original structure. The result was to preserve an industrial appearance while providing an interesting modern space. The remaining trusses that supported the shed were removed, and the supporting columns were reduced to one story and used as structural supports for a new promenade along both sides of the central atrium. The enclosed atrium faces northward and, at the reduced height of two and one-half stories, is reasonably economical to operate. New brick-and-glass cladding typical of modern office buildings encloses the rest of the back facade, replacing original glass roll-up doors that had opened into the train shed.

Another 44-foot, five-story section of the train shed at one end of the building was preserved to accommodate an exit stairwell; this space also serves as a main air shaft feeding rooftop mechanical units. The stairwell is enclosed by three existing brick- and terra-cotta-clad walls and a new glass curtain. Designers were able to reduce the requirements for steel by shoring up the existing concrete beams that support the terra-cotta walls with brick-enclosed steel truss columns.

Efforts to economize and to fast track predemolition investigation led to some surprises when construction began to uncover more of the building's history. For example, about 18 inches of cinder-like fill material was discovered on one end of the concrete roof. At some point, the material had been placed on the roof to create a pitch before tiling, and the roof had been replaced several times thereafter. When designers removed the reroofing material down to the original tile, they discovered distances between the tile and the concrete ranging from 12 to 24 inches. This difference in elevation meant that connections to the rooftop HVAC system had to be extended and the HVAC support system enlarged, in some areas by as much as two feet. Designers left this fill material in place and covered the original tile with a new membrane.

Several storage sheds and lean-to buildings behind the main building were demolished to increase the area for tenant parking. A reproduction of one of the original one-story storage buildings now houses a cafeteria and multipurpose space.

Accommodating parking required creative design and engineering. The site was too small to provide adequate surface parking, and adding structured parking proved to be too expensive. The solution was to use 80 parking spaces at an off-site lot owned by MIT three blocks away. An on-call taxi service shuttles users between the building and the off-site parking lot. Each tenant is assigned a prorated number of parking passes, leaving it to the tenant to determine how to allocate the spaces to its employees. Parking spaces are generally charged to the tenant at $60.00 per month for on-site spaces and $40.00 per month for off-site spaces. MIT estimates that at least 20 percent of the employees in the building commute on public transportation; in fact, the property's accessibility to public transit was an important factor in the lead tenant's decision to locate in the building.

Interior Construction

The building's interior was in excellent structural condition, and interior support columns required no repair or replacement. The 23-foot spacing of the columns was particularly suitable for office use, but because the previous use had not required level floors, it was necessary to top the floors with poured concrete to make them even.

The building's outdated mechanical systems were replaced with two new gas-fired boilers and eight new rooftop HVAC units. So that the building could be marketed as an office and biotech facility, standard office mechanical systems were installed to gave tenants the flexibility to improve the systems as needed. Space on the roof was also provided for tenants to add their own air-handling equipment.

Sewer and water lines were completely replaced; two separate water lines were installed. One line feeds

640 Memorial Drive before and during redevelopment.

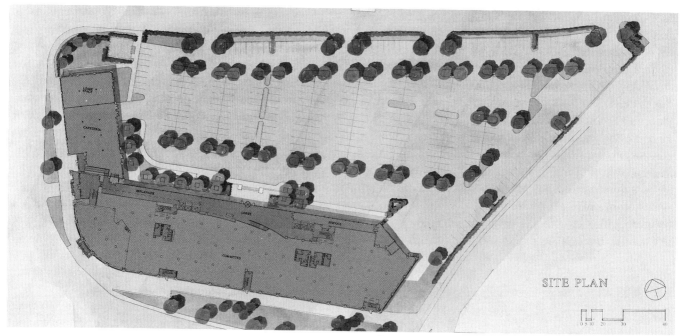

Site plan.

domestic uses, such as bathrooms and water fountains; the other feeds the building's sprinkler system. Because of low water pressure, pumps had to be installed along with the sprinkler system. To comply with the Massachusetts Water Redevelopment Authority's mandate that all new construction and some redevelopment projects install separate sewer and stormwater drainage, separate stormwater lines were also installed at 640 Memorial Drive. Because of the intended use as biotech laboratories, an acid neutralization system was also installed in the sewer system.

Given the age and previous industrial uses of the building, the need for environmental mitigation was surprisingly small. A limited amount of asbestos and some lead paint were found and removed. Two 20,000-gallon oil tanks located in a storage bunker were also removed.

To accommodate the varying sizes and changing space needs of the targeted startup biotech companies, the building was designed to accommodate tenants of 5,000 square

feet to more than 70,000 square feet. One elevator core would normally suffice for a building the size of 640 Memorial, but because of the building's long, rectangular shape, a central elevator core would have resulted in long walks for some tenants. Instead, two elevator cores were located in the former train shed, one-quarter of the way from each end of the building. This solution eliminated the need for long entry corridors and provides tenants with individual identities, good visibility, and easy public access. As a result, net rentable square feet as a proportion of gross building area is over 90 percent on the floors where tenants are located.

Leasing/ Operations

Early rents were in the targeted range, and by the time the last two deals were signed, they had moved somewhat ahead of pro forma estimates. As of mid-1996,

the property ranked at the top of the local market. The typical lease is for ten years, although MIT expects that some tenants might need to buy out their positions because of rapid growth. Tenants are charged a net rate for services with negotiated add-ons. For the tenants at 640 Memorial Drive, the ability to meter electricity individually and contract for specialized cleaning services is an important amenity.

Experience Gained

▼ As an education and research institution, MIT was able to take advantage of its knowledge of emerging trends within the biotech industry, giving the university a competitive advantage in the commercial marketplace.

▼ Given the limited financial resources available to startup biotech companies, MIT's ability to finance tenant improvements played an invaluable role in al-

▼ Project Data

Land Use Information

Site Area: 5.3 acres
Gross Building Area: 236,250 square feet
Net Rentable Area (NRA): 187,201 square feet
Typical Floor Area: 37,105 square feet
Floor/Area Ratio: 1.02
Building Height: 5 stories

Land Use Plan

	Acres
Buildings	1.0
Parking Structures	0.0
Paved Areas (surface parking/roads)	4.0
Landscaped Areas	0.3
Total	5.3

Tenant Information

Percent of NRA Occupied: 100%
Annual Rents: $22.00–32.00 per square foot (base rent: $10.00–13.50 per square foot plus amortization of tenant improvements equaling $12.00–22.00 per square foot)
Average Length of Lease: 5–10 years
Typical Terms of Lease: Triple net
Typical Tenant Size: 6,800–74,000 square feet[1]
Number of Tenants: 6

Tenant Size (square feet)	Number of Tenants
5,000–10,000	2
10,000–50,000	3
>50,000	1
Total	6

Redevelopment Cost Information

Site Acquisition Cost		$1,600,000

Base Building Cost

Sitework	$	702,509
Concrete		801,289
Masonry (restoration)		958,791
Masonry (new)		617,538
Steel		1,123,419
Roofing		271,850
Doors/windows		1,406,859
Walls/partitions		900,130
Flooring		263,420
Painting		185,388
Elevators		573,633
Plumbing/fire safety		580,288
HVAC		2,707,088
Electrical		813,944
Total		$11,906,146

Tenant Fitup	$5,995,914

Soft Costs

Architectural/engineering	$1,109,027
Project management	126,730
Leasing/marketing	727,857
Legal/accounting	153,449
Taxes/insurance	636,360
Construction interest/fees	970,410
Total	$3,723,833
Total Redevelopment Cost	$23,225,893
Redevelopment Cost (excluding tenant fitup) per Net Square Foot	$92.00

Annual Operating Expenses (1995)

Taxes	$ 482,994
Insurance	13,104
Services	44,928
Maintenance	119,809
Janitorial	35,568
Utilities	387,506
Management/payroll	149,760
Miscellaneous/cafeteria	44,928
Total	$1,278,597
Annual Operating Expenses per Net Square Foot	$6.83

Developer

Massachusetts Institute of Technology Real Estate Office
238 Main Street, Suite 200
Cambridge, Massachusetts 02143
617-253-1483

Architect

Tsoi/Kobus & Associates
P.O. Box 9114
One Brattle Square
Cambridge, Massachusetts 02238
617-491-3067

Development Schedule

Site Purchased: 1956
Planning Started: 1987
Construction Started: 1991
Leasing Started: 1990
Project Completed: March 1994

Note:
[1] A majority of the building is a combination of office and laboratory space. Two tenants totaling 14,500 square feet occupy only office space.

lowing the university to capture pent-up demand for office and laboratory space in the Boston metropolitan market.

▼ The sturdy concrete frame building was very compatible with its new use. This compatibility, together with careful value engineering and tightly monitored construction costs, enabled MIT to redevelop the project for less than new construction would have cost, thereby being able to offer desirable, competitively priced space.

▼ The distinctive history of the building—both its design and original use—worked together to define a strong marketing image for the property.

▼ Sometimes it is cost-effective in the long run to incorporate a more expensive design solution to meet the expectations of prospective tenants. At 640 Memorial Drive, for example, installing two elevator cores when one would have sufficed increased the net rentable area and improved the project's marketability. To en-

sure adequate convenient parking, MIT provided supplemental off-site parking, even though it entails more intensive attention to parking management than normal.

▼ Construction contingencies to cover the unexpected should be more generous when adapting an existing building to a new use, particularly if original construction drawings are not available.

Trump International Hotel and Tower

New York, New York

A luxury apartment and hotel condominium building on the edge of Central Park is being built around the steel shell of a 52-story "white elephant" office tower. The existing building's facade was replaced by a multifaceted curtain wall made of bronze-colored glass, stainless steel, and aluminum.

The former Gulf & Western Building, long past its useful life as an office skyscraper but blessed with a privileged location on Manhattan's Columbus Circle, is being stripped down to its 52-story steel skeleton, reclad in bronze-tinted glass, and transformed into a luxury apartment and hotel condominium complex.

The Trump International Hotel and Tower (TIHT), which is expected to be completed in mid-1997 (the hotel by late 1996), is an adaptive use development of unusual scale. The $250 million project is a joint venture of Galbreath Company, Trump Organization, and General Electric Pension Trust.

The first third of the redeveloped TIHT will comprise a 168-unit condominium hotel with studio, one-, and two-bedroom suites. The remaining two-thirds will contain 158 luxury condominium apartments. Separate hotel and apartment entrances and lobbies will open onto Central Park. A ground-floor restaurant will be located on a wedge-shaped terrace facing Columbus Circle on the southern end of the building. A small public park, designed by Thomas Balsley and Phillip Johnson, will border the western side of the building.

The Site

Built in 1968 as the Gulf & Western Building and later renamed the Paramount Building, the 538,700-square-foot international-style office building presented the development team with an exceptional opportunity for adaptive use.

The towering office skyscraper became outmoded soon after its completion because of a poorly conceived architectural and engineering plan. Ironically, many of the faults that had reduced its commercial value enhanced the building's residual value and potential for reuse. A key advantage in reuse is the building's floorplates, which, at 13,000 square feet, are much smaller than floorplates in modern office towers (optimally 20,000 square feet or more). The smaller floorplates, however, are well suited for residential use.

Located on Columbus Circle, a prominent site on the southwest corner of Central Park, the building commands magnificent views

A rendering of the project, which is scheduled to be completed in two stages. The hotel condominium units, a restaurant, and a health club were expected to open in late 1996, residential condominum units in mid-1997.

of Central Park and Manhattan. Near Lincoln Center, the Fifth Avenue shopping corridor, and the Broadway theater district, the building was ideally suited for conversion to a hotel and luxury condominiums.

The Gulf & Western Building was originally developed under a New York City zoning variance that allowed a significant height and setback bonus. By reusing the existing office tower's steel superstructure, the developers were able to use the original height and setback bonuses, which allow an FAR that would never receive public approvals today.

Project Initiation

General Electric Investment (GEI) assumed ownership of the building in February 1993 as part of a foreclosure on a 19-property portfolio that GEI had financed for a syndication put together by First Winthrop. Upon assuming ownership of the underperforming Columbus Circle asset, GEI was faced with numerous challenges for repositioning the building in a soft Manhattan commercial real estate market:

▼ A significant number of soon-to-expire leases, including the property's anchor tenant, Viacom, which occupied over 400,000 square feet (a majority of the building);
▼ The building's upper floors' tendency to sway up to two feet in high winds;
▼ Relatively small floorplates, which were too small for most commercial applications;
▼ High levels of asbestos fireproofing material throughout the building;
▼ Obsolete mechanical systems.

In May 1993, GEI secured the real estate advisory services of Galbreath

Company to evaluate the alternatives to sale of the building. The objectives of the analysis were to consider the building's alternative uses, define its highest and best use, and evaluate the balance between risk and return for GEI.

Galbreath assembled a multidisciplinary team of consultants, including a mechanical engineer, a structural engineer, a residential architect, a construction expert, a hospitality consultant, zoning and environmental attorneys, and marketing experts. The team studied the pricing, absorption, zoning, development costs, financing options, and marketing considerations for seven different "as-of-right" redevelopment alternatives, evaluating each alternative on a leveraged and an unleveraged basis. Galbreath's study recommended three redevelopment alternatives for GEI's consideration: Class A office space and luxury residential condominiums; luxury residential apartments and a hotel; corporate suites and luxury residential apartment condominiums.

According to Galbreath's study, at the time of the evaluation neither office nor apartment rents in Manhattan's real estate market could, by themselves, support the project's renovation costs or GEI's yield and risk profile.

In December 1993, with Galbreath's feasibility and market analysis in hand, GEI issued requests for proposals (RFPs) to nine of the country's largest development companies, calling for the submittal of redevelopment proposals that incorporated one of the three identified alternatives. Guidelines for the RFPs included three participation options for developers, including a joint venture, fee development, and asset acquisition.

After much thought and consideration, Trump Organization and Galbreath Company joined forces to file a joint development proposal. The Trump-Galbreath team strongly believed that the most viable strategy to turn the building around was to convert the asset into a luxury apartment and hotel condominium complex. (This decision was based on a combination of factors, including the functional obsolescence of the building as a commercial asset, the soft office market in midtown Manhattan, and entitlement/regulatory considerations.) Initial studies indicated that financial returns for this alternative could be enhanced if the building's hotel units were purchased as condominiums rather than rented conventionally by the day.

After evaluating the proposals, GEI and its CEO Dale Frey selected the Trump-Galbreath team for the creation of a joint venture. The TIHT joint venture redevelopment initiative is being financed by the GE Pension Trust and developed by Trump Organization and Galbreath Company. The Trump-Galbreath partnership is a 50–50 joint venture that has assumed an equity stake in the project. To date, the project's various divisions of equity are considered proprietary information. The team has been able to successfully benefit from each player's individual experiences in large-scale urban redevelopment and reuse.

Public Approvals

The regulatory setting surrounding the development of TIHT was unusual. The Gulf & Western Building was constructed pursuant to a permitted variance issued by the New York City Board of Standards and Appeals in 1968. At the time the building was originally planned, designed, and constructed, it was generally perceived that the triangular shape of the Columbus Circle site prohibited the development of a conventional high-rise office tower without violating the height and setback standards dictated by the NYC zoning ordinance. The building's original developer, however, was able to successfully negotiate waivers from some of those regulations and receive a significant height and setback bonus in exchange for the financing and development of the Columbus Circle Rotunda and subway station.

By developing a subway entrance on site, the developer took advantage of standard floor/area bonuses then available in the NYC zoning ordinance. The height and setback bonus allowed the original designers of the Gulf & Western Building to achieve an FAR of 17.18 at a height of 52 stories. By comparison, today a newly constructed building on the Columbus Circle site could not exceed an FAR of 15 under NYC's current zoning and building codes

Handling the high volume of materials and personnel being moved in and out of the building during demolition and construction required additional hoisting equipment.

and would probably be restricted to no more than 29 stories to reduce the effects of shadows on the adjacent Central Park. The former Gulf & Western Building's spectacular views, safe from future obstruction, add enormously to the structure's value as a residential asset.

Given the regulatory constraints associated with new construction, the TIHT development team chose to rehabilitate the building. Article V of the NYC Zoning Resolution establishes that a nonconforming building can stay in use so long as the degree of nonconformance does not increase. The TIHT development strategy, therefore, was to use the Gulf & Western Building's superstructure while completely redeveloping the building's interior, exterior, and systems. By stripping the obsolete office tower to its steel frame/superstructure, the development team was able to take advantage of the existing building's nonconforming height and setback standards and redevelop the asset as of right, thereby significantly expediting the predevelopment regulatory approval and public review process for the project.

The TIHT development team worked closely with the NYC Building Department to establish criteria by which to evaluate the reuse of the highly visible building. Other than for structural enhancement, the development team was not permitted to build beyond the configuration of the existing building envelope. For example, approval was granted to attach several triangular light-reflective prisms to TIHT's exterior curtain wall for structural stabilization. The prisms are a major design feature of an entirely new curtain wall, designed by architect Phillip Johnson. The new curtain wall was slightly outside the building envelope granted by the origi-

The Gulf & Western Building before redevelopment.

nal Board of Standards permit but did not add floor area.

The project's unusual mix of uses was driven by market and regulatory considerations. The New York State Multiple Dwelling Law and the NYC zoning code limit residential floor area on most single-zoning lots to an FAR of 12. Given the existing building's FAR exceeding 17, the development team was fortunate that both the NYC zoning code and the predevelopment market studies supported the adoption of a hotel use for the "nonresidential" component of the structure at 5.1 FAR. At 171,930 square feet, the condominium hotel will represent a total of 26 percent of the building's total square footage. Regulatory provisions also require separate entrances and front desks for each of the building's components.

Redevelopment Process

Converting the Gulf & Western Building into the TIHT has involved stripping the existing building to its steel superstructure and removing

and replacing all exterior walls, windows, and major building systems.

In large-scale adaptive use projects like TIHT, the presence of cranes and hoisting equipment is an extremely important consideration throughout demolition and construction. To handle the high volume of materials and personnel being moved into and out of the building, additional equipment has been integrated throughout the construction site.

Demolition, asbestos removal, and refireproofing were conducted simultaneously and were completed in approximately six months (requiring over 2,500 truckloads of debris). Demolition and removing asbestos began before Viacom's departure from the building, requiring a significant portion of the demolition and removal to be coordinated with the tenant's gradual departure. With this scenario and the significant amount of sprayed-on asbestos fireproofing on columns and beams in the building, the development team was required to carefully monitor indoor air quality and create several environmentally sound buffer zones throughout the property. All demolition and asbestos removal was accomplished for approximately $20.00 per square foot.

The Gulf & Western Building was notorious throughout New York real estate circles for its tendency to sway in high winds, the result of its asymmetrical design. The building's wobbling caused cracks in elevator cores, stairwells, and floors, and the shifting of glass and curtain wall panels. While all high-rise buildings are designed to be dynamic, less movement typically is tolerated in residential towers. Consequently, the project's engineers worked to reduce chronic sway and eliminate further structural damage. Engineers tried 12 to 14 different design permutations before they successfully devised a system to stabilize and stiffen the building that achieved the developers' goals. Concrete sheer walls were added to the structural steel building. In addition to stiffening the building, they provide the added advantage of soundproofing between individual apartments. Numerous design/engineering teams, including engineers from GE and the University of Illinois, evaluated all structural engineering considerations. TIHT's design was tested and evaluated by two independent wind tunnel testing organizations. The construction schedule was an important consideration in the selection of the concrete sheer wall stabilization system. The technique used for stabilization gave the developers increased flexibility and control over construction timing and sequencing, which would not have been feasible otherwise. In addition, the building's new curtain wall was designed to reduce wind stress, thereby increasing stabilization. According to the development team, the redeveloped building will have the lowest movement-to-height ratio of any New York high-rise building.

The existing dark and dated facade was replaced by a multifaceted curtain wall made from bronze-colored glass, stainless steel, and aluminum. The curtain wall, which was ordered in December 1994, was installed from October to December 1995. Given the various challenges of putting a new curtain wall on an existing building, the design and construction management team spent a great deal of time and resources planning for the design and installation of the curtain wall. Because the curtain wall needed to be designed, fabricated, and ready for installation before demolition, the construction team's ability to take

Located on Columbus Circle, a prominent site on the southwest corner of Central Park, Trump International Hotel and Tower commands unparalleled views of Central Park and is close to many of Manhattan's attractions.

accurate measurements was significantly impaired. As a result, an extraordinary level of flexibility and tolerances was devised for determining the number and location of anchors on the curtain wall. Having extensive experience in large-scale rehabilitation, the TIHT construction team recognized that the building's remaining structural components (such as the floor slab) contained extensive variations and damage caused from preexisting holes, penetrations, and other conditions. In an effort to minimize variations and uncertainties in the floor slab, two inches of concrete

fill was added to the existing floor slab before the installation of construction finishes.

With the reduction in demand for the elevator as a result of converting the building from commercial to residential use, the developers were able to reduce the number of elevators on the side of the building facing Central Park, shifting the core of the building to the west and increasing the number and percentage of salable square feet facing the park.

New mechanical systems were installed that allow the hotel and residential components to operate

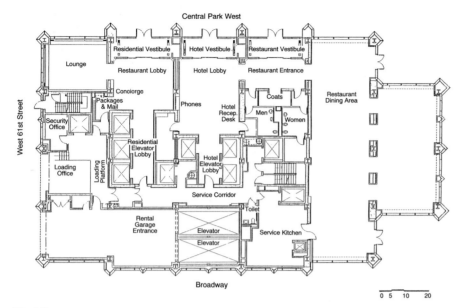

First floor.

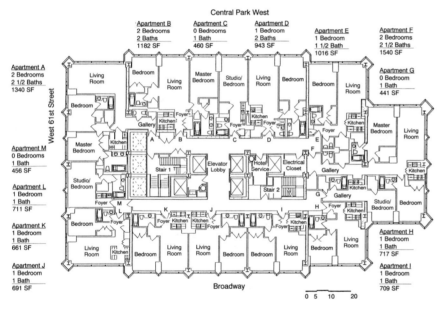

Typical residential floor.

independently—an especially important factor because the hotel will be completed approximately six months before the residential component.

Interior Design

Many of the building's physical attributes were advantageous for the new use, including increased depth from core, high slab-to-slab floor heights, and the original steel su-

perstructure and curtain wall construction, thereby creating a real estate product with considerable market differentiation. The structure's relatively small floorplates (13,000 square feet) and the location of structural columns made the building well suited for conversion to luxury residential/hotel use. The interior design team, led by architect Costas Kondylis, was able to achieve an efficient layout in which the typical floor plan

yields a net to gross floor/area ratio that exceeds 89 percent.

By taking advantage of the building's depth from core, the designers were able to create luxury amenities, including walk-in closets, dressing rooms, his and her master bathrooms, eat-in kitchens, service entrances, and large foyers and entrance galleries. The building's high slab-to-slab height (typical in many commercial structures) allowed ten- to 15-foot finished ceiling heights. In the New York market, these features are usually found only in prewar apartment buildings, which often lack extensive modern amenities.

The building's steel structure and design of the curtain wall allowed the designers to make the most of window surface area. Rooms throughout the building will have window bays reaching up to nine feet. Eighty percent of all units will have views of Central Park. To maximize each unit's view corridor, the interior design team located all the living room interiors at the corner of the building.

The residential condominium units, which will average 2,100 square feet, will range from one- to five-bedroom units. Condominium hotel units, which average approximately 825 square feet, will range from studios to two-bedroom units.

To date, the project's total redevelopment cost is estimated at approximately $380 per gross square foot. Both the residential and hotel units will have similar construction costs per square foot, although the hotel will also incur costs for furniture, fixtures, and equipment.

Marketing

The joint venture development team adopted the Trump name early in

▼ Project Data

Land Use Information

Site Area: 31,349 square feet
Gross Building Area (GBA): 538,700 square feet
Total Residential Condominium Units Planned: 158
Total Hotel Condominium Units Planned: 168
Retail Net Rental Area: 20,855 square feet
Building Height: 52 stories
Typical Floor Size: 13,451 square feet
Floor/Area Ratio: 17.18

Building Plan

	Square Feet (GBA)
Residential	394,866
Hotel	171,931
Retail	20,855
Circulation and Common Areas	69,614
Storage	1,434
Total	658,700

Residential Condominium Unit Information

Unit Type	Unit Size (square feet)	Number of Units Planned
One-Bedroom	1,290–1,440	9
Two-Bedroom	1,600–2,255	74
Three-Bedroom	2,000–4,400	65
Four-Bedroom	4,400–4,500	5
Five-Bedroom	5,500–5,540	5
Total Units		158

Range of Initial Sale Prices: $800–1,400 per square foot

Hotel Condominium Unit Information

Unit Type	Unit Size (square feet)	Number of Units Planned
Studio	440–460	38
One-Bedroom	660–1,016	90
Two-Bedroom	1,182–1,340	40
Total Units		168

Range of Initial Sale Prices: $700–1,200 per square foot

Projected Redevelopment Cost

Acquisition Cost	$ 60,000,000
Direct Construction Costs	130,000,000
Soft Cost	60,000,000
Total Redevelopment Cost	$250,000,000

Total Projected Redevelopment Cost per Gross Square Foot (GBA): $380

Retail Tenant Information

Number of Tenants: 2 (auto rental garage and restaurant)
Tenant Size: Restaurant: 10,000 square feet
  Auto Rental Garage: 15,000 square feet
Expected Average Annual Rent: Restaurant: $30.00 per square foot
Expected Annual Operating Expense: $2,500,000

Owner

General Electric Pension Trust
3003 Summer Street
Stamford, Connecticut 06904-7900

Developers

The Galbreath Company
437 Madison Avenue
New York, New York 10022

The Trump Organization
725 Fifth Avenue
New York, New York 10022

Architects

Philip Johnson, Ritchie &
  Fiore Architects
885 Third Avenue
New York, New York 10022-4834

Costa Kondylis Architects
3 West 18th Street
New York, New York 10011

Structural Engineer

The Cantor Seinuk Group, P.C.
600 Madison Avenue
New York, New York 10022-4834

Mechanical Engineer

I.M. Robbins, P.C.
310 Madison Avenue
New York, New York 10017

Construction Manager

HRH Construction Corporation
909 Third Avenue
New York, New York 10022

Development Schedule

Site Purchased: February 1993
Planning Started: June 1993
Construction Started: July 1995
Sales Started: September 1995
Hotel Condominiums, Restaurant, Health Club, and Auto Rental Garage Completed (projected): November 1996
Residential Condominiums Completed (projected): July 1997

the development process to capture the enhanced marketability associated with Trump's name and prestigious luxury residential properties. (Informal estimates say that the Trump name alone can add up to $100 per square foot to the price of a residential property in the New York City market.)

The project will be one of the only properties in Manhattan to integrate luxury residential and hotel condominiums; therefore, a major component of the marketing campaign for TIHT is to promote the mutually beneficial and synergistic relationship between the hotel and residential components.

The for-sale condominium hotel units will provide prospective owners and frequent New York visitors with a flexible alternative to conventional hotel accommodations or apartment ownership. They will allow corporate and individual owners to take advantage of hotel-style services, as well as the ability to rent their unit when not in use and to recover a percentage of the unit's maintenance and operational expenses. Owners of the condominium hotel units will also be able to take advantage of certain commercial real estate tax abatements that are part of a New York City industrial and commercial incentive program.

TIHT apartment residents will be able to take advantage of the numerous amenities and services of a five-star hotel. The building will include many luxury amenities, including a health club with a 55-foot swimming pool, a four-star restaurant, a car rental facility, and a business center. A substantial percentage of TIHT's prospective residents will most likely be foreign owners who visit Manhattan regularly.

With an investment of approximately $2 million in a storefront sales office, the developers expect to close on approximately 70 percent of the units before the completion of construction, which is scheduled for July 1997. (As of March 1996, only the residential condominiums were being offered for sale.) With the sale of over $125 million in residential units and four price increases over six months, the project is currently considerably ahead of its pro forma absorption rates. Sale prices have ranged from $800 to $1,400 per square foot.

Experience Gained

▼ In converting the building from commercial to residential/hotel use, the developers were able to take advantage of a former commercial building's physical attributes, including increased depth from core, high slab-to-slab floor heights, and the original steel superstructure and curtain wall construction, creating a real estate product that will undoubt-edly achieve considerable market differentiation.

▼ Originally concerned about the exorbitant cost estimates associated with the building's renovation (including asbestos removal and structural engineering), the development team proved that doing one's homework can pay off. The extensive predevelopment study conducted by Galbreath Company provided the development team with realistic market and development cost assumptions and accurate pro forma projections, thus minimizing the risk typically associated with adaptive use development projects. To date, the project's development costs (both hard and soft) are within 3 percentage points of predevelopment projections.

▼ The developers avoided much of the risk and entitlement constraints typically associated with large-scale urban development by taking advantage of the existing building's height and setback bonuses.

▼ When putting together the development team, the joint venture partnership handpicked not only the consulting firms, but also the professionals within each prospective firm, thus creating a confident and experienced team that the developers felt comfortable with from the very beginning.

The Carriage Works

Atlanta, Georgia

Reincarnated from a 1907 buggy factory, the Carriage Works building appeals to tenants looking for distinctive, nontraditional office space in downtown Atlanta.

Originally a turn-of-the-century manufacturing facility and most recently warehouse space, the Carriage Works today is a 62,556-square-foot commercial office building. Completed in 1992, the project represents the first in Winter Properties's vision for the revitalization of a neglected area near downtown Atlanta into a new arts district. The project is within minutes of the CBD, midtown, and Georgia Tech University.

Winter Properties, Inc., purchased the property in June 1988, planning to convert the building into loft hous-

ing. After failing to obtain debt financing for this use, Winter began renovating the building with its own money, hoping to secure financing once the project was under development. Eventually, the company did obtain bank financing but for conversion to office use rather than loft housing as originally planned. Today, the building is the cornerstone of an award-winning office and arts complex created from historic three- and four-story brick warehouses. It also is home to the Winter Group of Companies, Inc.,

the Georgia Arts Council, and several other arts-related and high-tech tenants. The Carriage Works galvanized the area for further redevelopment, creating a burgeoning arts district.

Building History

Built in 1907 and located on Means Street near downtown Atlanta, the Carriage Works was originally the home of the Atlanta Buggy Company, a second-generation descendant of the Georgia Buggy Company founded in the mid-1890s. The building served as a full assembly plant, manufacturing wheels and bodies for painting, upholstering, and assembly. In 1913, Atlanta Buggy Company filed for bankruptcy, and the building reverted back to the original owners.

Between 1928 and 1940, Block Candy Company occupied the building. In 1951, Mouchet Corporation, dealers in textile salvage that had been a tenant in the building since 1944, purchased the building. The building's most recent use was as a warehouse. In 1988, after standing vacant for ten years, the building was purchased by Carriage House Associates, a joint venture of Carriage Works Partners and Marietta Atelier, Inc. (owned by Bob and Arnie Silverman of the

Winter Group of Companies), for $950,000. In May 1989, an agreement was reached for Carriage House Associates to own 100 percent interest in the building now known as the Carriage Works.

Project Feasibility And Financing

Winter Properties chose to redevelop the Carriage Works building largely because of its historic value and downtown location. A predevelopment market analysis indicated a strong demand for housing in the downtown area generated by the increasing number of Atlanta residents seeking a more urban lifestyle. The developer felt that converting the building to loft housing could satisfy part of that demand. But the apparent dilapidated condition of the building and the fact that the market for loft housing in Atlanta was untested prevented Winter from securing financing for that use.

Winter Properties continued to believe in the project's potential and proceeded to renovate the building for housing, investing $1.5 million of equity resources and hoping it could subsequently obtain financing. A big boost to the project's ultimate success came in 1991 when the Nexus Contemporary Arts Center located its new home across the street from the Carriage Works building in four contiguous warehouses bought from Winter Properties. With financial assistance from community development block grants, Nexus was able to complete its renovation in 1992 and open what is now the Nexus Gallery and Nexus Press. The arts center acted as an anchor for the Carriage Works, helping to attract tenants to the building and interest from artists in the area.

Eventually, Winter was able to secure financing to complete the project but under a different scenario. Barnett Bank of Florida, the 13th bank the company approached, agreed to provide $2.5 million in financing to complete construction of the project. The bank believed, however, that in-town loft housing posed too much risk and made the financing contingent on the building's conversion to a commercial

office building. Winter agreed and proceeded with the renovation and conversion to a commercial office building, knowing the project would offer an alternative to typical cookie-cutter office buildings common in most downtowns. Winter Properties sensed a demand for distinctive, economically priced office space that would appeal to Atlanta's growing creative, high-tech community. The company felt it

Although the building was structurally sounder than its decrepit exterior suggested (top), jackposts were used to shore up weak sections of the building during renovation (bottom).

could attract this niche market by creating appealing office space in a historic building.

Given the building's historic significance, the developer was able to secure federal rehabilitation tax credits, and a facade easement to the Georgia Trust for Historic Preservation qualified as a charitable contribution for tax purposes. In addition, the city agreed to freeze annual property taxes for nine and one-half years. Because of these financial incentives, the low acquisition cost, and judicious control over the cost of renovation, the Carriage Works achieved a profitable cash flow at only 60 percent occupancy. The building is currently operating profitably, at full occupancy.

Structural Renovation

The L-shaped, 62,556-square-foot brick building is on a 154,000-square-foot site. One leg of the "L" measures 160 feet long by 86 feet wide and is on four levels with a partial basement. Attached to the larger wing by a two-foot-thick brick wall, the building's smaller wing is 126 feet long by 80 feet wide and contains three levels with a full basement. The interior of the building is all wood, consisting of one- and two-foot beams and four- by six-inch tongue-and-groove flooring spanning ten-foot bays. One industrial-sized elevator inside an oversized shaft served the building in its former uses.

Because the building stood vacant for a decade before its renovation and appeared to be in serious disrepair, Winter commissioned its architect and structural engineer, MSTSD Architects, to thoroughly evaluate the structure before be-

Allowing timbers, brick, and other original construction materials to show through emphasizes the historic character of the building.

ginning any real planning for the project. Fortunately, the analysis revealed the structure to be only moderately deteriorated. Nevertheless, structural failure during construction was a major concern for both the developer and the lender. In fact, approximately 30 percent of the building's beams and timbers needed to be replaced. Weak sections of the building were supported using screwjacks, while replacement timbers were installed from the basement to the roof. This approach effectively prevented any structural failure during the renovation.

Previous warehouse operations had caused the building's floors to sag. Although for the most part the floors were structurally sound, they could vary as much as four to six inches within a ten-foot span. As a result, the greatest structural engineering challenge the project team faced was to level the floorslabs to a degree that was suitable for

a modern commercial office with heavy use of electronic equipment. A large area of the flooring around the existing elevator shaft and its supporting columns was rotten and had to be completely replaced. Other smaller sections of the floor had to be replaced as well. Lightweight concrete was poured onto all the floors to make them level; the concrete provided the added benefit of enhanced soundproofing between the floors.

The building's roof also was in poor condition and had to be replaced. The project team discovered that, several times throughout the building's history, the existing roof had been left in place while another roof was installed over top of it, resulting in roofing material eight to ten inches thick. Structural enhancements to the roof also were necessary. The wood and steel trusses supporting the roof of the short leg of the building lacked any lat-

The Carriage Works's 2,400-square-foot lobby is also used by one of the building's office tenants as a gallery.

eral bracing and needed supports. Because the trusses would remain open to view, the new lateral bracing was designed to be compatible with the existing trusses.

Interior Renovation

Whenever possible, the designers attempted to leave the existing wood structure and metal beams intact and untouched. Some replacement was necessary, however, resulting in a striking contrast between the old and new components of the building. This approach, besides being aesthetically pleasing, was also cost-effective. Brick walls and even old fire mains in the building were left exposed, emphasizing the building's age and patina. A wall painting on the third floor with "Atlanta Buggy Company" on it was left in place, mak-

ing the Carriage Works's history even more accessible to its new office tenants.

The existing elevator shaft on the west side of the building was removed and converted into an exit stairwell. A new elevator shaft was created in a more convenient area near the new lobby entrance and core building elements. The new oversized lobby, measuring nearly 2,400 square feet, is used by one of the building's tenants, the Georgia Council for the Arts, as a gallery to exhibit works by local artists.

The building's outdated mechanical systems were completely replaced and new electrical wiring, plumbing, and sewer lines installed. The majority of the fire-sprinkler lines could be reused, however. As had been indicated in a predevelopment study, no environmental problems materialized during the renovation with the exception of some asbestos on the roof.

Lacking windows, the basement of the building could not be leased as office space, but Winter converted it into a private health club for tenants' use. The club includes exercise equipment and separate showers for men and women.

Exterior Renovation

The original brick facade needed extensive cleaning, pointing, and replacement. Because the designers were able to illustrate the brick exterior in fine detail, the contractor was able to provide accurate price estimates for the work necessary to stabilize the exterior wall.

Most of the windows in the building were deteriorated and needed replacement. Over 80 percent of the existing windows were replaced with similar-style white aluminum windows with mullions that matched the existing mullions.

A considerable amount of site work had to be done to make the area suitable for a commercial office development. For instance, much of the soil on the site was inadequate for the construction of surface parking and landscaping, necessitating the removal of a large amount of soil. Backfill piled as high as the first floor of the building also had to be removed. Railroad tracks surrounding the property were removed to make much-needed room for parking and landscaping.

To enhance security for the building and its tenants, a ten- to 12-foot concrete wall was erected around the entire site. The city granted Winter permission to close off Means Street at its western end to further enhance the area's security. The city also agreed to change the name of a connecting two-block strip to Means Street, which helps facilitate

▼ Project Data

Land Use Information

Site Area: 3.5 acres
Gross Building Area: 62,556 square feet
Net Rentable Area (NRA): 60,098 square feet
Typical Floor Size: 18,000 square feet
Floor/Area Ratio: 0.41
Building Height: 4 stories, plus basement
Total Parking Spaces: 223 spaces

Land Use Plan

	Acres
Buildings	.75
Paved Areas (surface parking/roads)	2.00
Landscaped Areas	.75
Total	3.50

Office Tenant Information

Percent of NRA Occupied: 100%
Annual Rents: Approximately $11.00–14.00 per square foot
Average Length of Lease: 5–7 years
Typical Terms of Lease: Full service
Average Tenant Size: 3,000 square feet
Largest Tenant Size: 28,000 square feet

Office Tenant Size (square feet)	Number of Tenants
<5,000	12
5,000–10,000	3
>10,000	1
Total	16

Owner/Developer

Winter Properties, Inc.
330 Means Street
Suite 110
Atlanta, Georgia 30318
404-223-5015

Architect

MSTSD, Inc., Architects
1401 Peachtree Street, N.E.
Suite 460
Atlanta, Georgia 30340
404-876-6040

Development Schedule

Site Purchased: June 1988
Planning Started: January 1991
Construction Started: April 1991
Leasing Started: November 1991
Project Completed: January 1992

Redevelopment Cost Information

Site Acquisition Cost	$945,000

Site Improvement Costs

Excavation	$ 50,000
Grading	60,000
Sewer/water/drainage	30,000
Paving	100,000
Curbs/sidewalks	30,000
Landscaping/irrigation	60,000
Fees/general conditions	70,000
Fencing, etc.	100,000
Total	$500,000

Construction Costs

Superstructure	$ 250,000
HVAC	300,000
Electrical	260,000
Plumbing/sprinklers	225,000
Elevators	70,000
Fees/general conditions	300,000
Finishes	60,000
Graphics/specialties	10,000
Other	25,000
Total	$1,500,000

Soft Costs

Architecture/engineering	$ 95,000
Project management	50,000
Leasing/marketing	15,000
Legal/accounting	10,000
Taxes/insurance	25,000
Title fees	7,000
Construction interest and fees	70,000
Other	40,000
Total	$312,000

Total Redevelopment Cost	$3,257,000
Redevelopment Cost per Net Square Foot	$54.00

Annual Operating Expenses (year one)

Taxes	$ 12,000
Insurance	9,000
Security	78,000
Maintenance	15,000
Janitorial	30,000
Utilities	68,000
Legal	2,000
Management	31,000
Miscellaneous	18,000
Total	$263,000

Annual Operating Expenses per Net square Foot	$4.38

access to the site, as the property is not on a main street.

Community Benefits

Ironically, the redevelopment of the Carriage Works has generated demand among artists for the loft housing that Winter initially wanted to develop, prompting the conversion of many surrounding structures into loft housing developments. Winter Properties has so far successfully redeveloped three properties in the Means Street area, two of them containing loft housing. As artists, arts organizations, and emerging high-tech businesses continue to be attracted to this formerly run-down area, wider revitalization is assured.

Experience Gained

▼ Bring experienced construction professionals on board as soon as possible to review design plans for costs and engineering feasibility.
▼ Make accurate drawings of existing conditions to aid the contractor in the initial stages and facilitate more reliable cost estimates.
▼ Build in a higher contingency factor for adaptive use projects than for new construction.

Denver Dry Goods Building

Denver, Colorado

The landmark Denver Dry Goods Building department store in the heart of downtown Denver was saved from destruction and transformed into a mixed-use development.

For nearly 100 years, the Denver Dry Goods department store served as the retail heart of downtown Denver. Built in 1888 and added onto three times over the years, the 350,000-square-foot "Denver Dry" was the city's premier department store for generations of Denver residents. But as fortunes changed, the building was sold in 1987 and the store closed.

With the beloved Denver Dry running the risk of becoming a parking lot, the Denver Urban Renewal Authority (DURA) stepped in and purchased the building in 1988. After several false starts, DURA selected the Affordable Housing Development Corporation (AHDC) as project developer, and together DURA and AHDC have managed to resurrect the Denver Dry, fashioning it into a vibrant mixed-use project of affordable and market-rate housing, retail shops, and office space. The key to Denver Dry's resurrection was an echo of its past: just as the building was built in in-

crements, so its reconstruction and reuse were accomplished piece by piece. The mammoth structure was broken down, figuratively and legally, into smaller condominium units to provide for more manageable and financeable packages of development. In these smaller pieces, separate housing, retail, and office units could be planned and then variously bundled into financing and construction packages.

The Site and Building

The Denver Dry Goods Building occupies the entire frontage of California Street from 15th Street to 16th Street. The building has a strategic location: it sits where the 16th Street pedestrian/transitway mall joins the new light-rail system, which began operation in fall 1994. The Denver Dry also links the convention center, retail business district, and downtown hotels.

The Denver Dry Goods Building was erected in 1888 as a three-story structure occupying half of the California Street frontage closest to 16th Street. The red brick, sandstone, and limestone structure was designed by Frank D. Edbrooks, the architect of several notable Denver buildings, including the historic Brown Palace

Over 30 coats of white lead-based paint were removed to expose the original brick, sandstone, and limestone exterior of the building.

mitments. Out of these failed attempts, however, a new concept emerged: breaking the building down into smaller pieces. The plan that ultimately took shape provided for three development phases, two of which have been completed. The first phase, completed in October 1993, consisted of 51 units of affordable and market-rate rental housing, 73,370 square feet of retail space, and 28,780 square feet of office space. The second phase, consisting of an additional 42,000 square feet of retail space, was completed in May 1994. The final phase of redevelopment will provide 66 luxury condominium units. BCORP Holdings, Inc., the owner/developer of the final phase, began construction in late 1995 and was expected to complete the units in December 1996.

Hotel. In 1898, a fourth story was added to the original structure, and in 1906, a six-story addition was constructed on the 15th Street side of the original building. In one last expansion, in 1924, an additional two stories were constructed on top of the original building, which became the location of the Denver Tearoom.

proximately half the purchase price, and the remainder was financed by a consortium of local banks and union pension funds.

Over the next two years, several developers responded to DURA's requests for proposals, offering a variety of adaptive use schemes, including a retail mall, a hotel, an aquarium, movie theaters, and upscale housing, but none were able to obtain leasing or financing com-

Planning, Design, And Renovation

The first phase of development concentrated on the 15th Street building and one floor of the 16th Street building. DURA sold two floors of the building to Robert Waxman

Redevelopment Strategy

The city of Denver regarded the preservation of the Denver Dry Goods Building as critical to the health of downtown The department store had closed, and the vacated building was becoming an eyesore threatened with demolition. In the depressed real estate market of the late 1980s, no private buyer emerged to save the Denver Dry. As a last resort, the city of Denver and DURA stepped in and purchased the building for $6.9 million. The city financed ap-

The fifth floor of the Denver Dry during its conversion to rental apartments.

Shannon Sperry, DURA

Shannon Sperry, DURA

The basement, first floor, and second floor are occupied by major retail tenants. Shown above is the interior of Media Play on the first floor of the 16th Street building; original column capitals were retained.

Camera Company, a strong local retailer that has been in the downtown market for 30 years, to install Waxman's Camera and Video in the basement and on the first floor. National retailer T.J. Maxx, enticed by low rent and an escalator that provided direct access from the street to the second floor, committed to taking most of the second floor of the 15th Street and 16th Street buildings. The remainder of the second and third floors of the 15th Street building was improved for office use, and the top three floors of the building were renovated into a mix of market-rate and low-income housing units. The housing takes advantage of its high elevation and the building's large windows to afford spectacular views of Denver and the Rocky Mountains beyond. Construction of this phase lasted ten months.

Shannon Sperry, DURA

One of the fourth-floor rental units.

During the second phase, which took seven months to complete, the first floor and basement of the 16th Street building were converted to retail space and leased by Media Play.

The remaining portions of the 16th Street building, the third through sixth floors, are being converted into condominium units during the final phase of redevelopment.

Renovating the exterior of the building included removing over 30 layers of white lead-based paint to expose the building's original orange-red brick, sandstone, and limestone surface. This process took eight months to complete at a cost of $800,000. The original wood windows were renovated and retrofitted with double-pane glass. In addition, new canopies and signs were installed.

The interior of the Denver Dry was gutted except for historic elements. Architectural plans for the reconfiguration of the approximately 50,000-square-foot floorplates took advantage of the many existing elevator cores to dedicate individual elevators for the housing and offices. New, direct access was provided to the second-floor retail space.

Significant fire and safety improvements were made all at once

Shannon Sperry, DURA

The four upper floors of the 16th Street building are being converted to luxury condominium units. The legendary two-story Denver Tearoom, built on top of the Denver Dry in the 1920s, is being converted to condominium units with balconies.

▼ Project Data

Land Use Information

Site Area: 1.15 acres
Gross Building Area: 350,000 square feet

Building Plan

	Square Feet
Office	28,780
Retail	115,370
Residential (rental)	47,235
Residential (for sale)	77,000
Circulation and Common Areas	81,615
Total	350,000

Residential Unit Information

Rental Units:

Unit Type	Number of Units	Floor Area (square feet)	Monthly Rent per Unit
Affordable:			
One-Bedroom	31	590–950	$440–540
Two-Bedroom	9	1,100–1,400	$523–623
Market-Rate:			
One-Bedroom	2	890–950	$800–850
Two-Bedroom	9	1,100–1,265	$995–1,050
Total	51		

For-Sale Units:

Unit Type	Number of Units Planned	Floor Area (square feet)	Price Range per Unit (all units)
One-Bedroom	19	794–1,189	
Two-Bedroom	46	874–2,027	$140,000–230,000
"Historic"	1	3,900	
Total	66		

Commercial Tenant Information

Average Annual Rents:
Office: $12.74 per square foot
Retail: $10.00 per square foot

Average Annual Retail Sales: $250–650 per square foot

Length and Type of Leases:
Office: 10–15 years full service
Retail: 15–20 years triple net

Redevelopment Cost Information

Site Acquisition Cost			$6,900,000[1]

	Phases I and II	Phase III Pro Forma	Total
Construction Costs			
Superstructure	$ 7,050,000	$1,500,000	$ 8,550,000
HVAC	2,150,000	860,000	3,010,000
Electrical	1,500,000	730,000	2,230,000
Plumbing/sprinklers	1,100,000	1,087,000	2,187,000
Fees/general conditions	975,000	460,000	1,435,000
Graphics/specialties	100,000	53,000	153,000
Tenant finishes	5,600,000	1,705,000	7,305,000
Total	$18,475,000	$6,395,000	$24,870,000
Soft Costs			
Architecture/ engineering	$ 860,000	$ 185,000	$1,045,000
Leasing/marketing	530,000	960,000	1,490,000
Legal/accounting	600,000	65,000	665,000
Taxes/insurance	90,000	60,000	150,000
Construction interest and fees	1,175,000	580,000	1,755,000
Other	1,500,000	305,000	1,805,000
Total	$4,755,000	$2,155,000	$6,910,000

Total Redevelopment Cost: $38,680,000

---

for the entire building. In addition, new HVAC and electrical systems were installed and tenant finishes constructed for the first and second phases. Evaporative coolers were installed in lieu of central air conditioning in the apartments, and city steam was used for heating.

For the housing component, the challenge for designers was to use the deep bays of the existing space and bring light to the deep interiors. Solutions included constructing wide hallways with adjacent leasable storage units and providing clerestory windows to light interior bedrooms. For the office space, the greatest challenge was to provide space for new HVAC systems while respecting the high window openings of the historic structure. Designers decided to construct dropped soffits in part of the space while maintaining the original 18-foot-high ceilings along window walls and other significant areas.

Financing

Twenty-three separate sources of funding were pieced together to finance the several uses and phases

▼ Project Data *(continued)*

Major Sources of Financing

Affordable Housing Development Corporation
Colorado Historical Society
Colorado Housing and Finance Authority/Bank One
Denver Dry Retail II, L.P.
Denver Housing Trust Council
Denver Urban Renewal Authority
Dominion Bank
Federal National Mortgage Association
First Bank of Republic Plaza
First Interstate Bank of Denver (Norwest)
Rocky Mountain Investors
Tax credit purchasers
United Bank of Denver
U.S. Department of Housing and Urban Development
Women's Bank

Sponsor

Denver Urban Renewal Authority
1555 California Street, Suite 200
Denver, Colorado 80202
303-295-3872

Architect

Urban Design Group
1621 18th Street, Suite 200
Denver, Colorado 80202

Developers

Affordable Housing Development Corporation
33 Katonah Avenue
Katonah, New York 10536
914-232-1396

BCORP Holdings, Inc.
250 15th Street, Suite 202
West Vancouver, B.C. V7T2X4
604-926-8109

Development Schedule

Site Purchased: July 1988
Planning Started: July 1988
Construction Started: January 1993
Sales/Leasing Started: July 1993
Phase I Completed: October 1993
Phase II Completed: May 1994
Phase III Completed: December 1996 (projected)

Note:
[1]Includes $900,000 for asbestos removal.

---

of the project. Financing sources included pension funds, state bond issues, tax increment bonds, Urban Development Action Grants, the sale of low-income housing and rehabilitation tax credits, loans and equity investments from public agencies and private nonprofit organizations, private bank loans, and developer equity.

Organizationally, the development of the first phase was split between two limited partnerships: the Denver Building Housing Ltd. and the Denver Dry Retail L.P. Denver Building Housing Ltd. was responsible for development of the 51 units of rental apartments and office space for the Denver Metro Convention and Visitors Bureau. This partnership was made up of two entities, the Federal National Mortgage Association, which purchased the tax credits providing equity for the deal, and the Denver Dry Development Corporation, a nonprofit corporation formed by DURA. The partnership selected AHDC and its president, Jonathan F.P. Rose, as the fee developer for these portions of the project.

Denver Dry Retail L.P. was responsible for developing the entire second floor of the building, consisting of the T.J. Maxx store and office space for DURA. The Denver

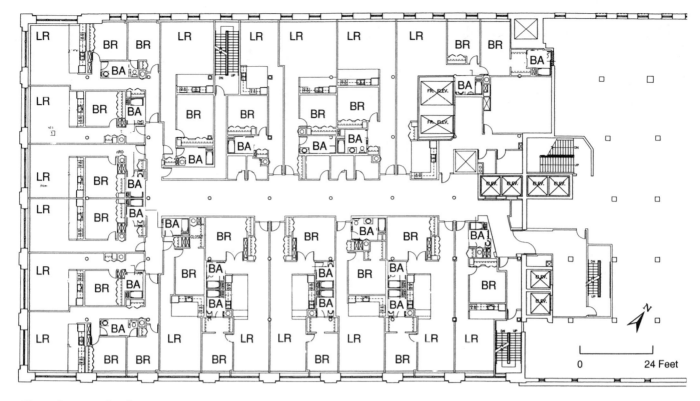

Floor plan—rental units.

Dry Retail Corporation, an affiliate of AHDC, is the general partner of Denver Dry Retail L.P. The team for the second phase of development consists of a single limited partnership, the Denver Dry Retail II, L.P., also an affiliate of AHDC. This partnership was responsible for the development of the Media Play store in the basement and on the first floor of the 16th Street building.

The adaptive use of the Denver Dry Goods Building has been successful for both the developers and the city of Denver. The two national retailers that leased space in the project are the first large national retailers to locate in downtown Denver

in ten years. The housing component, which was fully leased in just two months, now has a 200-person waiting list and has acted as a catalyst for six other residential projects in downtown Denver. More generally, renovation of the Denver Dry was the impetus for eight other historic renovation projects in downtown Denver.

Experience Gained

▼ While large, unconventional adaptive use projects like the

Denver Dry Goods Building might not be feasible when viewed as a whole, redefining the project into smaller components and packages could allow for a variety of development and financing options.

▼ Housing can be a valuable partner in a commercial project, because it provides a 24-hour presence and stimulates an active retail environment.

▼ A public/private partnership, such as the one between DURA and AHDC, can be most successful when the approach is open on both sides and the parties work by consensus.

Preservation Park

Oakland, California

Preservation Park is adjacent to Oakland's recently developed federal office complex. Sixteen dilapidated Victorian residences from scattered locations were brought to the two-block site and renovated for use as offices and conference space.

Today, after some false starts, Preservation Park does indeed have a new life: in all, 16 structures have been renovated, providing offices for 47 nonprofit organizations and related businesses. Collectively, the structures provide 55,604 rentable square feet of space: 47,015 square feet for office tenants, 7,612 square feet in separate leasable meeting and conference areas, and 977 square feet of retail space.

The adaptive use plan for Preservation Park focused on an often neglected market segment: nonprofit, public-benefit organizations. Within this market segment, the developers of Preservation Park focused on four types of nonprofit organizations: social service, environmental, educational, and cultural.

The Site

Preservation Park occupies most of a two-square-block site from 12th to 14th Streets in downtown Oakland. Bordering the site to the east is a recently constructed high-rise federal office building that is part of Oakland City Center, a multiblock, multiuse office and retail redevelopment project. Immediately to the west of the site is the Grove Shafter Freeway (I-980), whose construction provided eight of Preservation Park's historic houses.

In its 125-year history, Preservation Park has experienced changes common to many urban areas. The community started in the 1870s as an upscale residential neighborhood made up of elaborate Victorian houses. By the 1970s, however, many of the large houses had been subdivided into rooming houses, and the neighborhood had deteriorated into what planners at the time considered "redevelopment material." All but five of the structures on the two-block site were demolished. The construction of the Grove Shafter Freeway adjacent to the site of Preservation Park also threatened to destroy a significant percentage of the neighborhood's historic Victorian houses. To preserve these historic structures, the city of Oakland created a public/private partnership to relocate the endangered buildings and to renovate the regrouped residential structures for new life as a "business neighborhood."

Several of the project's historic structures have raised first floors. Access for wheelchairs is provided by an elevated boardwalk at the rear of each building.

Construction of the freeway entailed truncating 13th Street and resulted in a dead end within the site of Preservation Park. Seizing the opportunity, project designers cut a new internal street into the site (Preservation Park Way) perpendicular to 13th Street and joined the two streets with a traffic circle anchored by a historic cast-iron fountain relocated from another site.

The five structures north of 13th Street all remain in their original locations. The 11 structures that were relocated to the parcel were sited south of 13th Street, with the larger, more imposing structures situated to the exterior of the

block and the smaller structures set in, facing Preservation Park Way. The Oakland Redevelopment Authority (ORA) orchestrated and financed transportation and siting of the historic buildings.

Redevelopment Process

In 1982, the project's original developer, Preservation Ventures, began renovation of the five Victorian houses already on the site, aiming to lease the renovated structures as commercial office space. Preserva-

tion Ventures, a real estate syndication formed by the Northern California Black Chamber of Commerce, used federal historic rehabilitation tax credits as a source of equity to redevelop the site's five original structures. By 1986, however, with renovation of the five structures nearly completed, none of the office space had been leased, and it was becoming clear that the developer would not be able to complete the project. Adding to Preservation Ventures's difficulties were changes in the federal tax code and regulatory stipulations making it difficult to secure tax credits for the rehabilitation of structures that had been relocated, creating a financial shortfall for the redevelopment of the 11 relocated houses.

Preservation Ventures's difficulties concerned both the city of Oakland, which had sponsored and partially financed the project, and Bramalea, Inc., the Toronto-based developer of the adjacent City Center project, which saw a lingering eyesore at its back door. As a result, Bramalea agreed to assist the city in completing the project in 1986 after Preservation Ventures bowed out. The condition on Bramalea's involvement, however, was that Preservation Park's development concept be changed to an office and con-

A building known as "the White House," before and after adaptive use renovation.

ference center for nonprofit organizations. The developer believed that nonprofit organizations would be more willing to occupy unconventional office space in a gentrifying neighborhood.

With this new plan and an infusion of additional financing from the city of Oakland and the U.S. Department of Housing and Urban Development, Bramalea took over the development, management, and leasing of the project, donating its executive services to the city. Bramalea's construction initiatives, which included the renovation and refurbishment of 11 historic structures and limited on-site improvements, were completed by 1991. The project was fully leased 18 months later. A successor to Bramalea—CMA Asset Managers, Inc.—remains as management and leasing agent.

To enhance internal circulation throughout the project's two-square-block site, a new street and circular turnaround were constructed.

Design and Construction

The 16 historic structures at Preservation Park, built between 1870 and 1911, represent the breadth of styles popular in that period—Italianate, stick, Queen Anne, colonial revival, and English arts and crafts. Renovation included new mechanical and electrical systems, seismic bracing, sprinklers, improved access for the disabled, and interior and exterior restoration. New concrete foundations were required for the relocated structures.

The elaborately detailed building exteriors received the most extensive restoration. Original Victorian gingerbread detail was patched and repaired, and the structures were repainted in classic Victorian colors. Exterior porches and steps, many of which could not be salvaged when the buildings were relocated, were authentically reconstructed

when documentary evidence was available and rebuilt in the period style when it was not.

Much of the deteriorated interior finish was replaced with new materials to maintain a workable budget for the project. Interior window casings and other highly noticeable details, however, were retained and restored where possible.

The most challenging issue of the renovation was designing accessibility for the disabled. By the nature of their Victorian designs, most of the structures had raised first floors, accessible only by a series of steps up to a porch or landing. The solution to this problem, developed by the Architectural Resources Group, the project architect, was to construct an elevated pathway at the rear of the houses. This new pedestrian circulation system, designed as a boardwalk, provides a code-compliant route to the main level of each house and an accessible connection between houses. To minimize the impact of the raised walkway, the guardrails and walk-

ways are built of wood compatible with the buildings' architecture, and the area is landscaped with flowering vines.

Financing

ORA acquired the site for approximately $1.25 million as part of a larger redevelopment and site acquisition project. Financing for the original Preservation Ventures project (pre-Bramalea) included approximately $1.9 million in equity generated by historic rehabilitation tax credits and loans from ORA. ORA provided an additional $4 million in financing (a ten-year note) at the time Bramalea joined the project.

In addition to these sources of financing, Preservation Park (as a nonprofit, community-benefit project) was able to garner a significant amount of donated services and materials. Bramalea, for example, contributed approximately $1 million of in-kind services to the project and arranged for substantial con-

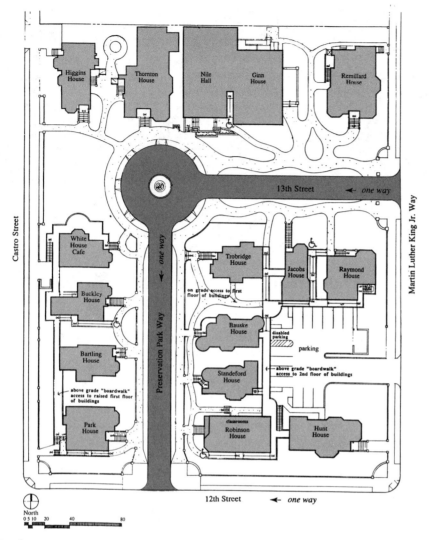

Site plan.

tributions from a variety of other suppliers and contractors.

Marketing and Leasing

To develop its marketing strategy, Bramalea first surveyed nonprofit organizations to pinpoint their space needs and rents. The survey and a direct-mail campaign were the principal methods of introducing the project to the nonprofit community in the initial phases. Word of mouth

soon overtook those methods, however, and has been the principal source of new tenants ever since.

All units were rented over a planned 18-month period. By allowing that amount of time, Bramalea was able to select the tenants it wanted. Generating a positive cash flow after debt service, the project's revenue provides income to offset ongoing costs of property management and capital improvements.

To provide business services for the nonprofit tenants (including a cafe and printing/copying services), space at Preservation Park was re-

served for several commercial tenants. Lower lease rates are offered to nonprofit organizations, higher ones to commercial tenants.

Preservation Park's conference and banquet facilities generate a valuable revenue stream while giving the project good market exposure. The conference center (which in 1995 housed 691 meetings for nonprofit organizations and 112 meetings for other businesses) has proven to be a valuable amenity for Preservation Park tenants as well as the surrounding business community. The centerpiece of the conference center, the 3,200-square-foot Nile Hall, can accommodate meetings of up to 150 people and receptions for up to 200 people.

Experience Gained

▼ The renovation of historic residential buildings for office space works well for the nonprofit sector, as such tenants tend to be smaller and do not require the larger and more regular footprints of traditional office space.

▼ The establishment of a stand-alone conference center at Preservation Park has worked well, both for the project's economics and for the needs of its nonprofit tenants. The conference center also serves as a marketing tool and source of public identity for the project.

▼ Through the creation of a public/private redevelopment initiative, Bramalea was able to assist the community by providing expertise in real estate development and management while simultaneously working to ensure the successful development and ongoing management of the neighboring project it owns.

▼ Project Data

Land Use Information

Site Area: 2.5 acres
Net Rentable Area (NRA):
　　Offices: 47,015 square feet
　　Retail Space: 977 square feet
　　Meeting Rooms: 7,612 square feet
　　Total: 55,604 square feet
Typical Floor Size: 1,000 square feet
Building Heights: 2–3 stories
Total Parking Spaces: 16

Office Tenant Information

Percent of NRA Occupied: 100%
Rents: Approximately $12.60–16.90 per square foot
Average Length of Lease: 1–3 years
Typical Terms of Lease: Adjusted annually based on CPI (3 percent minimum)
Average Tenant Size: 850 square feet
Largest Tenant Size: 5,657 square feet

Office Tenant Size (square feet)	Number of Tenants
<5,000	45
5,000–10,000	2

Retail Tenant Information

Percent of NRA Occupied: 100%
Number of Tenants: 2
Average Tenant Size: 977 square feet

Redevelopment Cost Information

Site Acquisition Cost	$1,250,000[1]
Site Improvement Costs	$1,746,349[2]

Construction Costs

Shell	$5,515,137
Tenant improvements	125,751
Graphics/specialties	187,526
Other	25,004
Total	$6,853,418[3]

Soft Costs

Architecture/engineering/consultants	$ 546,874
Project management	300,000
Leasing/marketing	358,515
Legal/accounting	124,527
Construction interest and fees	35,417
Operating loss reserve	(291,691)
Other	212,017
Total	$1,285,659

Total Redevelopment Costs	**$11,135,426**
Construction Cost per Net Square Foot	**$123**

Annual Operating Expenses

Taxes	$ 23,389
Cleaning	32,185
Mechanical maintenance	8,966
Elevator	900
Security	37,076
General building	124,723
Administration	161,342
Energy	45,560
Nonrecoverable	43,500
Total	$477,641

Owner

City of Oakland
1333 Broadway, Suite 900
Oakland, California 94612
510-238-3692

Development Manager

Bramalea, Inc.
1111 Broadway, Suite 1400
Oakland, California 94612
510-464-8200

Architect

Architectural Resources Group
Pier 9, The Embarcadero
San Francisco, California 94111
415-421-1680

Property Manager

CMA Asset Managers, Inc.
500 12th Street, Suite 210
Oakland, California 94612
510-874-7808

Development Schedule

Site Purchased: Mid-1970s (as part of a larger redevelopment area)
Planning Started: Mid-1970s
Construction Started: 1982
Leasing Started: 1991
Project Completed: October 1991

Notes:
[1]Based on a percentage of a larger land acquisition and redevelopment initiative spearheaded by ORA.
[2]Bramalea was responsible for $496,349 of total site improvement costs.
[3]Preservation Ventures funded approximately $1 million of the project's construction costs, which is included in the total.

Part 3

Profiles

Described in the following pages are 83 adaptive use projects from throughout the country, representing a broad range of old and new uses and a diversity in size, cost, and financing techniques. Emphasis is on projects undertaken since the late 1980s that did not benefit from public sector financing that is no longer available, such as urban development action grants.

Project descriptions and tables are based on information supplied by the owners, developers, or architects in response to a survey conducted by the Urban Land Institute. Questionnaires were sent to representatives of projects recommended by *ULI Market Profiles* authors as being outstanding adaptive use projects recently completed in their local markets. Projects are described in a brief analysis, focusing on building type, construction characteristics, and general adaptability to new uses.

Catalog entries are arranged according to the original use of the building. The five categories covered are commercial buildings (mostly retail and office buildings); factories, warehouses, and industrial buildings; public buildings (including schools, churches, firehouses, civic buildings, and train and bus stations); cultural buildings (mostly theaters); and residences and hotels. Projects within each category are listed alphabetically.

Tables at the end of each category include the economics and physical redevelopment work involved in converting the buildings to new uses. For purposes of comparison, costs are broken down into acquisition (building and land) and redevelopment (construction, professional services, financing, and other). When costs per square foot were not provided, an approximate figure was computed by dividing redevelopment costs by gross build-ing area. Estimates derived in this way are indicated by parentheses. A dash in any column indicates the information was not available.

Appendix A contains cross-references of projects described in Parts 1, 2, and 3, arranged according to old uses, new uses, and geographic locations.

Original Use: Commercial Buildings

1. AEtna Health Plans Headquarters at Blue Hen Corporate Center
Dover, Delaware

Original Use: Regional mall anchor store, 1960s

New Use: Office, 1994

Developer: Blue Realty Corporation, New York

Architect: Gensler and Associates, New York

Conversion: This project demonstrates that outdated, underperforming shopping malls can be renovated and repositioned to provide excellent low-cost corporate office space. AEtna Health Plans needed extra space with more technological amenities. Time and money were also important considerations. By converting a structurally sound but vacant 90,000-square-foot, one-story mall anchor store into Class A office space, Blue Realty Corporation, owner/developer of the underused mall, was able to offer AEtna superior office space at lower cost. The building conversion, which took only four months, provides 11-foot ceilings, a large lunchroom, bright and open office space, access to retail shops, and a convenient location near two major highways.

The redevelopment of a vacant 90,000-square-foot anchor store into Class A corporate office space was the first phase of transforming a failing shopping center into a corporate office center.

Redevelopment of the vacant anchor store for AEtna was the first phase of a major repositioning of the 470,000-square-foot former Blue Hen Mall. Blue Realty has since converted the remaining vacant 80,000-square-foot anchor store to office space for NationsBank, and another 18,000 square feet has been converted to a daycare center. The owner/developer is currently negotiating terms for 210,000 square feet with three potential corporate tenants.

2. Blueprint Furniture
Los Angeles, California

Original Use: Bank, 1931

New Use: Furniture store, 1988

Developer: Hyon Chough, Los Angeles

Architect: Projects Architecture, Culver City, California

Conversion: Designed, engineered, and drawn in ten days, this conversion of a 12,500-square-foot 1930s moderne-style bank building provided the tenant a quick, cost-effective solution for urgently needed showroom space. All nonoriginal external layering was stripped away from the structure to expose the cast-in-place concrete frame and timber truss ceiling. A brick and glass storefront added to the building in the 1960s was demolished and the clearspan frame replaced with 3/8-inch-thick glass. Tough, inexpensive industrial materials were used throughout the interior for their color and textural qualities —sandblasted and exposed concrete, exposed or galvanized steel, white drywall. Removal of the dropped ceiling revealed an expansive well-preserved timber truss ceiling. The tenant-financed improvements to the building cost $100,000 ($8.00 per square foot).

3. Canned Foods, Inc., Corporate Offices
Berkeley, California

Original Use: Auto dealership, 1934

New Use: Office and retail space, 1992

Developer: Read Investments, Berkeley

Architect: The Ratcliff Architects, Emeryville, California

Conversion: Canned Foods Company relocated its headquarters to an existing auto dealership building renovated and adapted into new offices. The designers created a comfortable office environment by taking advantage of the building's barrel-vaulted ceiling and its network of bowstring trusses, and by installing skylights. The original two-story, 20,000-square-foot warehouse was enlarged to 42,000 square feet, incorporating new office and retail space. The extremely deteriorated building required extensive redevelopment throughout, at a cost of $4.7 million ($110 per square foot).

4. Dallas Area Rapid Transit (DART) Headquarters
Dallas, Texas

Original Use: Department store, 1964

New Use: Office, 1992

Developer: Woodbine Development Corporation, Dallas

Architect: Corgan Associates Architects, Dallas

Conversion: With leases soon expiring in three of its office buildings, DART wanted to consolidate its headquarters into one downtown building close to a rapid-transit station. The Baptist Foundation of Texas, which manages endowment funds for various Baptist institutions, believed that a vacant 436,634-square-foot department

The owner of a vacant 28-year-old department store in downtown Dallas (top) teamed with Woodbine Development to redevelop the building to meet DART's office needs. Turnkey redevelopment cost for the ready-to-operate office building and parking garage (bottom) totaled $21 million (less than $49.00 per square foot).

store in its control could be converted to supply the office space DART needed. DART ultimately entered into a lease/purchase agreement with the foundation (with financing by the seller) for a completely renovated, ready-to-operate office building, including modular furniture and other tenant improvements, for a turnkey price of $21 million, less than $49.00 per square foot. The agreement was contingent upon the building's being ready for occupancy 11 months after construction began, a target that was met with one week to spare. Design and preconstruction consulting fees came to $1.4 million, base building and tenant improvements to $11.5 million. The 28-year-old building required extensive renovation inside and out, including installation of energy-efficient mechanical systems, modifications to comply with the Americans with Disabilities Act, additional restrooms, and structural capacity to accommodate two additional floors. The building now has 281,754 square feet of office space on four levels and 146,000 square feet of parking on two underground levels.

5. Dallas Education Center
Dallas, Texas

Original Use: Department store, 1954

New Use: College, 1994

Developer: Centre Development Company, Inc., Dallas

Architect: GREENarc Corp., Dallas Meckfessel Associates, Dallas

Conversion: Three of the eight floors of this 200,000-square-foot department store were converted into college classrooms at a cost of $38.00 per square foot. The building was structurally sound, but the interior had deteriorated since its construction in the 1950s. New mechanical systems were installed, and extensive interior construction and environmental remediation were required. The building was acquired for $300,000; redevelopment cost for 46,198 square feet of the building totaled $1.75 million. The project was financed through private equity and civic and institutional donations.

6. DePaul Center
Chicago, Illinois

Original Use: Department store, 1914

New Use: Offices, retail space, classrooms, 1993

Developer: DePaul University, Chicago

Architect: Daniel P. Coffey & Associates, Ltd., Chicago

Conversion: Previous plans by the city to convert the abandoned Goldblatt department store in downtown Chicago into a library were abandoned, and the building was slated for demolition. DePaul University stepped forward with a plan to purchase the 11-story, 650,000-square-foot building and redevelop it as a mixed-use center to be occupied by DePaul and speculative office and retail tenants. For $95.00 per square foot, DePaul transformed the eroded structure into a vibrant multipurpose commercial center that includes 65,000 square feet of retail space, 225,000 square feet of office space, and 300,000 square feet of academic and administrative support space. In addition to the interior renovation, a new facade, minipark, and skybridge to adjacent buildings were added. The building was purchased for $3 million and redeveloped for $62 million, with financing from the university and city-backed tax-exempt bonds.

7. Georgia State University, College of Business Administration
Atlanta, Georgia

Original Use: Bank headquarters/office building, 1901

New Use: Georgia State University, College of Business Administration building, 1993

Developer: Board of Regents, The University System of Georgia, Atlanta

Architect: Georgia State University Office of Planning and Facilities, Atlanta

Conversion: After merging with C&S National Bank in 1990, NationsBank constructed a new 50-story office building and donated its turn-of-the-century headquarters building to Georgia State University. The 14-story, 196,417-square-foot building (originally ten floors and added onto later) now houses faculty from the College of Business Administration. Because the new use was so compatible with the old use, only minor redevelopment work was needed. Total redevelopment cost was $2 million ($11.00 per square foot). As part of the deal, NationsBank has a 60-year, $1.00-per-year (plus operating costs) lease on 20,000 square feet of the building to use as a branch office.

8. Hagerstown Telework Center
Hagerstown, Maryland

Original Use: Department store, furniture store, circa 1930

New Use: Telework center, 1995

Developer: City of Hagerstown, Maryland

Architect: Kurt Cushwa, Hagerstown

Conversion: The city of Hagerstown was able to purchase and assemble several downtown parcels for redevelopment. One parcel contained a former department store whose second floor the city converted into a 7,200-square-foot telework center, one of four demonstration sites to establish telework centers for federal workers. The telecenter has 35 workstations with copiers, fax machines, a teleconference room, and a break area. Federal workers can be connected to their offices from this remote location without commuting to Washington, D.C., or Baltimore. The property, vacant since 1957, needed a substantial amount of redevelopment work. The interior was completely rehabilitated, new mechanical systems installed, and the roof replaced. The ground floor and basement of the building have been converted to state offices and a ballet school. Redevelopment costs for the telework center totaled $385,000 ($53.00 per square foot). The project was financed through general obligation bonds, a community development block grant, and funds allocated from a government demonstration program.

9. Pembroke Square at Peabody Place
Memphis, Tennessee

Original Use: Department store, 1900

New Use: Apartments, office and retail space, 1996

Developer: Belz Enterprises, Memphis

Architect: Hnedak Bobo Group, Memphis

Conversion: Pembroke Square is one of four adaptive use buildings at Peabody Place, an eight-block urban mixed-use project developed by Belz Enterprises in downtown Memphis (also see project numbers

A view of the former Goldsmith's department store in downtown Memphis being redeveloped for a mix of new uses.

16, 71, and 75). Formerly a 235,000-square-foot, eight-floor department store with offices on the upper floors, Pembroke Square now contains 45 rental apartment units, 110,000 square feet of office space (ten tenants), and approximately 60,000 square feet of specialty shops and restaurants on the lower levels. Although equipped with modern amenities, the newly renovated interiors still retain the character of the old department store, as many of its historical and architectural features were restored. Although both the exterior and the interior needed extensive redevelopment work, the configuration of the existing building was quite compatible with the new uses. The developer purchased the building for $75,000 and redeveloped it for $20 million ($85.00 per square foot). The project was financed using developer equity and a commercial bank.

10. Philadelphia Arts Bank
Philadelphia, Pennsylvania

Original Use: Bank and office space, 1928

New Use: Performing arts theater, 1994

Developer: University of the Arts, Philadelphia

Architect: Mitchell Kurtz Architects, New York

Conversion: A former bank building now houses a nonprofit rental theater and rehearsal hall, providing greater Philadelphia's performing arts community with a downtown venue located on the Avenue of the Arts corridor. Although the three-story, 21,000-square-foot building was very sound, extensive interior alterations and new mechanical systems were necessary to accommodate the new use. Now the former banking hall is occupied by a 238-seat theater and rehearsal hall. A 1,000-square-foot cafe/gallery complements the theater. The building was acquired for $700,000 and redeveloped for $3.8 million ($181 per square foot). The project was financed with a grant from the William Penn Foundation.

11. Solomon Schechter Day School
Northbrook, Illinois

Original Use: Office building, circa 1982

New Use: School, 1994

Developer: Pickus Construction, Waukegan, Illinois

Architect: Phillip Kupritz & Associates, Chicago

Conversion: Adaptive use renewed the economic value of this vacant early 1980s office building while providing reasonably priced space for a private school. The two-story office building required extensive exterior renovation, site restoration and landscaping, new interior construction, and new mechanical systems. As a fairly modern building, it did not require environmental remediation. The 110,000-square-foot building was acquired for $1.7 million and redeveloped for $6.4 million ($58.00 per square foot).

12. The Exchange Building
San Antonio, Texas

Original Use: Office, 1925

New Use: Apartments and retail, 1994

Developer: Exchange Building Limited, San Antonio

Architect: Lake/Flato Architects, San Antonio

Conversion: With a sizable inventory of 1920s and 1930s buildings downtown, the city of San Antonio supported the conversion of the ten-story Exchange Building into 42 affordable apartments and ground-floor retail space. The building, which had sat vacant for ten years because its footprint was too small for contemporary office use, was purchased for $650,000 by developer Tom Guggolz and his partners David Lake and Ted Flato (principals of Lake/Flato Architects). The interior of the building was gutted to expose the concrete structure, the dropped ceiling removed, and the historic lobby restored.

As part of its exterior renovation, The Exchange Building's concrete-stone and aluminum storefronts were replaced with fixed glass. The ground floor, designated as retail space, is currently occupied by a restaurant and a grocery/delicatessen.

Piping for the new sprinkler system and electrical conduit were left exposed to closely replicate the "raw" appearance of the original 1925 finish and to meet the budget of $44.00 per square foot. Compact fluorescent lights, ceiling fans, operable windows, and individual utility meters were installed to save energy. The average unit is 600 square feet, although one large penthouse unit was also constructed. The reluctance of banks to make loans in an unproved downtown housing market made financing difficult, but the adaptive use project was eventually financed through a combination of the developer's equity, the San Antonio Housing Trust's limited partner equity, state tax-exempt revenue bonds for affordable housing, a ten-year tax abatement for historic city properties, the federal rehabilitation tax credit, and a facade easement to a local preservation organization. Flexibility on the part of the city's building and fire code inspectors also aided in the project's completion.

13. The Olympia Apartments
Miami, Florida

Original Use: Office and retail space, 1926

New Use: Residential and retail space, 1996

Developer: The Cornerstone Group, Coral Gables, Florida

Architect: Cityscapes, Inc., Miami

Conversion: This ten-floor, 55,000-square-foot office building, a registered historic landmark, was converted into 80 affordable apartment units with 3,600 square feet of ground-floor retail space. The building is leased from the city of Miami and was financed with federal rehabilitation tax credits, a community development block grant, HUD HOME funds, and bank loans. Remodeling the storefront had to comply with strict guidelines for renovation of historic properties. To accommodate the new use, the entire interior was demolished and new mechanical, electrical, and plumbing systems installed.

14. The Suite Hotel at Underground Atlanta
Atlanta, Georgia

Original Use: Office building, 1915–1917

New Use: Hotel, 1990

Developer: Phillips International, Atlanta

Architect: AiGroup/Architects, Atlanta

Conversion: Lack of money and a shortage of steel during World War I halted construction of this 17-floor office building at the sixth floor. The truncated steel frame building functioned as an office until the late 1980s, when the Rouse Company's plans for the Underground Atlanta Entertainment Complex recommended changing the use to a hotel. A Japanese investment firm purchased the building from the city of Atlanta for $1.1 million (including air rights) and assembled a development team to convert it to an all-suite hotel. The plan called for adding 11 new floors to the structure, but without information on the existing building's foundation, the project was as much a technical feat as it was an aesthetic challenge. Construction began in 1989 by adding wind bracing throughout the existing structure and 11 new floors framed by steel. The existing building's column layout was not well suited for the hotel use, but the structural system of the new floors had to be loaded at the same locations to minimize loading on the foundation. The original 45,000-square-foot building now encompasses 127,500 square feet; it houses 157 hotel suites and meeting rooms. Underground Atlanta provides restaurants, entertainment lounges, and specialty shops. The $14.2 million redevelopment took 11 months and was completed early and under budget. The project was financed through private equity and a conventional construction loan, with a permanent loan obtained during construction.

15. Tower Lofts
Chicago, Illinois

Original Use: Wieboldts department store, 1916, and adjacent store annex, 1920

New Use: Loft condominiums, townhouses, retail store, grocery store, and parking, 1996

Developer: LR Development Company, Chicago

Architect: HSP/Ltd., Chicago

Conversion: Tower Lofts incorporates the adaptive use of the original seven-story, 170,000-square-foot Wieboldts department store, an annex constructed in 1920 for furniture sales, a tunnel between the two buildings, and an adjacent parking lot. The former department store building was well suited for its new uses: 80 loft condominiums offering views of the Chicago skyline (average sale price $150,000) and a 65,000-square-foot Service Merchandise store. The tunnel connecting the former department store and the basement of the annex were converted to underground parking for the loft residents. The annex building was demolished, and a new, 31,500-square-foot Whole Foods grocery store was constructed on the site. Forty-seven townhouses (average sale price $250,000) and a parking garage were constructed on the old Wiebolts parking lot. The developer acquired the property for $8 million; redevelopment cost $26 million ($72.00 per square foot). The project was funded through the developer's equity, a bank construction loan, and tax increment bond financing.

16. 50 Peabody Place
Memphis, Tennessee

Original Use: Furniture store and warehouse, 1890

New Use: Office and retail space, 1995

Developer: Belz Enterprises, Memphis

The contemporary new offices created inside this 100-year-old furniture store are open and filled with natural light.

Architect: Hnedak Bobo Group, Memphis

Conversion: Considering its advanced years, this late 19th century furniture store and warehouse was in fairly good condition before it was adapted for multiple new uses. One of four redeveloped buildings at Peabody Place (also see project numbers 9, 71, and 75), the five-story, 70,000-square-foot building contains 40,000 square feet of office space, 10,000 square feet of retail space, and 10,000 square feet for other uses. The building's small floorplates were well suited for office and retail space designed for smaller tenants but still required extensive exterior, structural, mechanical, and interior work. The developer purchased the building for $75,000; redevelopment cost $5 million ($72.00 per square foot). Sources of financing included a bank loan and a community development block grant.

Figure 3-1. Project Economics (Originally Commercial Buildings)

Catalog Number and Project Name	Year of Conversion	Gross Area (square feet)	Building Acquisition Cost	Approximate Redevelopment Cost	Cost per Square Foot	Source of Financing	Rental Rates
1 AEtna Health Plans Headquarters at Blue Hen Corporate Center	1994	90,000	–	–	–	–	Office—$12–15 psf
2 Blueprint Furniture	1989	12,500	Leased	$100,000	($8)	Privately financed by tenant	–
3 Canned Foods, Inc., Corporate Offices	1992	42,000	–	$4,700,000	($110)	–	Owner-occupied
4 DART Headquarters	1992	436,636	$21 million turnkey project	–	$48	Seller financing	Owner-occupied
5 Dallas Education Center	1994	200,000	$300,000	$1,750,000	$38[a]	Private equity, institutional and civic donations	–
6 DePaul Center	1993	650,000	$3,000,000	$62,000,000	($95)	Bonds	–
7 Georgia State University	1993	196,417	Donation	$2,000,000	($11)	State of Georgia	Office—owner-occupied; other—$1 psf + operating costs
8 Hagerstown Telework Center	1995	7,200	–	$385,000	$53	Various sources of public financing	Telework offices—$11 psf
9 Pembroke Square at Peabody Place	1996	235,000	$75,000	$20,000,000	$85	Developer equity, commercial bank	Office—$14 psf; retail—$15 psf
10 Philadelphia Arts Bank	1994	21,000	$700,000	$3,800,000	($181)	Foundation grant	Owner-occupied
11 Solomon Schechter Day School	1994	110,000	$1,700,000	$6,400,000	($58)	Commercial bank	Owner-occupied
12 The Exchange Building	1994	41,000	$675,000	$1,800,000	($44)	Developer equity, tax-exempt revenue bonds, San Antonio Housing Trust limited partner equity, tax credits, property tax abatement	42 rental apartments—$395–1,050/month
13 The Olympia Apartments	1996	55,000	40-year lease	–	–	Federal tax credits, CDBG, HOME, and commercial bank	Retail—$60 psf; 80 housing units—$258–444/month
14 The Suite Hotel at Underground Atlanta	1990	127,500	$1,100,000	$14,200,000	$120	Private equity; commercial bank construction loan and permanent financing	–
15 Tower Lofts	1996	360,300	$8,000,000	$26,000,000	$72	Developer equity, commercial bank, tax increment bond financing	–
16 50 Peabody Place	1995	70,000	$75,000	$5,000,000	$72	Commercial bank, CDBG	Office—$15 psf; retail—$20 psf; other—$10 psf

Note: Figures in parentheses were derived from other data. A dash indicates data were not available or not applicable.
[a]Cost for 46,198 square feet.

Figure 3-2. Redevelopment Work (Originally Commercial Buildings)

Catalog Number and Project Name	New Use	Exterior Restoration	New Exterior Construction	Structural	Mechanical	New Interior Construction	Environmental Remediation	New Facilities, Parking	Site Restoration
1 AEtna Health Plans Headquarters at Blue Hen Corporate Center	Office	Extensive	Moderate	Moderate	Extensive	Extensive	Moderate	Extensive	Extensive
2 Blueprint Furniture	Furniture store	Moderate	Minor	Minor	Minor	Moderate	Minor	Minor	Minor
3 Canned Foods, Inc., Corporate Offices	Office and retail	Extensive	Extensive	Extensive	Extensive	Extensive	Extensive	Extensive	Extensive
4 DART Headquarters	Office	Extensive	Extensive	Moderate	Extensive	Extensive	Moderate	Moderate	Minor
5 Dallas Education Center	College classrooms	Minor	Minor	Moderate	Extensive	Extensive	Extensive	Extensive	Minor
6 DePaul Center	Office, retail, and classrooms	Extensive	Extensive	Moderate	Extensive	Extensive	Minor	Minor	Minor
7 Georgia State University	School offices	Minor	None	None	Moderate	Minor	Minor	None	Minor
8 Hagerstown Telework Center	Telework office	Minor	Extensive	Moderate	Extensive	Extensive	Minor	Minor	Minor
9 Pembroke Square at Peabody Place	Apartments, office, and retail	Extensive	Extensive	Extensive	Extensive	Extensive	Moderate	Minor	Minor
10 Philadelphia Arts Bank	Performing Arts Center	Minor	Moderate	Extensive	Extensive	Extensive	Moderate	–	Minor
11 Solomon Schechter Day School	School	Extensive	Extensive	Moderate	Extensive	Extensive	Minor	Moderate	Extensive
12 The Exchange Building	Apartments	Moderate	Minor	Extensive	Extensive	Extensive	Extensive	Minor	Minor
13 The Olympia Apartments	Residential and retail	Moderate	Extensive	Minor	Extensive	Extensive	Minor	Minor	–
14 The Suite Hotel at Underground Atlanta	Hotel	Minor	Extensive	Extensive	Extensive	Extensive	Minor	Minor	Minor
15 Tower Lofts	Loft condominiums and retail	–	Extensive	Moderate	Extensive	Extensive	Moderate	Extensive	Extensive
16 50 Peabody Place	Office and retail	Extensive	Moderate	Extensive	Extensive	Extensive	Moderate	Minor	Moderate

Note: A dash indicates data were not available or not applicable.

Original Use: Factories, Warehouses, and Other Industrial Buildings

17. Atherton Mill
Charlotte, North Carolina

Original Use: Manufacturing, 1916

New Use: Office and retail space, 1993

Developer: MECA Properties, Inc., Charlotte

Architect: Narmour Associates, Charlotte

Conversion: Atherton Mill is one of several adaptive use buildings located in Charlotte's historic south end. Originally a factory manufacturing textile ventilation equipment, the building now contains 16,500 square feet of office space with four tenants and 32,234 square feet of retail space leased to seven tenants. Although the building was only moderately deteriorated, extensive redevelopment was required to turn it into modern commercial space, especially in the interior. New parking facilities and landscaping were also required. Redevelopment took longer and cost more money than originally anticipated, but because no acquisition cost was incurred (the property has been owned by the same entity since it was built in 1916), the cost of redevelopment totaled only $2.3 million ($38.00 per square foot).

The renovation of this former cable car power station into a library and technology center for Baruch College (left) included a careful restoration of the brick exterior. The photo on the right, taken during cleaning of the facade, reveals the effect of 100 years of grime.

18. Baruch College New Campus Library and Technology Center
New York, New York

Original Use: Power station for the Lexington Avenue streetcar line, 1895

New Use: College library and technology center, 1994

Developer: City University of New York, New York

Architect: Davis, Brody & Associates, New York

Conversion: This old streetcar power station traded in its cable lines for fiber-optic lines in an award-winning adaptive use renovation. The 100-year-old building now serves as the library and technology center at Baruch College, equipped to support 1,700 computer workstations and seat 1,450 students. The conversion required substantial interior and exterior work. An existing central light well was converted into an enclosed, skylit atrium. Additions, which increased the size of the eight-story structure from 300,000 square feet to 330,000 square feet, include a new second floor inserted in the former engine room and a partial ninth floor above the original roof. While the original cast-iron structure and masonry-vault floors look the same, much of the interior looks new. Major interior work included the installation of a new elevator core, a central mechanical plant, and telecommunications infrastructure. The $218 per square foot cost of redevelopment was financed by the New York State Dormitory Authority.

19. Circle City Industrial Complex
Indianapolis, Indiana

Original Use: Manufacturing, 1927–1969

New Use: Distribution warehouse, 1994

Developer: B&E Realty, Indianapolis

Architect: Brese Associates, Indianapolis

Conversion: Despite severe dilapidation, this old manufacturing center was very well suited for conversion to a distribution warehouse. The original 80,000-square-foot structure was added to several times, growing to an eventual 569,000 square feet. Thirty-three tenants now occupy the redeveloped facility. The building needed considerable exterior renovation and new mechanical systems but only moderate environmental remediation and interior construction. The developer acquired the property for $800,000 and redeveloped it for $2.2 million ($4.00 per square foot).

20. Citadel
Commerce, California

Original Use: Factory, 1929

New Use: Office and retail space, 1991

Developer: Copley Commerce Telegraph #1, Commerce

Architect: Widel Partnership, Los Angeles

Conversion: The ziggurat castle facade and 1,700-foot-long "Assyrian" wall surrounding this former tire factory were local landmarks that the developer capitalized on to convert a 1920s tire factory into a mixed-use facility. Located on a 40-acre

The marketing value of this distinctive local landmark and its proximity to a freeway were key incentives for the developer to convert the badly eroded, contaminated former tire factory into an office and retail center.

A three-building lithograph plant where California fruit labels were printed until the 1950s now contains 127 live/work loft condominiums. The former plant's five-story clock tower (shown on the right) was incorporated into the new rooftop penthouse, providing a 360-degree panoramic view of the San Francisco Bay and city skyline.

site adjacent to a major freeway, the project includes 270,000 square feet of office space and 146,000 square feet of retail space. The original five-story factory was extremely deteriorated, and large sections of it had to be demolished and replaced with new construction.

21. ClockTower Lofts
San Francisco, California

Original Use: Lithograph plant, 1907, 1920, 1938

New Use: Live/work loft condominiums, 1992

Developer: McKenzie, Rose & Holliday Development Company, San Francisco

Architect: David Baker Associates Architects, San Francisco

Conversion: This project is one of several warehouse and factory buildings in San Francisco's south of market area (known as SOMA)

that have been adapted for new uses. The 230,000-square-foot former factory complex included one three-story, 125,000-square-foot brick and timber building; a six-story, 70,000-square-foot concrete building; and a 15-story, 35,000-square-foot steel frame clock tower. The developer reused all three existing buildings. The clock tower includes 127 live/work lofts, ranging from 600 to 5,000 square feet and arranged around a sizable shared courtyard. Because the existing building configuration was so complex, each loft plan is different. The project includes a 40,000-square-foot parking garage. The developer acquired the buildings for $7 million; redevelopment totaled $20 million ($75.00 per square foot). Financing came from private sources.

22. Deer Island Reception/ Training Building

Boston, Massachusetts

Original Use: Steam pumping station, 1894

New Use: Office and meeting facilities, 1994

Developer: Massachusetts Water Resources Authority, Boston

Architect: Tsoi/Kobus & Associates, Cambridge, Massachusetts

Conversion: This award-winning (for preservation and design) restoration of a late 19th century steam pumping station preserved the building's historically significant engineering and architectural features while blending 18,000 square feet of modern office, meeting, and training space throughout the structure. The project is part of a regional wastewater treatment facility located on Deer Island in Boston Harbor. The red brick Romanesque facility was in poor condition before reuse

This 19th century steam pumping station was saved from total collapse (top) and rehabilitated for productive use as an office, conference, and training facility (bottom).

and required major exterior restoration, environmental remediation, site restoration, interior construction, and installation of a new mechanical system. The $5.9 million cost of redevelopment ($328 per square foot) was financed through public funds.

23. Good Samaritan Mental Health Center

Puyallup, Washington

Original Use: Manufacturing, warehouse, 1940–1945

New Use: Mental health clinic, 1993

Developer: Good Samaritan Community Health Care, Puyallup

Architect: McGranahan Partnership, Tacoma, Washington

Conversion: This extremely eroded 24,000-square-foot warehouse required extensive work to convert it into an outpatient mental health center and offices. Despite the constraints of working with the existing structure, the building's layout was quite compatible with its new use; space was converted at a cost of $130 per square foot. The owner acquired the building for $700,000 and redeveloped it for $2.4 million using internal funds.

24. Great Mall of the Bay Area

Milpitas, California

Original Use: Automobile manufacturing plant, 1955

New Use: Retail outlet mall, 1994

Developers: Ford Motor Land Development Corporation, Dearborn, Michigan; Petrie Dierman Kughn, McLean, Virginia

Architect: Wah Yee Associates, Farmington Hill, Michigan

Conversion: After producing automobiles and trucks for nearly 30

years and then sitting idle for a decade, this 2.1 million-square-foot former assembly plant has been transformed into a 1.6 million-square-foot retail outlet mall. In 1992, after cleaning up environmental problems and exploring various alternatives for redevelopment, Ford Motor Land Development Corporation teamed up with retail developer Petrie Dierman Kughn to convert the surplus property to a shopping mall. Aptly designed around a travel theme, the mall includes 1.3 million square feet of retail space housing large anchor tenants, smaller off-price stores, restaurants, a food court, and entertainment facilities. The developers made a great effort to retain as much of the existing structure as possible while providing appropriately sized retail spaces and well-balanced parking fields. To accommodate additional parking, it was necessary to demolish 500,000 square feet of the original building before construction could begin. True to their objective of reusing as much material as possible, the project team was able to salvage 12,000 tons of steel, tin, and copper and recycle over 75,000 cubic yards of asphalt and concrete. A major challenge was completing the project within 15 months from the start of demolition to open before the holiday shopping season. Despite the unexpected need to

The interior of the Great Mall of the Bay Area gives no hint that it was originally an automobile assembly plant.

145

incorporate seismic upgrading into the schedule, the project was completed on time. The mostly internally financed project totaled $94 million ($61.00 per square foot).

25. Harris County Jail Expansion
Houston, Texas

Original Use: Cold-storage warehouse, 1926

New Use: Jail, 1991

Developer: City Partnership, Houston

Architect: Morris Architects, Houston

Conversion: Converting a 350,000-square-foot cold-storage warehouse into a 650,000-square-foot jail offered Harris County a quick, cost-effective solution to overcrowd-

This 4,000-bed jail was converted from a cold-storage warehouse. The jail's brick facade, lined with artificial windows, is intended to resemble nearby university buildings. Only about 14 percent of the glass used in the windows is actual vision glass.

The jail's reception area.

ing. Two double-height maximum-security floors were built on top of the existing six-story warehouse to provide space for 4,000 beds. To adequately strengthen the roof structure of the warehouse for the new floor loads, concrete floor topping was added to the existing roof concrete slab. So that the facility would blend in with the surrounding university buildings and gentrified industrial buildings, artificial windows were added to the brick facade, creating the illusion of an office building. Redevelopment costs totaled $85 million, or $20,000 per bed—one-half the national average. The county acquired the vacant warehouse for $6 million. A nonprofit corporation established by the county hired Facilities Development Group (based on a competitive design-build proposal) as the jail's development manager on a fee basis. The project was financed through tax-exempt revenue bonds.

26. Hart Brewery & Pub
Seattle, Washington

Original Use: Warehouse, 1913

New Use: Brewery and pub, 1995

Developer: Harold Hill & Company, Mercer Island, Washington

Architect: Mesher Shing & Associates, Seattle

Conversion: Barley and hops are the active ingredients that transformed this former shipping warehouse into a popular microbrewery. The brick and timber warehouse was basically sound but had to undergo extensive interior construction; improvements were also necessary for parking, landscaping, and site restoration. The microbrewery now occupies 17,000 square feet of the building, and a 270-seat pub with retail store occupies another 6,000

One-of-a-kind space for a microbrewery and pub was created from an 80-year-old warehouse in the heart of Seattle.

square feet. Construction costs of $4 million ($174 per square foot) were financed through a bank.

27. Indiana Farm Bureau Insurance Headquarters
Indianapolis, Indiana

Original Use: Manufacturing, 1922

New Use: Office, 1992

Developer: Mansur Development Corporation, Indianapolis

Architect: Ratio Architects, Indianapolis

Conversion: This endeavor transformed a defunct 1920s rubber tire manufacturing facility into a vibrant top-quality corporate headquarters

Just a few years ago, Indiana Farm Bureau Insurance's thoroughly 1990s corporate headquarters building (top) was a contaminated, crumbling eyesore of an abandoned factory complex near downtown Indianapolis. After extensive environmental cleanup and demolition of nearly 40 smaller structures on the site, the original main plant was stripped to its reinforced concrete frame and transformed into corporate offices.

for Indiana Farm Bureau Insurance. The project first required massive demolition and cleanup of the asbestos, petroleum, and PCBs prevalent throughout the site. Cleanup and site demolition alone took 18 months and $2 million to complete. After cleanup, restoration began on the 250,000-square-foot, five-floor, cast-in-place concrete building. The building's 16-foot ceilings allowed for raised flooring for electrical and communications systems and dropped ceilings for mechanical systems. A three-story atrium was cut from the floor slabs, reflective windows were installed, and the exterior was finished in brick and precast Portland concrete. In addition to satisfying the owner's office

space requirements, the insurance company leases more than 100,000 square feet of space to outside tenants. At a cost of $138 per square foot, the project was completed for about the same price as a new high rise. The Indiana Farm Bureau believes, however, that in addition to providing Class A office space and amenities, recycling the existing building demonstrated an investment in and commitment to the city.

28. King Plow Arts Center
Atlanta, Georgia

Original Use: Farm equipment manufacturing plant, 1914 and 1936

New Use: Live/work art studios, 1995

Developer: King Shaw, Atlanta

Architect: Smith-Dahlia Architects, Atlanta

Conversion: After more than 80 years of manufacturing farm plows, the farm crisis during the 1980s put the company out of business, leaving the factory abandoned and deteriorating. In 1990, the owners designed a plan to transform the historic 11-building complex totaling 165,000 square feet into an affordable live/work arts community for commercial, performing, and visual arts. The plant contained two types of buildings. The first, built about 1900, has large arched windows and doorways with massive oak and heart pine timber beams. The second, built in 1936, has large steel beams, windows, skylights, and clerestories. The expansive open spaces, high ceilings, and large windows made the buildings ideal for use as lofts and studios for artists. The project, which required substantial mechanical, interior, environmental remediation, and site restoration work, was divided into five phases over five years. The project now includes 30 lofts, 80,000 square feet of office

space, and 10,000 square feet of retail space. Redevelopment cost $7.25 million ($44.00 per square foot). The project was financed through private sources and conventional bank loans.

29. LIVINGreen
Omaha, Nebraska

Original Use: Light industrial, 1912

New Use: Showroom, offices, and warehouse, 1994

Developer: Jeffery Zindel, Omaha

Architect: Randy Brown, Omaha

Conversion: Over the years, this 13,320-square-foot building had more than ten industrial uses, the last of which was as a warehouse. It now serves as the office headquarters, showroom, and warehouse for a business dealing in house plants. Gutting the warehouse exposed the original terrazzo floor, heavy brick walls, steel post and beam supports, and bowstring roof trusses, which were used in the final design. New mechanical, electrical, and plumbing systems were installed, and once-tarred-over skylights were cleaned to allow natural light to reach the plants. Redevelopment emphasized recycling existing materials; for example, existing tin ceilings and existing light fixtures were taken down and reinstalled in the private offices. Existing doors and windows were likewise relocated. Despite its advanced state of disrepair, the building's open design made it suitable for its new use. With redevelopment costing only $215,000 ($16.00 per square foot), this adaptive use provided the company with flexible and distinctive space at an affordable price.

30. Magnolia Station
Dallas, Texas

Original Use: Petroleum products processing and distribution center, 1911–1917

New Use: Apartments, 1994

Developer: Bennett Miller Co., Ltd., Dallas

Architect: In-house

Conversion: One developer saw opportunity others had overlooked in this vacant seven-building industrial complex. The 80-year-old low brick buildings, used by an oil company as a processing and distribution center, have been converted to out-of-the-ordinary, affordable apartments in a convenient inner-city location. The developer left the exposed brick walls, concrete floors, and heavy columns in place to allow the original building to show through and give the units a simple industrial look. Costs were kept low by installing modular kitchens and cutting back on unnecessary frills. The buildings were extremely run-down and required extensive redevelopment for all aspects of construction. The buildings were acquired for $677,000; redevelopment cost $3.3 million ($54.00 per square foot). Funding the project was one of the biggest challenges; the developer eventually financed the project through private sources and heavily collateralized debt. Federal rehabilitation tax credits and a tax abatement from the city of Dallas boosted the economic bottom line.

31. Medical Biotechnology Center/University of Maryland Biotechnology Institute
Baltimore, Maryland

Original Use: Warehouse, 1914 and 1966

New Use: Research center, 1995

Developer: University of Maryland, College Park, Maryland

Architect: Davis Brody & Associates, New York

Conversion: This state-funded adaptive use initiative combined two existing warehouses into one structure to house the new 207,267-square-foot Medical Biotechnology Center. The open configuration of the warehouse buildings gave designers a great deal of flexibility and many options for creating the new space. The existing buildings were connected by an atrium that was constructed between the two structures. The facade was entirely redone with a brick and granite base, aluminum frame windows and curtain wall, and preformed metal siding and roofing. Redevelopment cost $182 per square foot.

32. Mercantile Stores Co., Inc., Corporate Headquarters
Cincinnati, Ohio

Original Use: Furniture warehouse, 1972

New Use: Office, 1992

Developer: Mercantile Stores Co., Inc., Fairfield, Ohio

Architect: Hixson, Cincinnati

Conversion: Once a 260,000-square-foot furniture store, the building now functions as the corporate headquarters for Mercantile Stores. The building was relatively new and required no structural work, but to make the transition from furniture store to corporate offices, extensive interior construction, parking improvements, and landscaping were necessary. A new $4.2 million, 30,000-square-foot corporate business university was added to the site. Both buildings incorporate the latest technology for energy management, multimedia presentations, and video conferencing. Mercantile acquired the warehouse for $4.1 million and redeveloped it for $26.5 million ($102 per square foot). A large portion of acquisition was financed through development bonds from the city of Fairfield; the rest of the acquisition and the redevelopment were funded internally.

33. Nexus Contemporary Art Center
Atlanta, Georgia

Original Use: Garage, 1923

New Use: Art gallery/artist studios, 1993

Developer: Nexus, Atlanta

Architects: Peter H. Hand and Associates, Inc., Atlanta; Irv Weiner and Associates, Atlanta

Conversion: This 26,311-square-foot truck garage and 10,500-square-foot courtyard converted into an art gallery with studios provided the impetus for the redevelopment of downtown Atlanta's west quadrant. It took creative design and extensive interior construction and mechanical work to configure the new space within the existing building. Nexus acquired the property for $350,000 and redeveloped it for $1.3 million ($38.00 per square foot). Sources of financing included a community development block grant, the Fulton County Arts Council, the Kresge Foundation, and the Whitehead Foundation.

34. O'Hern House
Atlanta, Georgia

Original Use: Factory, 1905

New Use: Single-room-occupancy housing, 1993

Developer: Project Interconnections, Inc., Atlanta

Architect: Cordell W. Ingram, Atlanta

Conversion: By using eight sources of public and private financing, the developer was able to convert an 80-year-old shoe factory into 76 units of rental housing for mentally ill homeless people. Job training, counseling, and other services for residents are available on site. The four-floor, 26,500-square-foot building was structurally sound but lacked appropriate mechanical systems and had to be gutted for rehabilitation. The brick exterior of the building required only minor cleaning and new windows. The building was acquired for $213,570; redevelopment cost close to $3 million ($110 per square foot). Among the several sources of funding were a community development block grant, affordable housing subsidies, the sale of rehabilitation and low-income tax credits, and private contributions.

35. Perkins Building
Tacoma, Washington

Original Use: Newspaper publishing plant, 1903

New Use: School, 1990

Developer: Richard Eberharter, Tacoma

Architect: Roger Williams, Seattle

Conversion: The owner/developer of this turn-of-the-century building presented the University of Washington with a cost-effective and timely solution to its need for temporary classroom space. While a new campus was being constructed several blocks away, the developer converted the 7fi-floor newspaper publishing plant into an interim campus that the university will lease for seven years. Another 6,000 square feet of retail space is leased to three tenants. The building was structurally sound, but the interior and mechanical systems needed extensive renovation. The 76,000-square-foot building was acquired for $700,000 and redeveloped for $1.1 million ($15.00 per square foot).

36. Port of Seattle Headquarters, Pier 69 Renovation
Seattle, Washington

Original Use: American Can Company, early 1930s

New Use: Port of Seattle administrative headquarters, 1993

Developer: Port of Seattle, Washington

Architects: Hewitt-Isley Architects, Seattle; Gensler & Associates, San Francisco; Karen Gunsel, Interior Design, Seattle

Conversion: After sitting idle for more than a decade, the Pier 69 warehouse was purchased by the Port of Seattle to use as its headquarters. Earlier attempts by private developers to convert the waterfront structure into offices, retail space, and a parking lot were confounded by the building's trapezoidal design and large columns throughout the interior. For the Port of Seattle, however, these obstacles became opportunities. Designers used the open space to create an office without walls to complement the Port's non-hierarchical organizational structure. Even so, the project entailed comprehensive interior, exterior, and mechanical restoration. A two-story atrium was added to provide natural light, and a new 400-foot-long "creek" running the length of the building acts as an acoustic buffer to muffle noise inside the office and from nearby streets and trains. After examining several alternatives, including moving to office space in downtown Seattle or near Seattle-Tacoma International Airport, the Port found that adapting the old cannery was the most economical option. The Port purchased the 210,000-square-foot structure on the pier for $3.1 million, $150,000 below its appraised value. Redevelopment cost $33 million ($157 per square foot) and was financed through a tax levy. The Port leases 38,000 square feet of office space to private users and the dock space to commercial fishing vessels.

37. Potrero Square Lofts
San Francisco, California

Original Use: Warehouse and factory, 1910

New Use: Residential, 1994

Developer: Mission–701 Minnesota, San Francisco

Architect: Pyatok Associates, Oakland, California

Conversion: While half the original 68,900-square-foot warehouse was removed to create five courtyards for the 58 condominiums, mezzanines in each unit and a new garage under the building increased its overall size to 75,000 square feet. The conversion, which required extensive exterior and interior construction, was completed for $13.3 million ($177 per square foot). The new garage and seismic retrofits complicated conversion, but overall the new use was very compatible with the old.

38. Q.F.C. #807 at University Village

Seattle, Washington

Original Use: Dairy plant, 1956

New Use: Retail space, 1996

Developer: Q.F.C., Inc., Bellevue, Washington

Architect: Lee Crowthers, Bellevue, Washington

Conversion: This former dairy plant now provides 119,000 square feet of retail space for seven tenants. Reusing the two-story building required considerable demolition (some of the interior walls that had to be removed were eight-inch-thick concrete) and removal of asbestos and lead-based paint. Q.F.C.'s construction team used a special piece of equipment that pulverized the concrete walls, turning them into gravel that could be used as a sub-base for the new floor. The owner/developer acquired the plant for $8 million and converted it for $5 million ($42.00 per square foot) with equity financing.

39. San Francisco Bar Pilots Station House

San Francisco, California

Original Use: Warehouse, 1932

New Use: Office headquarters, 1990

Developer: San Francisco Bar Pilots, San Francisco

Architect: David Baker Associates Architects, San Francisco

Conversion: The San Francisco Bar Pilots Station House is the adaptive use of a warehouse into headquarters for the association of ship captains who pilot ocean-going ships through the treacherous waters of the San Francisco Bay. The existing concrete warehouse, built in 1932, is located at the end of Pier 9 on the San Francisco waterfront. In addition to offices, the new pilots

The 19,000-square-foot headquarters for the San Francisco Bar Pilots was constructed inside the shell of an existing 110,000-square-foot waterfront warehouse (top). The reception area of the new inner building (bottom) looks out onto the exposed concrete walls and corrugated galvanized steel panels of the original warehouse.

station contains dispatch and chart rooms, a conference room, bunk rooms, a nautical library, and boat maintenance facilities. Designed as a box within a box, the 19,000-square-foot pilots station was constructed inside the vacant 110,000-square-foot warehouse. The existing building's industrial concrete walls, steel panels and trusses, and steel sash windows were sandblasted and left exposed. Distinct from the existing shell, the new inner building is constructed of materials sympathetic to the original. A skylit forecourt demarcates the beginning of the new construction and sheds light into the interior of the old industrial building. With the exception of the interior, the original building required only minor renovation.

40. Shadeland Commerce Center

Indianapolis, Indiana

Original Use: Auto plant, 1954

New Use: Office and industrial space, 1991

Developer: First Highland Management and Development, Indianapolis

Architect: American Consulting Engineers, Indianapolis

Conversion: Structurally, this 1950s automotive plant was well suited for conversion to a warehouse/distribution center. Converting the 1.1 million-square-foot plant into 44,000 square feet of office space (four tenants) and 970,000 square feet of distribution space (six tenants) entailed extensive environmental remediation, site restoration, and interior renovation. The former plant's abundant parking was a plus. The developer purchased the building for $8 million and redeveloped it for $7 million ($6.00 per square foot). Construction loans came from commercial banks.

41. SODO Center

Seattle, Washington

Original Use: Catalog distribution center, 1912

New Use: Office, retail, and industrial space, 1996

Developer: Nitze-Stagen & Co., Inc., Seattle

Architects: Olson/Sundberg, Seattle; NBBJ, Seattle

Conversion: In December 1990, Nitze-Stagen & Co. could not pass up the opportunity to buy the nearly 2 million-square-foot Sears Roebuck & Co. regional catalog sales distribution center—the largest building in Seattle—for the bargain price of $12 million ($6.50 per square foot). While other investors and developers saw just another aging white elephant in an old industrial neighborhood, Nitze-Stagen realized its potential as a mixed-use center located near downtown at the center of a multimodal transportation hub. The redeveloped facility, renamed SODO Center, contains 1.9 million square feet of rentable space, including 1 million square feet of warehouse distribution and light industrial space (40 tenants), 300,000 square feet of office space (five tenants, including the corporate headquarters of Starbucks Coffee), 300,000 square feet of retail space (three tenants), and a 200,000-square-foot parking garage. The existing structure, originally built in 1912 with several additions, has required large-scale structural, mechanical, and interior redevelopment. The first stage of the conversion entailed removing the operating systems from the defunct Sears building. Tons of metal debris were recycled, two miles of conveyor belts were ripped out, and 80 tons of wood structures were removed. A substantial amount of redevelopment is still occurring with the tenants in place. Redevelopment cost as of mid-1996 was $30 million ($15.00 per square foot); the project was expected to be completed in late 1996 at a total cost of $52.5 million ($26.00 per square foot). In addition to private equity, project financing was obtained from Seattle First National Bank.

42. Sony Game Show Network Building
Culver City, California

Original Use: Auto repair shop/warehouse, circa 1930

New Use: Office, broadcast studio, 1994

Developer: Sony Pictures Entertainment, Culver City

Architect: Steven Ehrlich Architects, Santa Monica, California

The new skylight constructed on the roof of this 60-year-old bowstring truss industrial building creates a light-filled interior for the broadcasting operations of Sony's Game Show Network. Changing patterns of light are emitted from Michael Hayden's "Lumetric Sculpture" at the corner of the building.

Conversion: Open minds and creative design transformed a 1930s auto repair shop into this 1990s high-tech office and broadcasting center for Sony's all-digital Game Show Network. The existing 8,970-square-foot bowstring truss building was increased to 13,220 square feet after designers raised the roof, installed a skylight, and created a second-floor loft for executive offices. Sony requested that all of the production and broadcasting processes function in the open. Thus, key activities take place in the center of the building, a two-story atrium lit by the distinctive raised skylight, and support spaces are tucked around the atrium. Extensive renovation was required to restore structural integrity to the existing building and adapt it for the new use. Brick walls were reinforced, toxins, such as lead-based paint and asbestos, removed, and mechanical systems overhauled. To accommodate the network's sophisticated electronic technology, the concrete slab was ripped up

to add computer wiring, and several backup mechanical systems were installed.

43. Standish Village at Lower Mills
Boston, Massachusetts

Original Use: Mill, 1886

New Use: Housing for seniors, 1994

Developer: Standish Care Company, Burlington, Massachusetts

Architect: The Architectural Team, Chelsea, Massachusetts

Conversion: This historic 19th century textile mill was converted into 86 units of assisted-living housing for seniors. The existing 79,000-square-foot building had deteriorated, but its configuration was compatible with its new use. Environmental remediation, site restoration, and interior construction were the big-ticket items. New mechanical systems and parking facilities were also necessary. The mill was acquired for $1 million and redeveloped for $7.9 million ($100 per square foot). The project was financed with private equity, rehabilitation tax credits, and the HUD 232 program for boarding care facilities.

44. Telephone Factory
Atlanta, Georgia

Original Use: Manufacturing, 1936

New Use: Loft apartments, 1996

Developer: Industrial Conversion Enterprises, Atlanta

Architect: Brock Green Architects and Planners, Atlanta

Conversion: This adaptive use renovation is one of Atlanta's largest multistory loft conversions to date. The 130,000-square-foot building has 65 units of 1,100 to 2,300 square feet with full kitchens, baths, and new mechanical systems. Apartments rent for $850 to $1,800 per month. The historic old telephone equipment manufacturing and repair plant was in sound condition but had sustained superficial damage from vandalism. Although relatively little exterior or structural restoration was required, an extensive amount of interior renovation was necessary to create the apartment units. The building was acquired for $2 million, and redevelopment cost $5 million ($54.00 per square foot). The project was financed through tax-free municipal housing bonds and equity capital raised from the sale of rehabilitation tax credits.

45. The Florentine
Seattle, Washington

Original Use: Railroad warehouse, 1906

New Use: Condominiums and retail space, 1991

Developer: Alexander & Ventura, Seattle

Architect: In-house

Conversion: The adaptive use of this four-story, 226,400-square-foot railroad warehouse into 116 condominiums with 12,000 square feet of ground-floor retail space helped revitalize Seattle's historic Pioneer Square district. Major structural, exterior, and interior work was required, including seismic upgrading, but environmental contamination was minor. The addition of a fifth floor for more condominium units on top of the building brought the size of the project to 310,000 square feet. The project was completed for $61.00 per square foot. The building was acquired for $6 million, and redevelopment cost $13 million. Financing came from Security Pacific Bank.

46. The Portorino
Seattle, Washington

Original Use: Warehouse, 1918

New Use: Retail space and condominiums, 1990

Developer: Alexander & Ventura, Seattle

Architect: In-house

Conversion: This four-floor warehouse was transformed into 37 condominiums with 6,500 square feet of ground-floor retail space. A fifth floor was added to the building for townhouse condominiums, increasing the size of the original 41,320-square-foot structure to 55,320 square feet. Although the new use was very compatible with the layout of the existing building, the structure was extremely eroded and needed substantial exterior restoration, new interior construction, and mechanical systems upgrading. The building was purchased for $750,000 and redeveloped for $2.4 million ($57.00 per square foot). The developer obtained a construction loan from Key Bank.

47. The Seed Factory
Atlanta, Georgia

Original Use: Warehouse, 1913

New Use: Loft apartments, 1994

Developer: Seed Partners, Atlanta

Architect: Smith Dalia Architects, Atlanta

Conversion: The conversion of this four-story, 43,200-square-foot warehouse into 18 loft apartments was completed for only $32.00 per square foot. Extensive interior alterations and new mechanical systems were needed, but the concrete slab construction, sound condition, and configuration of the warehouse made the renovation easier. The open loft apartment units range from 1,100 to

2,200 square feet and rent for $900 to $1,450 per month. The building was acquired for $340,000 and redeveloped for $1.1 million ($32.00 per square foot). Financing came from a heavily collateralized mini-perm loan from a local bank.

48. The Shop at Whitinsville
Whitinsville, Massachusetts

Original Use: Manufacturing, 1847–1921

New Use: Light industrial and office, 1989

Developer: Whitinsville Redevelopment Trust, Whitinsville

Architect: In-house

Conversion: This 1.5 million-square-foot textile mill was saved from collapse and redeveloped into a multitenant mixed-use facility. The building's 20 tenants represent a mix of light manufacturing, warehouse, and office uses. On average, lease rates are $2.00 per square foot. The brick and timber building was in fairly sound condition before the renovation and had very little environmental contamination. All mechanical systems were replaced and separate electrical metering installed. Sixty truck docks were constructed, and some parts of the structure were demolished to provide better access to the building. Conversion reduced the size of the building to 1.2 million square feet. The developer acquired the building for $1.5 million and redeveloped it for $6 million ($5.00 per square foot) with private financing.

49. Wynkoop Brewing Company/Wynkoop Mercantile Lofts
Denver, Colorado

Original Use: Warehouse and showroom, 1899

New Use: Brewpub and loft condominiums, 1992

Developer: John Hickenlooper, Denver

Architect: Blue Sky Studios, Denver

Conversion: The federal rehabilitation tax credit boosted the economic viability of reusing this turn-of-the-century warehouse, showroom, and offices for a mercantile company. The redeveloped structure includes a brewpub, jazz club, billiards hall, and banquet facility encompassing 36,000 square feet. Thirteen loft condominiums cover the remaining 36,000 square feet. Much attention was given to preserving interior architectural details, such as the original pressed tin ceiling, seven-foot arched windows, and maple floors. Extensive site restoration, mechanical systems replacement, and interior construction were required. The five-story, 72,000-square-foot building was acquired for $1.2 million and redeveloped for $4 million ($55.00 per square foot). Financing was difficult to obtain because of the mixed-use nature of the project but was finally secured through a combination of private sources, commercial banks, and a Small Business Administration loan.

50. Zipangu Restaurant
Santa Monica, California

Original Use: Mechanics garage, 1910

New Use: Restaurant, 1990

Developer: Kishi Han, Santa Monica

Architect: Projects Architecture, Los Angeles

Conversion: This Japanese/Italian restaurant combines many original features of the existing structure with new construction and materials. The badly decayed 3,500-square-foot garage was gutted and stripped to the brick walls, concrete slab floor, and wood ceiling. The building was also retrofitted with seismic improvements and features to accommodate the disabled. The tenant-financed redevelopment totaled $350,000 ($100 per square foot).

51. 355 Bryant Street Lofts
San Francisco, California

Original Use: Warehouse, 1916

New Use: Live/work loft condominiums, 1992

Developer: McKenzie, Rose & Holliday Development Company, San Francisco

Architect: David Baker Associates Architects, San Francisco

Conversion: Like many other warehouses and factories in San Francisco's SOMA district, this abandoned building was boarded up for nearly 20 years until the zoning was changed to allow live/work spaces. Built in 1916 as an electrical equipment distribution warehouse, this four-story, 85,000-square-foot brick and timber structure was in very sound structural condition.

One of 44 live/work loft condominium units created from a four-story distribution warehouse.

The load-bearing exterior walls, internal column and beam structural system, and high ceilings made the building particularly well suited for live/work condominiums. The renovated building has 44 loft units and a 1,000-square-foot lobby. Extensive structural, mechanical, and new interior construction was required to accommodate the new use. The building was acquired for $2.8 million and redeveloped for $5.8 million ($68.00 per square foot). The project was privately financed.

52. 601 Fourth Street Lofts
San Francisco, California

Original Use: Warehouse, 1915

New Use: Live/work condominiums, 1990

Developer: McKenzie, Rose & Holliday Development Company, San Francisco

Architect: David Baker Associates Architects, San Francisco

Conversion: This structurally sound three-story, 120,000-square-foot concrete warehouse sat vacant for years, adding to the decline of the once thriving commercial neighborhood. When zoning codes were changed to accommodate live/work spaces in San Francisco's SOMA district, the developer brought life to this and other nearby buildings (also see project numbers 21 and 51). The old warehouse now accommodates 85 live/work condominium loft units and has a 30,000-square-foot parking garage. Designers worked with and emphasized the existing structure's construction and building materials; no two units are alike. The developer acquired the property for $5.7 million and redeveloped it for $8.1 million ($68.00 per square foot) with private financing.

Figure 3-3. Project Economics (Originally Factories, Warehouses, and Other Industrial Buildings)

Catalog Number and Project Name	Year of Conversion	Gross Area (square feet)	Building Acquisition Cost	Approximate Redevelopment Cost	Cost per Square Foot	Source of Financing	Rental Rates
17 Atherton Mill	1993	60,000	Already owned	$2,300,000	($38)	Private equity	Office—$9–14 psf; retail—$7.50–12 psf
18 Baruch College	1994	330,000	–	–	$218	Dormitory Authority of the State of New York	Owner-occupied
19 Circle City Industrial Complex	1994	569,000	$800,000	$2,200,000	($4)	Developer equity	$2.60 psf
20 Citadel	1991	420,000	–	–	–	Developer equity, commercial bank	Office—$22 psf NNN; retail—$24 psf
21 ClockTower Lofts	1992	280,000	$7,000,000	$20,000,000	$75	Private equity	–
22 Deer Island Reception/ Training Building	1994	18,000	–	$5,900,000	($328)	Bond issue, federal funding	Owner-occupied
23 Good Samaritan Mental Health Center	1993	24,000	$700,000	$2,400,000	$130	Internally financed	Owner-occupied
24 Great Mall of the Bay Area	1994	1,548,516	Developer already owned	$93,842,000	$61	Internal corporate financing; $7,000,000 reimbursement by city for off-site improvements	Retail—$22.80 psf
25 Harris County Jail Expansion	1991	650,000	$6,000,000	$85,000,000	$131 ($20,000 per bed)	Tax-exempt bonds	–
26 Hart Brewery & Pub	1995	23,000	Leased	$4,000,000	$174	Commercial bank	Retail and industrial— $7 psf
27 Indiana Farm Bureau Insurance Headquarters	1992	387,776	$4,769,000	$49,042,000	$139	AEtna Life Insurance	Office—$18 psf
28 King Plow Arts Center	1995	165,000	Already owned	$7,250,000	($44)	Private equity, commercial bank	$9–10 psf
29 LIVINGreen	1994	13,320	$125,000	$215,000	($16)	Private equity	Owner-occupied
30 Magnolia Station	1994	61,000	$677,500	$3,300,000	($54)	Private equity, collateralized debt, rehabilitation tax credit, property tax abatement	69 apartments—$1 psf
31 Medical Biotechnology Center	1995	207,267	–	–	$182	State funding	Owner-occupied
32 Mercantile Stores Co., Inc., Corporate Headquarters	1992	260,000	$4,100,000	$26,500,000	$102	Developer equity, development bonds	Owner-occupied
33 Nexus Contemporary Art Center	1993	34,039	$350,000	$1,300,000	($38)	CDBG, foundations	–
34 O'Hern House	1993	26,500	$213,570	$2,936,780	$110	Various public and private sources	76 residential units— $0–130/month/unit

Figure 3-3 *(continued)*.

Catalog Number and Project Name	Year of Conversion	Gross Area (square feet)	Building Acquisition Cost	Approximate Redevelopment Cost	Cost per Square Foot	Source of Financing	Rental Rates
35 Perkins Building	1990	76,000	$700,000	$1,100,000	($15)	–	Retail–$12 psf; school–$9.50 psf
36 Port of Seattle Headquarters	1993	210,000	$3,100,000	$33,000,000	($157)	Tax levy	Other uses–$16.50 psf
37 Potrero Square Lofts	1994	75,000	–	$13,263,000	($177)	–	–
38 Q.F.C. #807 at University Village	1996	119,000	$8,000,000	$5,000,000	($42)	Owner-financed	–
39 San Francisco Bar Pilots Station House	1990	19,000	Long-term lease	–	–	–	Owner-occupied
40 Shadeland Commerce Center	1991	1,100,000	$8,000,000	$7,000,000	($6)	Commercial banks	Office–$8.50 psf; industrial–$2.50 psf
41 SODO Center	1996	2,000,000	$12,000,000	$30,000,000 to date, $22,500,000 remaining	($15 to date, $26 estimated at completion)	Private equity, commercial bank	Office–$5 psf; retail–$10 psf; industrial–$3.50 psf; other–$140/month/stall
42 Sony Game Show Network Building	1994	13,220	–	–	–	–	Owner-occupied
43 Standish Village at Lower Mills	1994	79,000	$1,000,000	$7,900,000	$100	Private equity, HUD, rehabilitation tax credit	–
44 Telephone Factory	1996	130,000	$2,025,000	$5,000,000	$54	Equity from sale of tax credits and tax-free housing bonds	65 rental housing units–$850–1,800/month
45 The Florentine	1991	310,000	$6,000,000	$13,000,000	$61	Commercial bank	–
46 The Portorino	1990	55,320	$750,000	$2,400,000	$57	Commercial bank	–
47 The Seed Factory	1994	43,200	$340,000	$1,050,000	$32	Collateralized miniperm loan	18 loft apartments–$900–1,450/month
48 The Shop at Whitinsville	1989	1,200,000	$1,500,000	$6,000,000	$5	Privately financed	Industrial–$2 psf
49 Wynkoop Brewing Company	1992	72,000	$1,200,000	$3,950,000	($55)	Private equity, commercial bank, SBA loan	Retail–$3 psf
50 Zipangu Restaurant	1990	3,500	Leased	$350,000	($100)	Privately financed by tenant	–
51 355 Bryant Street Lofts	1992	85,000	$2,800,000	$5,800,000	($68)	Privately financed	–
52 601 Fourth Street Lofts	1990	120,000	$5,700,000	$8,100,000	($67)	Privately financed	–

Note: Figures in parentheses were derived from other data. A dash indicates data were not available or not applicable.

Figure 3-4. Redevelopment Work (Originally Factories, Warehouses, and Other Industrial Buildings)

Catalog Number and Project Name	New Use	Exterior Restoration	New Exterior Construction	Structural	Mechanical	New Interior Construction	Environmental Remediation	New Facilities, Parking	Site Restoration
17 Atherton Mill	Office/retail	Moderate	Minor	Minor	Extensive	Extensive	Moderate	Extensive	Extensive
18 Baruch College	Library	Extensive	Moderate	Extensive	Extensive	Extensive	Moderate	–	Moderate
19 Circle City Industrial Complex	Distribution warehouse	Moderate	Extensive	Minor	Extensive	Moderate	Moderate	Minor	Minor
20 Citadel	Office and retail space	Extensive	Extensive	Extensive	Extensive	Extensive	Extensive	Extensive	Extensive
21 Clock Tower Lofts	Live/work condominiums	Minor	Minor	Extensive	Moderate	Moderate	Minor	Minor	Minor
22 Deer Island Reception/ Training Building	Office and meeting facilities	Extensive	Extensive	Moderate	Extensive	Extensive	Extensive	Minor	Extensive
23 Good Samaritan Mental Health Center	Office	Extensive	Extensive	Extensive	Extensive	Extensive	Extensive	Extensive	Extensive
24 Great Mall of the Bay Area	Mall	Extensive	Moderate	Extensive	Extensive	Extensive	Moderate	Extensive	Extensive
25 Harris County Jail Expansion	Jail	Extensive	Extensive	Extensive	Extensive	Extensive	Moderate	Moderate	Extensive
26 Hart Brewery & Pub	Brewery and pub	Minor	Moderate	Minor	Moderate	Extensive	Minor	Moderate	Moderate
27 Indiana Farm Bureau Insurance Headquarters	Office	Extensive	Extensive	Extensive	Extensive	Extensive	Extensive	Extensive	Extensive
28 King Plow Arts Center	Live/work art studios	Moderate	Moderate	Moderate	Extensive	Extensive	Extensive	Extensive	Extensive
29 LIVINGreen	Showroom and offices	Moderate	Minor	Minor	Extensive	Extensive	Moderate	Moderate	Moderate
30 Magnolia Station	Apartments	Extensive	Extensive	Extensive	Extensive	Extensive	Extensive	Extensive	Extensive
31 Medical Biotechnology Center	Research center	–	Extensive	Extensive	Extensive	Extensive	–	Extensive	–
32 Mercantile Stores Co., Inc., Corporate Headquarters	Office	Moderate	Moderate	Minor	Extensive	Extensive	Minor	Extensive	Minor
33 Nexus Contemporary Art Center	Art gallery and studios	Moderate	Moderate	Moderate	Extensive	Extensive	Minor	Minor	Extensive
34 O'Hern House	Single-room-occupancy housing	–	Minor	Minor	Extensive	Extensive	Minor	–	–

Figure 3-4 (continued).

Catalog Number and Project Name	New Use	Exterior Restoration	New Exterior Construction	Structural	Mechanical	New Interior Construction	Environmental Remediation	New Facilities, Parking	Site Restoration
35 Perkins Building	School	Minor	Minor	Minor	Moderate	Extensive	Moderate	Minor	Minor
36 Port of Seattle Headquarters	Office	Extensive	Extensive	Minor	Extensive	Extensive	–	–	–
37 Potrero Square Lofts	Residential	Minor	Extensive	Extensive	Moderate	Extensive	Minor	Extensive	Minor
38 Q.F.C. #807 at University Village	Retail	Extensive	Extensive	Extensive	Extensive	Extensive	Extensive	Extensive	Extensive
39 San Francisco Bar Pilots Station House	Office	Moderate	Minor	Minor	Extensive	Extensive	Minor	Minor	Minor
40 Shadeland Commerce Center	Office and industrial	Extensive	Extensive	Moderate	Moderate	Extensive	Extensive	Moderate	Extensive
41 SODO Center	Office, retail, industrial	Moderate	Minor	Extensive	Extensive	Extensive	Moderate	Extensive	Minor
42 Sony Game Show Network Building	Broadcast studio, office	Extensive	Extensive	Extensive	Extensive	Extensive	Extensive	Moderate	Extensive
43 Standish Village at Lower Mills	Housing for seniors	Moderate	Moderate	Moderate	Extensive	Extensive	Extensive	Extensive	Extensive
44 Telephone Factory	Loft apartments	Moderate	Minor	Minor	Extensive	Extensive	Minor	Minor	Minor
45 The Florentine	Condominiums and retail space	Extensive	Extensive	Extensive	Extensive	Extensive	Minor	Extensive	Minor
46 The Portorino	Condominiums and retail space	Extensive	Moderate	Extensive	Extensive	Extensive	Minor	Minor	Moderate
47 The Seed Factory	Loft apartments	Moderate	Minor	Minor	Extensive	Extensive	Minor	Moderate	Minor
48 The Shop at Whitinsville	Light industrial and office	Moderate	Minor	Minor	Extensive	Moderate	Minor	Moderate	Moderate
49 Wynkoop Brewing Company	Loft condominiums and brewpub	Moderate	Minor	Minor	Extensive	Extensive	Minor	Minor	Extensive
50 Zipangu Restaurant	Restaurant	Extensive	Moderate	Moderate	Minor	Extensive	Minor	Minor	Minor
51 355 Bryant Street Lofts	Live/work condominiums	Moderate	Moderate	Extensive	Extensive	Extensive	Moderate	–	Moderate
52 601 Fourth Street Lofts	Live/work condominiums	Moderate	Minor	Extensive	Extensive	Extensive	Moderate	Extensive	Minor

Note: A dash indicates data were not available or not applicable.

Original Use: Public Buildings

53. BUS Wellness Center
Santa Monica, California

Original Use: Bus station, 1963

New Use: Fitness center, 1996

Developer: Richard Thayler and Brian Cinadr, Santa Monica

Architect: Steven Ehrlich Architects, Santa Monica

Conversion: This former Greyhound bus depot has been transformed into a bright fitness center, cafe, and boutique. Although the city-owned building was vacant and in decrepit condition, it had a distinctive identity and good parking. The building's current occupant (and project developer) recognized the building's potential and decided to convert it into the space for a fitness center it had been searching for. Early exploration of the 5,000-square-foot brick building revealed a beautiful tapered steel roof frame, which became a primary defining element in the conversion. Existing building materials—sandblasted brick walls, painted steel framing, drywall partitions, and the original terrazzo flooring—were used whenever possible. Sections of the floor removed for the installation of new plumbing and wiring were filled in with dyed concrete, which was also used as a leveling compound throughout the project. The tenant-financed redevelopment totaled $175,000 ($35.00 per square foot).

54. Fire Station #6
Atlanta, Georgia

Original Use: Fire station, 1894

New Use: Museum and office, 1995

Developer: Latco Construction Company, Atlanta

Architect: Paul Hatchett, Atlanta

Conversion: The National Park Service oversaw the conversion of a fire station that long served Atlanta's "old fourth ward" into a museum profiling the life of Dr. Martin Luther King, Jr., and the community in which he lived. The severely deteriorated landmark needed extensive structural rehabilitation, interior modifications, and removal of hazardous materials like asbestos. The city leases the 5,760-square-foot building to the National Park Service at no cost; it was redeveloped for $800,000 ($139 per square foot) using a congressional appropriation.

55. GlenCastle
Atlanta, Georgia

Original Use: Debtors prison, circa 1875

New Use: Single-room-occupancy housing, 1991

Developer: GlenCastle Constructors, Atlanta

Abandoned since 1925, this old debtors prison was resuscitated and adapted to provide transitional housing. The project was a labor of love made possible through donated professional services, labor, and materials.

Architect: Bradfield, Richards & Associates Architects, Inc., Atlanta

Conversion: Eight general contractors entered into a joint venture and offered their services pro bono to rejuvenate this castle-like debtors prison for a new use: 75 units of single-room-occupancy housing and small apartments for transitional housing. Abandoned since 1925, the three-story, 150,000-square-foot concrete building was worn to the bones but structurally sound. Converting it to housing required extensive exterior renovation, mechanical systems upgrading, and interior construction. The low redevelopment cost of $4 million ($27.00 per square foot) was achieved through donations of professional services, labor, some construction materials, and the building itself.

56. Jefferson County Memorial Forest Welcome Center
Fairdale, Kentucky

Original Use: School, 1914

New Use: Visitors center, 1994

Developer: Jefferson County, Louisville

Architect: Gerald Boston, Louisville

Conversion: Because of the dilapidated condition of this antiquated two-room schoolhouse, converting the building into a visitors center was not simple. Redevelopment work included exterior restoration, new mechanical systems, parking facilities, landscaping, and site restoration. The two-story, 3,672-square-foot welcome center is now a main focal point for the Jefferson County Memorial Forest, the country's largest urban forest. The project was financed through grants and government funding at a cost of $400,000 ($108 per square foot).

57. Lyman Hall at Georgia Institute of Technology
Atlanta, Georgia

Original Use: Adjoining classroom buildings, 1906 and 1926

New Use: Offices, 1991

Developer: Georgia Institute of Technology, Atlanta

Architect: Surber & Barber Architects, Atlanta

Conversion: By merging two old chemistry and physics classroom buildings, Georgia Tech created a new 42,000-square-foot administrative office building for the Department of Business and Finance. Work began by gutting both buildings to their shells, removing the auditorium-style lecture hall, restoring the exterior, and constructing a new main entry, fire stairs, and mechanical room. The second phase of the project consisted of renovating the interior and the mechanical, electrical, plumbing, and fire protection systems. The light well between the original buildings was enclosed and a three-story skylit atrium created. The state of Georgia financed the project, which cost $2.9 million ($68.00 per square foot).

58. Newburyport Firehouse
Newburyport, Massachusetts

Original Use: Meeting hall, public market, firehouse, 1823

New Use: Civic center/performing arts center, 1991

Developer: Society for Development of Arts and Humanities (SDAH), Newburyport

Architect: Schwartz/Silver Architects, Boston

Conversion: Throughout its 165-year history, this three-story, 18,000-square-foot building has served many purposes, including a town meeting hall and a fire station, which was abandoned in 1979. SDAH developed a plan to lease the building from the city and create a civic center emphasizing the performing arts. The building now houses a 200-seat theater with lobby and a first-floor restaurant. The venerable building needed major structural, mechanical, and interior work as well as environmental remediation. Total redevelopment cost was $2.3 million ($125 per square foot). The project was financed through a $1.8 million state grant and a fundraising drive by citizens to raise the additional $500,000.

59. Orchard Street Church
Baltimore, Maryland

Original Use: Church and school, 1882 and 1903

New Use: Office and museum, 1993

Developer: Baltimore Urban League, Baltimore

Architect: KC&M Architects, Baltimore

Conversion: The new office headquarters for the Baltimore Urban League and the African American Cultural Center and Museum is now housed in what used to be one of Maryland's oldest African American churches. Great effort was taken to preserve the architecturally and historically significant details on this 22,000-square-foot National Register property. The building was extremely eroded after two decades of neglect and required extensive renovation. The owner/developer acquired the church for $1.00, and redevelopment cost $4 million ($180 per square foot). Securing financing was a challenge, but the project was ultimately funded through public and private donations and a commercial bank loan.

60. Phelps Center
Seattle, Washington

Original Use: Exhibition hall, 1962

New Use: Performing arts center, 1993

Developer: Pacific Northwest Ballet, Seattle

Architect: NBBJ, Seattle

Conversion: After undergoing extensive renovations, this 1960s exhibition hall has acquired a modern appearance as well as a second primary use as home to the Pacific Northwest Ballet. The lower level of the building continues to serve as the Seattle Center Exhibition Hall. One and one-half floors of space were added within the shell of the column-free, 40-foot clear height building to create seven ballet studios, dressing rooms, offices, costume shops, and a ballet school. The facility is conveniently located adjacent to the Seattle Opera House, where the ballet company performs. Costs for the redevelopment totaled $8.5 million ($162 per square foot). The project was financed through public and private sources.

61. Ponce de Leon Clinic
Atlanta, Georgia

Original Use: Presbyterian headquarters, 1962

New Use: Medical clinic and offices, 1993

Developer: Fulton–De Kalb Hospital Authority, Atlanta

Architect: Jova, Daniels, Busby, Atlanta

Conversion: Adaptive use of this structurally sound but functionally obsolete brick office building resulted in one of the most comprehensive publicly funded outpatient HIV/AIDS treatment facilities in the country. The clinic uses only three of the building's seven floors;

the remaining four floors are planned for the clinic's future expansion. Initially, residents of the community were concerned about the impact the clinic would have on the development potential of the midtown neighborhood. After three years of operations, the well-maintained clinic is considered a good neighbor. The structure needed little exterior restoration, and it already had ample parking. Creative interior space planning was required to make the building accessible for the disabled; a new elevator was installed and the HVAC system refurbished. Redevelopment of this design-build project cost $3.5 million ($78.00 per square foot). The project, which took 30 weeks to complete, was funded by the Fulton –De Kalb Hospital Authority.

62. Pueblo Union Depot
Pueblo, Colorado

Original Use: Train depot, 1889

New Use: Office, retail, and residential space, restaurant and catering hall, 1996

Developer: Tim Miller and Katherine Miller, Pueblo

Architect: Michael Collins, Colorado Springs

Conversion: Constructed in 1889 as one of the largest train depots in the Midwest, Pueblo Union Depot is now a thriving mixed-use center that is credited with initiating the revitalization of Pueblo's Union Avenue historic district. In 1989, the owner/developer purchased the timeworn, four-story, 50,000-square-foot train depot and an adjacent 10,000-square-foot baggage cart shed from the Federal Deposit Insurance Corporation for $250,000. Phase one of the adaptive use project—redeveloping the train depot—was completed in 1992. The renovated depot has 10,000

square feet each of retail and office space (23 tenants combined), nine rental apartment units (11,650 square feet), a 6,000-square-foot banquet hall, and 4,000 square feet of restaurant space. Though structurally sound, the depot required new mechanical systems and substantial interior renovation. Care was taken to preserve as much of the existing facility as possible, including restoration of stained glass and wooden floors. Phase two— renovation of the adjacent 10,000-square-foot baggage cart building for a furniture store—was expected to be completed by mid-1996. The first $1 million of the $2.5 million total redevelopment cost ($50.00 per square foot) was funded by the owner/developer; locally owned Minnequa Bank of Pueblo financed the remainder.

63. Roosevelt Lofts
Atlanta, Georgia

Original Use: Public high school, 1924

New Use: Apartments, 1989

Developer: Roosevelt Associates, L.P., Atlanta

Architect: Surber & Barber Architects, Atlanta

Conversion: Federal rehabilitation tax credits helped make it financially feasible for the owner/developer to transform a school built in 1924 known as Girl's High School (later renamed Roosevelt High School) into a 111,200-square-foot apartment building. The 90 market-rate one- and two-bedroom apartments are located near downtown Atlanta. A lobby, lounge, swimming pool, and eight new two-bedroom townhouses were built behind the original school building. Emphasis was placed on preserving the building's architectural character. Corridor walls were relocated and original class-

room doors and transoms reused. Clay tile roofing, decorative gables, and the copper roof were carefully restored. To accommodate the new use, it was necessary to install modern mechanical, heating, plumbing, and electrical systems and a new elevator. Redevelopment costs totaled just over $4 million ($37.00 per square foot). The units, ranging from 650 to 1,100 square feet, began leasing at about $0.75 per square foot. A new owner of the project has since converted the original gymnasium behind the school building into 30 additional apartment units.

64. San Juan Brewing Company
Telluride, Colorado

Original Use: Train station, circa 1890

New Use: Restaurant and microbrewery, 1992

Developer: Wodehouse Builders, Telluride

Architect: Charles Cunniffe Architects, Telluride

Conversion: The preservation and adaptive use of this turn-of-the-century train station into an upscale restaurant with an in-house brewery required major redevelopment work and careful attention to preserving the structure's historic elements. Because the building was seriously eroded, the interior had to be stabilized with frames while the building was lifted and relocated. A basement was added, increasing the building's size to 4,185 square feet. After the structural, mechanical, and interior work was completed, the building was moved back to its original location. Redevelopment costs totaled $450,000 ($110 per square foot).

65. Schoolhouse Lofts
Atlanta, Georgia

Original Use: School, 1891

New Use: Loft apartments, 1993

Developer: John W. Ayers Schoolhouse Lofts, Inc., Atlanta

Architect: William C. Dorn, Atlanta

Conversion: The conversion of this 19th century schoolhouse into 11 loft apartments was accomplished for only $33.00 per square foot. The building was very solid but showed its age. Minimal exterior renovation was needed, but new mechanical systems were installed and a fair amount of interior construction done. The owner/developer acquired the 20,000-square-foot building for $175,000 and redeveloped it for $665,000. Construction was funded through private sources, and a bank provided permanent financing.

66. Tacoma Union Station
Tacoma, Washington

Original Use: Train station, 1911

New Use: Courthouse, 1992

Developer: City of Tacoma, Washington

Architect: Merritt & Pardini, Tacoma

Conversion: A citizen action committee to save this grand neoclassical train station began by trying to find a viable new use for the building; it eventually campaigned successfully to convert it into a federal courthouse. The city acted as its own developer, purchasing and redeveloping the station property. After design was completed, the city negotiated a lease with the General Services Administration to provide renovated facilities for the Western Washington Federal District Court and issued bonds for the purchase and redevelopment of the train station. The station's rotunda was restored to its original condition and remains a public gathering space. The public waiting spaces used during railroad days were changed to courtroom suites. A 120,968-square-foot modern addition to the original structure houses eight additional courtroom suites, increasing the project's size to 201,544 square feet. The addition uses similar architectural themes but is smaller in scale than the historic station. The station was acquired for $2.4 million and redeveloped for $56 million ($290 per square foot). The revitalized train station has galvanized redevelopment of other nearby older structures.

67. Welcome South Visitors Center
Atlanta, Georgia

Original Use: Bus station, circa 1960

New Use: Visitors center and retail space, 1995

Developer: Atlanta Convention and Visitors Bureau, Atlanta

Architect: Milton Pate & Associates, Atlanta

Conversion: Using corporate donations and public funding, the Atlanta Convention and Visitors Bureau was able to transform an outdated 23,000-square-foot Trailways terminal into a visitors center in nine months, in time for the Summer Olympic games. Two sets of large interior columns posed challenges for the architects, who had to incorporate them into the design of the exhibit area. Another challenge was the section of the floor that was raised three feet to accommodate buses. The difference in floor heights could not be incorporated into the design, so the raised floor had to be painstakingly leveled, a job made even more challenging in light of the tight schedule. The center now has an exhibition floor (where the raised floor was originally), a 57-seat theater, two retail areas, and a press facility for media representatives. The project's cost totaled $5.5 million ($239 per square foot).

68. YWCA of Metro Atlanta
Atlanta, Georgia

Original Use: Church, 1920

New Use: YWCA, 1991

Developer: YWCA of Greater Atlanta, Atlanta

Architect: Surber & Barber Architects, Atlanta

Conversion: The YWCA rescued this 16,790-square-foot former Baptist church built in the 1920s in one of Atlanta's oldest residential neighborhoods and adapted it to house a new YWCA branch. The facility offers daycare, after-school programs, adult education, and fitness classes. The old church required extensive redevelopment work inside and out but was very compatible with the new use in terms of building configuration. A new second floor "floats" within the volume of the original sanctuary, adding about 2,400 square feet of usable space. The stained glass windows were replaced with clear glass to allow more natural light, and a new fire stair and elevator were added to make the entire facility accessible to the disabled. Many of the existing building elements, including the tall windows from the sanctuary, portions of the original sanctuary floor, and interior columns and trim, were refurbished and reused. Redevelopment costs totaled $1.1 million ($57.00 per square foot).

Figure 3-5. Project Economics (Originally Public Buildings)

Catalog Number and Project Name	Year of Conversion	Gross Area (square feet)	Building Acquisition Cost	Approximate Redevelopment Cost	Cost per Square Foot	Source of Financing	Rental Rates
53 BUS Wellness Center	1996	5,000	Leased	$175,000	$35	Tenant/developer	–
54 Fire Station #6	1995	5,760	Leased	$800,000	($139)	Congressional appropriation	Owner-occupied
55 GlenCastle	1991	150,000	Donation	$4,000,000	$27	Donations	75 SRO units
56 Jefferson County Memorial Forest Welcome Center	1994	3,672	Already owned	$400,000	$109	Public funding	Owner-occupied
57 Lyman Hall at Georgia Institute of Technology	1991	42,000	Already owned	$2,861,400	$68	State of Georgia	Owner-occupied
58 Newburyport Firehouse	1991	18,000	Leased	$2,300,000	$125	Grants and fundraising	$1 psf
59 Orchard Street Church	1993	22,000	$1	$4,000,000	$180	State of Maryland, city of Baltimore, commercial bank, private donations	Owner-occupied
60 Phelps Center	1993	52,300	Leased	$8,500,000	$163	70 percent private, 30 percent public sources	–
61 Ponce de Leon Clinic	1993	45,000	–	$3,500,000	$78	Publicly funded	–
62 Pueblo Union Depot	1996	50,000	$250,000	$2,500,000	($50)	Owner's equity, commercial bank	Apartments—$550–750/month; office—$12 psf; retail—$10 psf; restaurants—$6 psf (all NNN)
63 Roosevelt Lofts	1989	111,200	–	$4,069,600	$37	Private equity, commercial bank, rehabilitation tax credit	90 rental units—$0.75 psf
64 San Juan Brewing Company	1992	4,185	–	$450,000	$110	–	Owner-occupied
65 Schoolhouse Lofts	1993	20,000	$175,000	$665,000	$33	Private and commercial bank	11 rental units—$800–1,400/month
66 Tacoma Union Station	1992	201,544	$2,350,000	$56,150,000	$290	City funds and bonds	$35.06 psf
67 Welcome South Visitors Center	1995	23,000	–	$5,500,000	($239)	Corporate, public, and private sponsors	Owner-occupied
68 YWCA of Metro Atlanta	1991	19,147	–	$1,102,000	$57	–	Owner-occupied

Note: Figures in parentheses were derived from other data. A dash indicates data were not available or not applicable.

Figure 3-6. Redevelopment Work (Originally Public Buildings)

Catalog Number and Project Name	New Use	Exterior Restoration	New Exterior Construction	Structural	Mechanical	New Interior Construction	Environmental Remediation	New Facilities, Parking	Site Restoration
53 BUS Wellness Center	Fitness center	Extensive	Minor	Moderate	Moderate	Extensive	Minor	Minor	Minor
54 Fire Station #6	Museum	Extensive	Extensive	Extensive	Extensive	Extensive	Extensive	Minor	Extensive
55 GlenCastle	Single-room-occupancy housing	Extensive	Minor	Moderate	Extensive	Extensive	Minor	Minor	Moderate
56 Jefferson County Memorial Forest Welcome Center	Visitors center	Extensive	Extensive	Moderate	Extensive	Moderate	Extensive	Extensive	Extensive
57 Lyman Hall at Georgia Institute of Technology	Offices	Extensive	Extensive	Moderate	Extensive	Extensive	Extensive	Minor	Minor
58 Newburyport Firehouse	Performing arts center	Moderate	Extensive	Extensive	Extensive	Extensive	Extensive	Minor	Extensive
59 Orchard Street Church	Office and museum	Extensive	Minor	Extensive	Extensive	Extensive	Extensive	Extensive	Moderate
60 Phelps Center	Performing arts center	Moderate	Moderate	Extensive	Extensive	Extensive	Extensive	Minor	Minor
61 Ponce de Leon Clinic	Medical clinic	Moderate	–	Minor	Extensive	Extensive	Minor	Minor	Moderate
62 Pueblo Union Depot	Office, retail, residential, restaurant	Moderate	Minor	Minor	Extensive	Extensive	Minor	Minor	Extensive
63 Roosevelt Lofts	Apartments	Moderate	Moderate	Minor	Extensive	Extensive	Extensive	Extensive	Moderate
64 San Juan Brewing Company	Restaurant/brewery	Moderate	Moderate	Extensive	Extensive	Extensive	Moderate	Moderate	Moderate
65 Schoolhouse Lofts	Residential	Minor	Minor	Minor	Extensive	Moderate	Minor	Minor	Moderate
66 Tacoma Union Station	Courthouse	Extensive	Extensive	Extensive	Extensive	Extensive	Moderate	Moderate	Moderate
67 Welcome South Visitors Center	Visitors center	Moderate	Minor	Moderate	Moderate	Extensive	Moderate	Minor	Extensive
68 YWCA of Metro Atlanta	YWCA	Extensive	Extensive	Extensive	Extensive	Extensive	Moderate	Extensive	Minor

Note: A dash indicates data were not available or not applicable.

Original Use: Cultural Buildings

69. Banana Republic at the Coliseum Theater
Seattle, Washington

Original Use: Theater, 1916

New Use: Retail space, 1994

Developer: Broadacres Properties, Seattle

Architect: NBBJ, Seattle

Conversion: Seattle's elegant old Coliseum Theater is thriving once again, but these days the customers try on clothing instead of watch movies. Banana Republic, the building's new tenant, targeted the Coliseum as its choice for a new downtown store because of its dramatic architecture, excellent location, and status as a community landmark. Built in 1916 during the era of grand movie theaters, the Coliseum began to go downhill with the growth of suburbs and multiple-screen cinemas. In 1985, the building ceased operating as a theater, although the sidewalk retail shops incorporated into the original design continued to operate. In 1990, the building owner began looking for an economically feasible way to revive the historic building. A long list of possible tenants came and, for various reasons, went, but Banana Republic was the choice because the retailer was willing to restore and renovate the building to the owner's satisfaction. Banana Republic achieved instant recognition among customers in its new location. Although the building was dilapidated in appearance, it was in fairly good structural condition. The most noticeable change to the exterior was renovation of the store's corner entrance in a style reflecting the original elaborate design before it was modernized in 1950. Inside, the theater's floors were leveled, its 80-foot ceil-ings were lowered, the large auditorium space was broken up into smaller rooms, and new mechanical systems were installed. Banana Republic occupies 16,000 square feet of the building's 28,000 square feet. (The original theater balcony is not used.)

70. Brook Theatre
Tulsa, Oklahoma

Original Use: Movie theater with office space and adjacent dry cleaners building, both 1940s

New Use: Office, retail, health club, and conference center, 1995

Developer: Stellar Commercial Corporation, Tulsa

Architect: Fritz Baily Architects, Tulsa

Conversion: Once in the heart of Tulsa's main retail district, this 50-year-old, 600-seat movie theater, deteriorated from absentee ownership and plagued by asbestos and a lack of parking, sat vacant for years. The new owner developed the 13,000-square-foot theater and an adjacent 5,800-square-foot dry cleaner into one mixed-use project. Because the theater is in a special use district with stringent zoning requirements, reusing the existing building shells truncated the approval process (compared to new construction), but virtually every other aspect of development is new. The dry cleaner was converted into a branch bank, with a drive-through bank cut into the ground floor of the theater building. A second floor was added to the theater to hold a health club, conference center, and offices. An elevator lobby to the second floor was constructed on the ground level of the theater, and the original lobby was converted to a restaurant with outdoor seating. The owner/developer purchased the buildings for $600,000; the tenants paid for $1.2 million of the $2.1 million redevelopment ($100 per square foot). The owner secured bank construction financing.

71. The Majestic Theatre at Peabody Place
Memphis, Tennessee

Original Use: Movie theater, 1913

New Use: Restaurant, estimated 1996

Developer: Belz Enterprises, Memphis

Architect: Hnedak Bobo Group

Conversion: The last of four existing buildings in the historic block of Peabody Place to be redeveloped (also see project numbers 9, 16, and 75), this well-used building was converted into a 9,000-square-foot, two-story restaurant and brewery (project completion was expected by late 1996). The most significant redevelopment work involved the construction of the new interior space and installation of new mechanical systems. The exterior was cleaned and many architectural features restored. The developer acquired the building for $200,000; redevelopment cost was projected to be $1.5 million ($165 per square foot). Private equity and a commercial bank were the primary sources of financing for the project.

72. The Rialto Theater
Atlanta, Georgia

Original Use: Movie theater, 1962

New Use: Center for the performing arts, 1996

Developer: Georgia State University, Atlanta

Architect: Richard Rothman and Gardner, Spencer, Smith & Associates, Atlanta

Conversion: Georgia State University took a long-term lease on this early 1960s movie theater and put it back into productive use as a center for the performing arts. The street-level lobby in the renovated Rialto leads up to a 1,000-seat performance hall. The basement includes instructional space for the Georgia State University School of Music. Redevelopment included raising the roof to provide more interior volume to improve acoustics and removing large amounts of asbestos. Because of its urban location, new parking facilities, site restoration, and landscaping were not required. Georgia State's redevelopment of the theater has provided a catalyst for further revitalization of the surrounding area. Total redevelopment costs were $8.9 million ($204 per square foot). The project was financed through Georgia State's capital campaign, a private foundation grant, and nonprofit corporate bonds.

Figure 3-7. Project Economics (Originally Cultural Buildings)

Catalog Number and Project Name	Year of Conversion	Gross Area (square feet)	Building Acquisition Cost	Approximate Redevelopment Cost	Cost per Square Foot	Source of Financing	Rental Rates
69 Banana Republic at the Coliseum Theater	1994	28,000	Lease	–	–	–	–
70 Brook Theatre	1995	20,000	$600,000	$2,100,000	$100	Local bank, tenant improvements	Office—$10 psf; retail—$12 psf; other—$10 psf
71 The Majestic Theatre at Peabody Place	1996	9,000	$200,000	$1,500,000	$165	Private equity; commercial bank	Restaurant/brewery—$21 psf
72 The Rialto Theater	1996	43,750	50-year lease	$8,930,000	$204	Private foundation grant, Georgia State University capital campaign, nonprofit corporate bonds	–

Note: A dash indicates data were not available or not applicable.

Figure 3-8. Redevelopment Work (Originally Cultural Buildings)

Catalog Number and Project Name	New Use	Exterior Restoration	New Exterior Construction	Structural	Mechanical	New Interior Construction	Environmental Remediation	New Facilities, Parking	Site Restoration
69 Banana Republic at the Coliseum Theater	Retail	Extensive	Moderate	Extensive	Extensive	Extensive	Moderate	Minor	Minor
70 Brook Theatre	Office, retail, health club	Extensive	Extensive	Extensive	Extensive	Extensive	Extensive	Extensive	Extensive
71 The Majestic Theatre at Peabody Place	Restaurant/brewery	Extensive	Moderate	Moderate	Extensive	Extensive	Moderate	Extensive	Moderate
72 The Rialto Theater	Performing arts center	Minor	Moderate	Moderate	Extensive	Extensive	Extensive	Minor	Minor

Original Use: Residences and Hotels

73. All-City Credit Union
Everett, Washington

Original Use: Residence, 1892

New Use: Credit union, 1992

Developer: All-City Credit Union, Everett

Architect: The Driftmier Architects, Kirkland, Washington

Conversion: The need for additional space prompted the All-City Credit Union to expand a 2,250-square-foot century-old historic house into a bank with drive-through facilities. The original two-story brick house was renovated and added onto to provide six teller stations, a lobby area, three drive-through lanes, a board room, and other office space. The credit union occupies 5,625 square feet of the building, with the remaining 1,125 square feet leased as office space. The original building's historic value was retained, while the 4,500-square-foot addition incorporates a modern design. The credit union redeveloped the property for a total cost of $615,000 ($91.00 per square foot).

74. Century Plaza Apartments
Washington, Pennsylvania

Original Use: Motel, 1967

New Use: Housing for seniors, 1994

Developer: Washington County Redevelopment Authority, Pennsylvania

Architect: Lorenzi, Dodds & Gunnill, Inc., Pittsburgh

Conversion: After the original owner's bankruptcy, the Washington County Redevelopment Authority, in southwestern Pennsylvania, saw an opportunity to convert this vacant 100-unit 1960s motel into affordable rental housing for seniors. Adding doors between adjacent motel rooms created 65 one-bedroom apartments, with one room left in its original configuration and the adjoining one converted into a kitchen/living room. The building was made accessible to the disabled, a new elevator was installed, and asbestos was removed. Giving the long, narrow building a residential feel was accomplished by replacing the parking lot with extensive landscaping, converting the reception and meeting rooms into a community area, installing pitched roofs, and adding brick facades. The building was acquired for $700,000 and redeveloped for $3.3 million ($55.00 per square foot). Funding was provided by HUD's Home Investment Partnership Program, community development block grants, and federal low-income housing tax credits.

75. Gayoso House at Peabody Place
Memphis, Tennessee

Original Use: Hotel and warehouse, 1892

New Use: Apartments and retail space, 1995

Developer: Belz Enterprises, Memphis

Architect: Hnedok Bobo Group, Memphis

Conversion: Once the hotel of choice for presidents, generals, and entertainers and later used as a warehouse, the Gayoso House now contains 156 affordable and luxury apartment units in two-story townhouse configurations. The first level of the six-floor building contains 20,000 square feet of commercial space for restaurants and small

This elegant late 19th century hotel building went through a long period of decline but has been reclaimed for apartments and ground-floor retail space.

specialty shops. The building is one component of Peabody Place in downtown Memphis, an eight-block mixed-use development that includes both adaptive use and new construction (also see project numbers 9, 16, and 71). Many of the historic building's original architectural features, including mosaic tile floors and stained glass windows, were restored. The existing building was in fairly good condition, and its configuration accommodated an efficient layout for the new apartments. Nevertheless, constructing the residential units and equipping them with modern amenities entailed extensive redevelopment work. The owner/developer acquired the hotel building for $75,000 and redeveloped it for $13 million ($62.00 per square foot). Project funding included bank financing and community development block grants.

76. Horine Manor House
Fairdale, Kentucky

Original Use: Residential, 1942

New Use: Meeting facility and office space, 1992

Developer: Jefferson County Fiscal Court, Louisville

Architect: Gerald Boston, Louisville

Conversion: The existing building in this adaptive use project was a

4,990-square-foot summer house, dating from the early 1940s, that had been donated to Jefferson County, Kentucky. Taking advantage of the former house's forest setting, the county adapted about half the space for use as a small conference center for retreats. In addition to use by the county, public organizations can rent the facility for $300 per day. The building was very solid, and aside from additional parking space, very little was done to the exterior. Considerable interior redevelopment, including all new mechanical systems, was necessary to fit the new conference center into the building. The county-funded redevelopment cost $120,000 ($42.00 per square foot).

77. Jerusalem House
Atlanta, Georgia

Original Use: House, circa 1920

New Use: Boarding apartments/ supportive housing, 1992

Developer: Jerusalem House, Inc., Atlanta

Architect: Surber & Barber Architects, Atlanta

Conversion: The nonprofit organization Jerusalem House, Inc., has converted a 6,500-square-foot single-family residence in the historic Druid Hills neighborhood of Atlanta to a supportive housing facility for up to 23 homeless people with AIDS and a resident manager. A three-story addition to the original 1920s house increased the usable space to 19,500 square feet. Jerusalem House accomplished its architectural, social, and economic objectives by blending the architectural character of the original house with the surrounding neighborhood and providing supportive housing that could be developed and maintained at a reasonable cost. Ample common areas, including a living room,

dining room, sunroom, and private outdoor spaces, create a noninstitutional environment. In the event that a cure for AIDS is found and Jerusalem House would no longer be needed, designers made it possible to easily convert the building to one- and two-bedroom apartments. The nonprofit owner/developer purchased the moderately deteriorated structure for $341,000. Redevelopment, including the new wing, extensive interior and mechanical work in the existing building, landscaping, and parking, cost nearly $1.5 million ($73.00 per square foot). Funding came from public and private foundations, grants, and contributions.

78. Medical Office
Smithtown, New York

Original Use: Inn, circa 1725

New Use: Medical office, 1994

Developer: Dr. Daniel Mayer, Smithtown

Architect: John Smits, Farmingdale, New York

Conversion: A physician has extended the useful life of this pre–Revolutionary War inn into the 21st century by adapting it to function as a private medical office. Although the layout of the 3,134-square-foot, 2fi-story structure was very compatible with its intended new use, it took a considerable amount of exterior and interior redevelopment work to accommodate the new use. To increase the amount of usable space, a loft was placed by the exit and a one-story waiting room added to the existing building, expanding the building's size to 4,250 square feet. Exterior work included replacing the roof, installing all new windows, landscaping the grounds, and expanding the parking area. The owner/developer purchased the building for $425,000 and redevel-

oped it for $375,000 ($88.00 per square foot). Financing included a commercial bank loan.

79. Medical Office
Smithtown, New York

Original Use: Farmhouse, private residence, circa 1726

New Use: Medical office, 1992

Developer: Dr. Richard Hamburg, Smithtown

Architect: John Smits, Farmingdale, New York

Conversion: This extremely deteriorated, 270-year-old, two-story farmhouse was saved from becoming a pile of rubble and is useful again as a private medical office. The project required extensive interior restoration and renovation. The existing 2,386-square-foot building was used for waiting areas and offices, and a new one-story, 1,363-square-foot addition with basement was constructed to house the examining and operating rooms. A 600-square-foot barn located on the site was also renovated for use as an art studio. Sitework, totaling $75,000, included lighting, a new parking area, and landscaping. The owner/ developer purchased the property for $400,000; the redevelopment cost of $400,000 ($91.00 per square foot) was financed with a bank loan.

80. Monte Cristo
Everett, Washington

Original Use: Hotel, 1925

New Use: Residential, office, retail, and art gallery, 1993

Developer: Lojis Corporation, Seattle

Architect: GGLO Architecture and Interior Design, Seattle

Conversion: By combining the sale of low-income and rehabilitation tax credits and leasing the ornate

The reincarnation of a long-vacant hotel into a mix of residential, retail, and commercial uses has helped galvanize the revitalization of downtown Everett.

lobby and mezzanine as office, retail, and gallery space, the owner/developer was able to renovate and convert this 70-year-old landmark hotel into an apartment building offering 69 one- and two-bedroom affordable units. Before the renovation, the 59,000-square-foot Italian second Renaissance–Revival–style hotel was in bad shape, having endured water damage, vandalism, and general deterioration for 20 years. Designing 69 units in a building designed for 140 hotel rooms with 11-foot by 13-foot column spacing and a rigorous window pattern (which offered no flexibility in a historic brick structure) created an additional challenge, but it resulted in highly marketable apartments with high ceilings and as many as six double-hung windows per unit. While removing a false ceiling in the hotel's ballroom, workers discovered an original stained glass skylight. Renovation included seismic upgrades, the installation of new mechanical, electrical, and plumbing systems, and accessibility for the disabled. The hotel was acquired for $617,700 and redeveloped for $7 million ($119 per square foot).

81. The Bellevue
Philadelphia, Pennsylvania

Original Use: Hotel, 1904

New Use: Hotel, office and retail space, athletic club, 1989

Developer: The Rubin Organization, Inc., Philadelphia

Architects: RTKL, Baltimore; Tom Lee Ltd., New York

Conversion: Until it closed in 1976 after 29 people died from what became known as "Legionnaires' disease," the Bellevue Stratford Hotel was Philadelphia's most elegant hotel. In 1978, The Rubin Organization acquired the 19-story French Renaissance building and tried unsuccessfully to restore it as a hotel. More than ten years later, Rubin completed a second and apparently successful attempt to bring

Philadelphia's legendary Bellevue Stratford hotel is now a mixed-use development called The Bellevue, combining retail, office, and hotel space.

its beautiful building to life again as a mixed-use development with an exclusive shopping center on the four lower levels, ten floors of office space, and seven floors containing a 173-room hotel and an athletic club. The building's exterior and many of the historic interior spaces had been restored during the previous hotel renovation and were essentially unchanged in the conversion to mixed uses. Most of the nonhistoric interior space, however, was remade to fit the new uses. Above its three-story base, the original hotel building was configured around two light wells. On the ten office floors, the open space was filled in with standard floors, creating additional usable space and a more efficient layout for offices. Each of the building's uses has a separate entrance. The complex and critically acclaimed conversion increased the size of the building from 554,200 square feet to 785,262 square feet. The building was acquired for $19 million and redeveloped for $150 million ($191 per square foot). Sources of financing included a first mortgage and a participating second mortgage.

82. The Kensington-Hobbs
Hobbs, New Mexico

Original Use: Hotel and banquet facility, 1965

New Use: Assisted living, 1990

Developer: Kensington-Hobbs Partners, Golden Valley, Minnesota

Architect: Robert Ready, Hopkins, Minnesota

Conversion: This 78-room hotel and banquet facility was easily converted to a 77-unit assisted-living facility. The original 65,000-square-foot building needed only minor refurbishing and remodeling but did require new mechanical and fire safety systems. Acquisition totaled

$190,000, redevelopment $1.2 million ($22.00 per square foot). The project was financed through bank loans and private investors.

83. 1340 North State Parkway
Chicago, Illinois

Original Use: Mansion, 1903–1914

New Use: Luxury condominiums, 1994

Developer: LR Development Company, Chicago

Architect: HSP Seglin Limited, Chicago

Conversion: The exquisite beaux arts architecture and rich history of this 30,000-square-foot mansion prompted several reuses as the building changed hands over the course of 90 years, including a private residence and surgeon's office, apartments, Hugh Hefner's Playboy mansion, classrooms, and dormitories. In 1989, the building was donated to the Art Institute of Chicago and ultimately sold to LR Development Company, which has converted it to seven luxury condominiums. Extensive restoration and construction were needed inside and out to create the custom units, which range from 3,400 to 7,400 square feet.

Figure 3-9. Project Economics (Originally Residences and Hotels)

Catalog Number and Project Name	Year of Conversion	Gross Area (square feet)	Building Acquisition Cost	Approximate Redevelopment Cost	Cost per Square Foot	Source of Financing	Rental Rates
73 All-City Credit Union	1992	6,750	Already owned	$615,000	$91	Owner-financed	Owner-occupied
74 Century Plaza Apartments	1994	60,000	$700,000	$3,300,000	($55)	CDBGs, Home Investment Partnership Program, and low-income housing tax credits	Rent based on income
75 Gayoso House at Peabody Place	1995	210,000	$75,000	$13,000,000	$62	Developer equity, commercial bank, CDBG	156 apartment units—$400–1,000/month; retail—$16 psf
76 Horine Manor House	1992	4,990[a]	Donated	$120,000	$42	County funding	$300/day
77 Jerusalem House	1992	20,000	$341,000	$1,471,415	($73)	Public, private foundations, religious institutions	Residential units—30 percent of gross income
78 Medical Office	1994	4,248	$425,000	$375,000	$88	Commercial bank	Owner-occupied
79 Medical Office	1992	3,749	$400,000	$400,000	($91)	Commercial bank	Owner-occupied
80 Monte Cristo	1993	59,000	$617,700	$7,000,000	($119)	Low-income housing and rehabilitation tax credits, Washington Community Reinvestment Association	Office/retail/gallery—$10 psf
81 The Bellevue	1989	785,262	$19,000,000	$150,000,000	($191)	First mortgage and participating second mortgage	–
82 The Kensington-Hobbs	1990	65,000	$190,000	$1,200,000	($18)	Private equity, commercial bank	–
83 1340 North State Parkway	1994	40,000	–	–	–	–	–

Note: Figures in parentheses were derived from other data. A dash indicates data were not available or not applicable.
[a]Only 2,850 square feet was adapted.

Figure 3-10. Redevelopment Work (Originally Residences and Hotels)

Catalog Number and Project Name	New Use	Exterior Restoration	New Exterior Construction	Structural	Mechanical	New Interior Construction	Environmental Remediation	New Facilities, Parking	Site Restoration
73 All-City Credit Union	Bank	Moderate	Extensive	Moderate	Moderate	Moderate	Minor	Extensive	Extensive
74 Century Plaza Apartments	Housing for seniors	Extensive	Minor	Minor	Extensive	Extensive	Minor	Extensive	Extensive
75 Gayoso House at Peabody Place	Apartments and retail	Extensive	Extensive	Extensive	Extensive	Extensive	Moderate	Moderate	Minor
76 Horine Manor House	Meeting facility and office	Minor	Minor	Minor	Extensive	Moderate	Moderate	Extensive	Moderate
77 Jerusalem House	Boarding apartments	Moderate	Extensive	Moderate	Extensive	Moderate	Extensive	Extensive	Extensive
78 Medical Office	Medical office	Moderate	Moderate	Moderate	Extensive	Extensive	Minor	Extensive	Extensive
79 Medical Office	Medical office	Extensive	Moderate	Moderate	Extensive	Extensive	Minor	Extensive	Extensive
80 Monte Cristo	Residential, retail, restaurant	Extensive	Minor	Extensive	Extensive	Extensive	Extensive	Minor	Minor
81 The Bellevue	Hotel, office, retail	Minor	Minor	Extensive	Extensive	Extensive	Extensive	Moderate	Minor
82 The Kensington-Hobbs	Assisted living	Minor	Minor	Minor	Extensive	Moderate	Moderate	Minor	Minor
83 1340 North State Parkway	Luxury condominiums	Extensive	Extensive	Extensive	Extensive	Extensive	Minor	Extensive	Extensive

Appendices

Appendix A

Cross-References

Appendix B

Selected References

General Information

Books/Monographs

Adaptive Reuse of Mental Health Facilities. Washington, D.C.: National Council for Urban Economic Development, 1993.

Brand, Stuart. *How Buildings Learn: What Happens after They're Built.* New York: Viking Penguin, 1995.

Breen, Ann. *Waterfronts: Cities Reclaim Their Edge.* New York: McGraw-Hill, 1994.

Cantacuzion, Sherban. *Re-Architecture: Old Buildings, New Uses.* New York: Abbeville Press, 1989.

Cecil Baker & Associates, Eugene LeFevre, and Center City District. *Turning On the Lights Upstairs: A Guide for Converting the Upper Floors of Older Commercial Buildings to Residential Use.* Philadelphia: Author, 1996.

Croft, Virginia. *Recycled as Restaurants: Case Studies in Adaptive Reuse.* New York: Whitney Library of Design, 1991.

Herbers, Jill. *Great Adaptations: New Residential Uses for Older Buildings.* New York: Whitney Library of Design, 1990.

Mack, Lorrie. *Art of Home Conversion: Transforming Uncommon Properties into Stylish Homes.* London: Cassell, 1995.

M/PF Research. *Adaptive Reuse of Commercial Real Estate in Over-supplied Markets.* Working Paper #602. Washington, D.C.: ULI–the Urban Land Institute, 1992.

National Audubon Society and Croxton Collaborative. *Audubon House: Building the Environmentally Responsible, Energy-Efficient Office.* New York: Wiley, 1994.

National Council for Urban Economic Development. *Neighborhood Economic Revitalization.* Washington, D.C.: Author, 1994.

——. *Urban Manufacturing: Dilemma or Opportunity?* Washington, D.C.: Author, 1994.

National Trust for Historic Preservation. *Reusing America's Tools: A Guide for Local Officials, Developers, Neighborhood Residents, Planners, and Preservationists.* Washington, D.C.: Preservation Press, 1991.

Robert, Philippe. *Adaptations.* New York: Princeton Architectural Press, 1991.

Schneekloth, Lynda H., Marcia F. Feuerstein, and Barbara A. Camagna. *Changing Places: Remaking Institutional Buildings.* Fredonia, N.Y.: White Pine Press, 1992.

Shopsin, William. *Restoring Old Buildings for Contemporary Uses.* New York: Watson-Guptill, 1989.

Smeallie, Peter H. *New Construction for Older Buildings: A Design Sourcebook for Architects and Preservationists.* New York: Wiley, 1990.

Journal Articles

"Adaptive Reuse: Vacant Office Buildings Becoming Apartments." *ENR–Engineering News-Record,* October 11, 1993, pp. 20–21.

Aldersey-Williams, Hugh. "New Leaf." *Architectural Record,* February 1994, pp. 112–17.

Allison, David. "Blending the Old and the New: 'Adaptive Reuse' Extends Life of Older Buildings." *Atlanta Business Chronicle,* October 7, 1994, p. 9.

"Alternative Mall Design Revitalizes Urban Brownfield Site." *Economic Developments,* February 15, 1995, p. 6.

Andorka, Frank H. "On a New Track." *Hotel & Motel Management,* January 22, 1996, p. 48.

Baker, Jon Alan. "Planning Important for Adaptive Reuse." *San Diego Business Journal,* June 13, 1994, p. 18.

Blaine, M. Cecile. "All's Fair in Love and War Games." *Mini-Storage Messenger,* July 1996, pp. 59–60.

Bordenaro, Michael. "Rail Station–to–Courts Conversion Stays on Track." *Building Design & Construction,* August 1993, pp. 30–34.

——. "Warehouse Renovation Arrests Jail's Cost." *Building Design & Construction,* April 1993, pp. 40–43.

Bruce, Robert. "Recycling Your Industrial Properties." *Journal of Property Management,* July/August 1995, pp. 44–47.

Butehorn, Ellie. "Savage Mill: No Run-of-the-Mill Renovation." *Corridor Real Estate Journal,* September 22, 1995, pp. A13–A19.

Campbell, Jan. "Is Your Building a Candidate for Adaptive Reuse?" *Journal of Property Management,* January/February 1996, pp. 26–29.

"Class B & C Office Buildings Making the Grade as Residences." *Building Design & Construction,* September 1995, pp. 12–13.

Colburn, Steven C. "Dealing with Older or Damaged Buildings: Rehabilitation vs. New Construction." *Journal of Real Estate Taxation,* Spring 1992, pp. 245–55.

"Commercial Reuse, New Construction Create Appeal." *Professional Builder,* December 1993, pp. 40–41.

"Community Eyesore Evolving into a School Building." *Building Design & Construction,* April 1994, p. 14.

"Converted Hotels Host Senior-Living Communities." *Building Design & Construction,* August 1994, pp. 9–10.

"Converting Hotels to Elderly Housing." *Real Estate Perspectives,* August 15, 1992, p. 5.

Cooper, W.K. "Amazonia: Breaking Down Barriers. With More Than $1 Million Invested in the Site, Sound Stewardship Argued for Adaptive Reuse." *Construction Specifier,* Vol. 47, No. 5 (1994), p. 102.

Cornish, Janet A. "Putting Old Buildings to Work." *Western Planner,* July/August 1992, pp. 10–12.

"Decaying Pier Gets a Life Preserver." *Building Design & Construction,* February 1996, p. 36.

Durand, Chris. "Bigger…And Better." *Spectrum,* September/October 1993, pp. 7–8.

Eaton, Maureen. "Historic Power Plant Goes High-Tech." *Building Design & Construction,* April 1995, pp. 42–45.

——. "New Faces for a Chicago Landmark." *Building Design & Construction,* June 1995, pp. 44–46+.

——. "640 Memorial Drive." *Building Design & Construction,* October 1993, pp. 32–36.

Eckstut, Stanton. "Circle Center, Indianapolis." *Urban Land,* February 1995, pp. 30–33.

Erlich, Gerald. "Rediscovering Historic Values in Denver." *Commercial Investment Real Estate Journal,* May/June 1996, pp. 26–29.

"Finding Uses for Surplus Corporate Buildings." *Building Design & Construction,* May 1994, p. 7.

"Focus On: Adaptive Reuse." *Architectural Record,* February 1995, p. 102.

Foong, L. Keat. "Home Economics." *MHN Multi Housing News,* November/December 1994, pp. 50–51.

Friedman, David J. "Financing Adaptive Reuse Properties in an Age of Tight Lending Practices." *Plants, Sites, and Parks,* January/February 1992, pp. 190–91.

"From Derelict to Dynamic: An Adaptive Reuse Case Study." *Development,* Winter 1995, pp. 30–31.

Green, Kay. "Adaptable Housing Makes Good Sense (and Dollars)." *Urban Land,* April 1992, p. 9.

Gregerson, John. "Carnation Building Reblooms as Spec Offices." *Building Design & Construction,* August 1993, pp. 44–46.

Guthrie, Margaret E. "Ventures: Run of the Mills." *Historic Preservation,* July/August 1992, pp. 22–23.

Hoch, Bruce. "Adaptive Reuse: Opportunities and New Challenges." *Corporate Real Estate Executive,* October 1994, pp. 30–31.

Hoyt, Charles K. "Blue Hen Corporate Center." *Architectural Record,* October 1995, pp. 106–7.

Hoyt, Charles K., et al. "Focus On: Turning Ordinary into Extraordinary." *Architectural Record,* February 1995, pp. 102–7.

Jonas, Marc. "Zoning and Adaptive Reuse: Making Redevelopment Worth Your While." *Commercial Investment Real Estate Journal,* Winter 1993, pp. 12–17.

Kennedy, Carolyn. "The Latest in Adaptive Reuse." *PAS Memo,* April 1992, pp. 1–4.

LaFreniere, Andrea. "In-Town Renovation Provides Attractive Apartment Living." *Professional Builder & Remodeler,* April 1993, p. 44.

Lake, David. "Solution File. The Exchange Building: From Offices to Apartments." *Urban Land,* April 1995, pp. 66–67.

Lambiase, Alan. "Adapting America's Industrial Heritage." *Commercial Investment Real Estate Journal,* Winter 1993, pp. 18–23.

"Large-Scale Rehabilitation Award: Schlitz Park. *Urban Land,* December 1993, p. 18.

Linn, Charles D. "Focus on 3 Rs: Rehabilitation, Renovation, Reuse." *Architectural Record,* January 1993, pp. 112–17.

"New Faces for a Chicago Landmark." *Building Design & Construction,* June 1995, p. 44.

Newman, Morris. "Ford Turns Old Auto Plant into Factory Outlet Center." *Real Estate Forum,* October 1993, p. 10.

Patterson, Maureen. "Great Mall of the Bay Area." *Buildings,* June 1995, pp. 48–50+.

"Recycling Obsolete Retail Centers." *Building Design & Construction,* August 1996, p. 9.

Russell, James. "A City in Limbo." *Architectural Record,* January 1993, pp. 102–7.

"Science Center to Set Up Shop in Former Marketplace." *Building Design & Construction,* March 1996, p. 14.

Seal, Kathy. "Hotels Find New Life as Senior-Housing Units." *Hotel & Motel Management,* December 14, 1992, p. 6+.

Selwitz, Robert. "Former Stockholm Prison 'Bars' Few from Entering." *Hotel & Motel Management,* May 24, 1993, p. 41.

——. "Trump to Turn Office Tower into Hotel/Condo Complex." *Hotel & Motel Management,* July 24, 1995, p. 3.

Stern, Julie D. "A Mixed-Use University Center." *Urban Land,* July 1994, pp. 10–11.

Stern, Martin. "Strings Attached: The Rehab of a Chicago Landmark." *Urban Land,* July 1994, pp. 25–28.

Sullivan, C.C. "Holiday Inn Downtown (New York, N.Y.)." *Buildings,* June 1994, p. 74+.

Tanner, Ted. "Union Station Reborn." *Urban Land,* December 1994, p. 13.

"Wall Street Woos Residential Developers." *Building Design & Construction,* January 1996, p. 16.

Watson, Tom. "Same Space, New Place." *Restaurant Business,* April 10, 1996, pp. 48–54.

Whaley, John W. "Bouncing Back from Defense Cuts." *Mortgage Banking,* May 1994, pp. 46–52.

Williams, Donald S., and Sally M. Dwyer. "Recycling Manufacturing Properties." *Urban Land,* January 1995, pp. 21–24.

"Winner: DMACC Polytechnic Campus." *Buildings,* June 1994, p. 66.

"Winner: Great Mall of the Bay Area." *Buildings,* June 1995, p. 48.

Wolff, Carlo. "From Downside to Upside." *Lodging Hospitality,* April 1996, pp. 41–44.

Wright, Gordon. "Auto Plant Remodeled into a Retail Mecca." *Building Design & Construction,* September 1995, pp. 48–50.

——. "Industrial Park Evolves from Recycled Auto Plant." *Building Design & Construction,* September 1993, pp. 54–56.

Reuse of Military Facilities

Journal Articles

Abramson, Dan. "The Brooklyn Navy Yard: Life after the Military Base." *Real Estate Forum,* August 1993, pp. 89–90+.

"Base Closings Pose Anxieties and Opportunities." *Building Design & Construction,* May 1995, p. 15.

"Best Examples in Reuse of Military Bases Aren't Disseminated Adequately." *Community Development Digest,* December 19, 1995, pp. 1–3.

"Commercial Wings Fly into Old Air Force Base." *ENR–Engineering News-Record,* January 30, 1995, p. 28.

Dorrier, Richard, and Laura Wiberg. "Military Base Closings Offer Reuse Opportunities." *Commercial Investment Real Estate Journal,* Winter 1993, pp. 24–30.

Feldtkeller, Andrews. "Converting Military Facility to an Urban Townscape." *Making Cities Livable Newsletter,* Vol. 4, No. 1–2, pp. 16–18.

Fisher, Bonnie. "Seizing the Opportunity in Military Base Closures." *Urban Land,* August 1993, pp. 11–15.

Goodkin, Sanford. "A Vision for Reuse." *Urban Land,* April 1994, p. 8.

Goodno, James B. "Former Subic Bay Navy Base Attracts Hotel Developers." *Hotel & Motel Management,* March 22, 1993, p. 4+.

Hankowsky, William P. "Military Base Reuse: The Philadelphia Story." *Urban Land,* October 1995, pp. 53–54+.

Maremont, Mark. "Lessons from the First Big Base to Go Dark." *Business Week,* April 5, 1993, p. 29.

Mulvihill, David A. "Do Military Base Closings Offer Development Opportunities?" *Urban Land,* August 1993, p. 44.

Murphy, Kevin D. "Making the Most of a Base Closing." *Governing,* September 1993, pp. 22–24.

Netter, Edith M., and W. David Stephenson. "Charlestown Navy Yard Reborn." *Urban Land,* October 1993, pp. 62–63.

"New Tenants Fuel Army Base Reuse." *Land Use Law Report,* February 7, 1996, p. 21.

Newman, Morris. "Base Reuse: Martin to Break Ground on Hamilton Project." *California Planning & Development Report,* March 1995, p. 4.

——. "Base Reuse: Toxic Cleanup Remains Biggest Base Issue." *California Planning & Development Report,* February 1995, p. 2.

Ordano, Jo-Ann. "Changing of the Guard at San Francisco's Presidio." *Urban Land,* July 1993, pp. 14–15.

Seal, Kathy. "Maine: Base Conversion Plan Includes Three Hotels." *Commercial Property News,* November 21, 1994, p. 8.

Seidman, Karl F. "Redeveloping Military Bases." *Economic Development Commentary,* Summer 1995, pp. 10–17.

Smith-Heimer, Janet, and David Shiver. "Progress in Bay Area Base Conversions." *Urban Land,* December 1994, pp. 38–41.

Venable, Tim. "Redeveloped Military Bases: Cold War Windfall of Business Sites." *Site Selection,* June 1994, pp. 556–64.

Federal Financing Resources

Books/Monographs

Affordable Housing through Historic Preservation: A Case Study Guide to Combining the Tax Credits. GPO stock no. 024-005-01148. Washington, D.C.: U.S. Dept. of the Interior, National Park Service, 1995.

Affordable Housing through Historic Preservation: Tax Credits and the Secretary of the Interior's Standard for Historic Rehabilitation. GPO stock no. 024-005-01163-3. Washington, D.C.: U.S. Dept. of the Interior, National Park Service, 1995.

Blumenthal, Sara K. *Federal Historic Preservation Laws.* Rev. by Emogene A. Bevitt. GPO stock no. 024-005-01124-2. Washington, D.C.: U.S. Dept. of the Interior, National Park Service, 1993.

Department of Human Services and Public Safety. *A Financing Tool for Affordable Housing: Housing Trust Funds.* Washington, D.C.: Metropolitan Washington Council of Governments, 1991.

Horbart, Susan, and Robert Schwarz. *Financing Multifamily Housing Using Section 42 Low-Income Housing Tax Credits.* Working Paper 654. Washington, D.C.: ULI–the Urban Land Institute, 1996.

Novogradac, Michael J., et al. *Low-Income Housing Tax Credit Handbook.* New York: Clark Boardman Callaghan Co., 1995.

Journal Articles

Belkowitz, David "Hidden Traps in HUD-Sponsored Low-Income Housing Loans." *Real Estate Review,* Spring 1995, pp. 71–73.

"Giving Investors a Stake in the Inner City: The Low-Income Housing Tax Credit." *Real Estate Finance Journal,* Fall 1995, p. 11.

Hobart, Susan, and Robert Schwarz. "Housing Credits: A Leading Financial Tool." *Urban Land,* November 1995, pp. 37–42.

Jacobs, Barry G. "IRS Clarifies Criteria for Tax-Credit Program." *National Real Estate Investor,* November 1994, p. 66.

Kaster, Lewis R. "New Audit Guidelines for Rehabilitation Tax Credit." *Journal of Taxation,* April 1995, pp. 225–26.

McKay, Kristine. "Take Credit: A Guide to Low-Income Housing and Rehabilitation Tax Credits." *Secondary Mortgage Markets,* Winter 1991/ 1992, pp. 14–17.

MacRostie, William G. "Historic Rehab Tax Credits." *Corporate Real Estate Executive,* June 1994, p. 37.

Miller, Jerrold L., and Ed Deck. "A Review of the Low-Income Housing Tax Credit." *Capital Sources for Real Estate,* January 1995, pp. 1–6.

Novogradac, Michael J., and Stephen B. Tracy. "The Low-Income Housing Tax Credit: Treatment of Land Preparation Costs in a Low-Income Housing Tax Credit Development." *Journal of Real Estate Taxation,* Winter 1996, pp. 156–60.

"Property Tax Tools Help Finance Downtown Preservation." *Downtown Idea Exchange,* December 15, 1992, pp. 4–5.

Schwartz, Robert S., and Joseph M. Lemond. "Low-Income Housing Tax Credit Basics and Financing." *Real Estate Law Journal,* Spring 1993, pp. 336–48.

Thorne-Thomsen, Thomas. "Low-Income Housing Tax Credit: Bridge Loan Opportunities." *Real Estate Finance,* Summer 1994, pp. 24–31.

Whetsell, Timothy, and Lisa Swenerton. "Projects That Qualify for Low-Income Housing Tax Credit Attract Developers and Corporate Investors." *Real Estate Newsline,* January/February 1995, p. 1+.

ULI Project Reference File Reports

ULI's Project Reference File (PRF) is a quarterly subscription service that provides current information on 20 outstanding development projects (five projects per quarter) for each PRF subscription year. Individual reports are also available. The following PRFs published since 1990 profile adaptive use projects.

"Audubon House." *ULI Project Reference File,* Vol. 24, No. 19, October–December 1994.

"Denver Dry Goods Building." *ULI Project Reference File,* Vol. 24, No. 17, October–December 1994.

"Federal Plaza." *ULI Project Reference File,* Vol. 23, No. 18, October–December 1993.

"Fisherman's Terminal." *ULI Project Reference File,* Vol. 20, No. 13, July–September 1990.

"Harborside Financial Center." *ULI Project Reference File,* Vol. 22, No. 6, April–June 1992.

"Mercy Family Plaza." *ULI Project Reference File,* Vol. 24, No. 10, April–June 1994.

"The Mill at Glenville." *ULI Project Reference File,* Vol. 22, No. 2, January–March 1992.

"Preservation Park." *ULI Project Reference File,* Vol. 26, No. 3, January–March 1996.

"Schlitz Park." *ULI Project Reference File,* Vol. 23, No. 16, October–December 1993.

"The Second & Pine." *ULI Project Reference File,* Vol. 23, No. 13, July–September 1993.

"640 Memorial Drive." *ULI Project Reference File,* Vol. 26, No. 4, January–March 1996.

"Tanner Market." *ULI Project Reference File,* Vol. 21, No. 14, July–September 1991.

"Truman Annex." *ULI Project Reference File,* Vol. 26, No. 14, July–September 1996.

"Union Station, Washington, D.C." *ULI Project Reference File,* Vol. 21, No. 15, July–September 1991.

"Warehouse Row." *ULI Project Reference File,* Vol. 20, No. 6, April–June 1990.

ULI Advisory Services Panel Reports

Advisory service panels are teams of ULI members that evaluate and make recommendations on land use issues presented by public or private sponsors. Each panel report outlines the project's history, the development question facing the sponsor, and the findings and recommendations of the panel. The following panel reports published since 1990 deal with the reuse of existing facilities.

Chanute Air Force Base, Rantoul, Illinois, April 1990.

Hughes Aircraft, Fullerton, California, October 1995.

Mare Island Naval Shipyard, Vallejo, California, January 1994.

Treasure Island, San Francisco, California, October 1996.

ULI InfoPackets

InfoPackets provide up-to-date information on more than 80 topics. ULI staff gather a broad range of views on one subject from numerous magazines, journals, and unpublished reports. The articles and reports are organized, compiled, and photocopied into 50- to 250-page books and updated annually. InfoPackets are available on the following subjects:

▼ Adaptive Use

▼ Inner-City Revitalization

▼ Low-Income Housing

▼ Military Installation Redevelopment